Baby Names 2016

Eleanor Turner

white
LADDER

Acknowledgments

I would like to extend my utmost gratitude to Michael Turner for his contribution; without him this book would have been much shorter. My thanks are also given to Beth Bishop and Hugh Brune at Crimson Publishing for their patience and guidance throughout this project. Finally, the greatest thanks go to my children, Owen Henri, Jasper Hugh, and Josie May. I fall more in love with them, and their names, every day.

This fifth edition published by White Ladder, an imprint of Crimson Publishing in 2015.

ISBN: 978 1 91033 604 5

Typeset by IDSUK (DataConnection) Ltd

Printed and bound in the United States of America by Edward Brothers Malloy, Michigan

Contents

A note on how to use this book

While the author and publisher acknowledge that baby names vary widely in spelling and pronunciation, this book lists each name only once: under the most common initial and spelling. If a name has a common alternate spelling with a different initial, it may also be listed under that letter.

Information relating to statistics and trends in baby names is based on the most recent data at the time of going to press.

Introduction

Did you know that the name Elizabeth is the most popular name for baby girls in the District of Columbia, but not anywhere else?

Did you know that your own political leanings affect the baby names you're most likely to pick?

Do you know why Princess Charlotte was given that name?

As daunting as it might sound at first, choosing a name for your baby is one of the most enjoyable, often hilarious, and best decisions you get to make as a new parent. You are being given free rein to get as creative as possible, to honor a family member or celebrity you love, or to find meaning in the dozens of names you've loved over the years. Who doesn't like the sound of that?

However, baby-naming is not without its pitfalls. Sometimes, choosing the right name is simply a case of hearing one you like and knowing instantly that you've chosen correctly. But for some parents the naming game gets far more complicated when they start trying to please parents, grandparents, friends, and siblings, while simultaneously trying to avoid names that could be shortened into ridiculous nicknames or would make for funny initials.

And here's another thing: you'll probably want to choose something unique, but not too unique, or something common, but not too common. A name could be inspired by an admired celebrity, a sports star, or an influential historical or political figure. It could come from the family tree, or follow a current baby-naming trend. You also need to make sure you love it—you and your baby will have to live with it forever! The possibilities are endless so it's understandable that it can send some parents into a tailspin.

Well, never fear. *Baby Names 2016* is here to take you through your options and solve your baby-naming dilemmas. It's updated annually, so it always includes the year's most popular names, celebrity choices, and names making a comeback. We've included dozens of lists to provide you with inspiration, and, of course, some downright kooky names children have been given over the years (usually by celebrities). Take a peek at the most up-to-date trends in baby naming, from the backlash against eccentric names to the return of the traditional, and some recent celebrity trends. Read about how movie stars and the characters they play influence what we name our children. Learn what teachers *really* think about the names in their classrooms, and discover whether Noah is still the most chosen US boys' name after knocking Jacob off the top spot last year.

Be sure to keep an eye out for all the facts and figures we've got for you—including what names are most popular around the world—so you can either go with the flow . . . or deliberately go against it.

This book is broken into two sections: the first deals with how to figure out what to name your child through a series of questions and suggestions, and the second gives you a meaning for each name you're considering. Many names are given added detail including fun facts, interesting trivia, and reminders of famous people who were given a name—or chose it for themselves. There's no right or wrong way to use this book, just as there's no right or wrong way to make your baby-naming decision. Remember, picking a baby name should be fun! Grab a pencil, dip in, and find some names you like. Use the tons of suggestions we've given you to work out if one of them is right for *your* baby.

Good luck!

part one

1 What was hot in 2015?

A flood of Noahs and Emmas

Noah, a name that didn't appear in the Top 10 charts until 2009, is once again at number one! Over 19,000 baby boys were given the Biblical name in 2015—which is 1,000 more than the year before.

This is made all the more incredible when you consider that, until two years ago, either Jacob or Michael had remained the top choice for parents of newborn baby boys in the US for over 50 years. Jacob has been given to more babies (4.86 million and counting), but Michael has claimed the top spot more often (44 times).

The average length of a baby name is six letters.

So where did the insurgent Noah come from? Back in 1960 Noah was down in a rather pathetic 668th position, but it hasn't just been a long slow haul of over 50 years for it to crawl its way to the top. In fact it's been more of a sprint finish, as Noah has jumped over 200 places since 1992.

Last year's edition of this very book forecast that Noah, which has seen resurgence in many Christian families, would become even more popular and remain at the top spot. Well whaddya know . . . we were right! Here at *Baby Names 2016* we like making predictions so much (and being proved right, naturally), that we are also predicting that Noah will remain in first place next year too. It's not just because movies like Russell Crowe's *Noah* have propelled Noah into the limelight—it's also because we are seeing a major shift throughout the country towards traditional names and names with history behind them.

You have to feel a little for poor Jacob. Not only has he been deposed two years in a row, he's slipped back into fourth place. Second place has been taken by Liam, and third is occupied by Mason. What's going on with boy names this year?

The Top 10 list for girls' names was a pretty similar story to the boys' list. Emma has made the jump into first place for the first time since 2008, and Sophia fell down to third place after a good few years running things from the top. Olivia has risen to second place now, which is the highest it's ever been. It's possible that it will either stay there or even climb to first place next year, but *Baby Names 2016* predicts it will not fall any further. Charlotte also made an appearance for the first time at number 10—no doubt inspired in part by the new Royal Princess (more on the royal baby on page 11, and Charlotte, below).

Top 10 baby boy names

1. Noah	6. Ethan
2. Liam	7. Michael
3. Mason	8. Alexander
4. Jacob	9. James
5. William	10. Daniel

Top 10 baby girl names

1. Emma	6. Mia
2. Olivia	7. Emily
3. Sophia	8. Abigail
4. Isabella	9. Madison
5. Ava	10. Charlotte

Traditional names continue to impress

What's interesting about recent trends is that no matter how many new and unusual names enter the most popular baby name lists each year, you will always see a large number of babies given the same familiar and traditional names of the past. The Top 10 names for both boys and girls seem to stay pretty fixed each year, and 2015 was no different.

The only newcomer to the Top 10 for boys' names last year was James, which was only just pushed out of the previous year's ranking into 13th place. Jayden, which was in ninth place in 2013, is now in 15th place beneath Aiden. Jacob, Michael, and William have all appeared in the Top 10 boys' names every year since 2006, and the girls' names Emma, Sophia, and Isabella have also stayed put.

We've also seen traditional names re-enter the charts; a wonderful example of this is the name Charlotte. Once a consistently popular name in the US, appearing exclusively in the Top 100 from 1908 to 1953, it had dropped to 309th place by 1982. However, in the last decade it's seen a massive increase in use, and last year clawed its way back to number 10. Once again, the team at *Baby Names 2016* spotted this trend in our previous edition and predicted Charlotte would be in the Top 10 in 2015. Of course, it was helped along by a certain royal baby, but who's to say the Duchess of Cambridge didn't peruse this very book when making her final decision?

Charlotte has now become so fashionable that even shortened versions of it are gaining momentum: Charlie entered the Top 1,000 for baby girls in 2005 and in just nine years has leapt over 700 places to 229th place. Charlie has also remained a steady favorite for parents of little boys, as the same name has climbed just over 200 spots since the year 2000 in the boys' charts.

More traditional names had dropped out of mainstream use by the 1980s and become vastly unpopular, but in the last ten years names ending in -a, -ie, -y, and -en have started to see a resurgence, particularly as a spelling option for parents who like the sound of a traditional name but want to give it a modern twist. Just take a look at the Top 10 (the first six spots for baby girls end in -a), or the highest climbers (six of the 10 biggest climbers end in either -a, -ie, -y, or a similar sound). Other old-fashioned names, such as Henry, Jasper, Hannah, Marilyn, and William, have climbed the popularity ranks in the Top 100 lists, along with their alternate spelling options of Henri, Jaz, Hanna, Mae, and Will.

The reign of eccentric names

Have you ever raised your eyebrows when you heard a friend's baby name choice? Statistics say you probably have. Research shows that we are seeing more variation in the names parents are choosing than ever before. In the 1950s, the Top 25 boys' names and the Top 50 girls' names were given to 50% of all babies born in that decade. To reach the same figure now, you would have to include the Top 154 boys' names and the Top 316 girls'. That's everything from Noah (1st) to Joel (154th), and Emma (1st) to Amanda (314th). In fact, if you look over the last decade, the percentage of babies given names in the Top 1,000 gets smaller every year: in 2005 75.5% of registered births appeared in the Top 1,000 names, but last year it was only 73.5%—and it gets smaller every year. This means that there is a far greater variety of names, spellings, pronunciations, and contracted names than ever before.

One explanation for this is that parents have begun to give their child a name *more* unusual than their own. A parent who has enjoyed their slightly unusual name will feel more confident about giving their offspring a unique name. This has been a rising trend since the 1990s, which would make sense, as children with eccentric names who were born in the early 1990s are now having children themselves. If this trend continues into 2016 and beyond, you can be sure that names will get stranger and stranger . . .

Some of the US's quirky baby names during the last year have included Austyn, Bo, Sincere, and Stetson for boys, and Jakayla, Jurnee, Princess, and Wynter for girls.

Every year the Social Security Administration releases a report on the biggest climbers and fallers, and most years these names tend to be the quirkiest. The names at the top of these lists have the greatest jumps in popularity, although it doesn't necessarily mean they are widely used across the USA. In fact, it's the opposite. The biggest climbers are always those further down the charts—if only 10 families chose a name last year, but then 20 families chose it this year, that's an increase of 100%. The same percentage increase for Noah would need an additional 19,000 families to choose the name. So a rarely used name can jump several hundred spots in a single year, despite only having a handful of families choosing it for their little ones. Make sense? No? Well, here's a short breakdown of the Top 10 names to jump up or down the charts anyway:

2015 biggest winners		2015 biggest losers	
Boys	**Girls**	**Boys**	**Girls**
Bode	Aranza	Bently	Miley
Axl	Montserrat	Damion	Karly
Gannon	Monserrat	Amare	Britney
Bodie	Maisie	Isiah	Kaya
Royal	Zendaya	Xavi	Nahla
Coen	Karter	Sidney	Rihanna
Anakin	Ariadne	Deegan	Kaylyn
Killian	Daleyza	Jair	Makena
Reyansh	Thea	Juelz	Karissa
Ronin	Remington	Corban	Sherlyn

So why do names increase or decrease so dramatically in a single year? Well, one thought for last year's crop of winners and losers is the popularity of two Latin American soap operas, with characters named Aranza and Montserrat—which explains the first three names for girls. Also, alpine skier Bode Miller had a turn in the spotlight recently, prompting many parents to pick his name for their sons. On the flip side, it's possible that as the antics of teenage popstar-turned-rebel Miley Cyrus have been noted and frowned upon by new parents, who don't want their own daughters to follow her lead. For more on how pop culture affects baby names, see page 35.

Epic kids need epic names

A fascinating trend over the last few years has been the increase in royal names, "epic" names, and car-themed names—particularly for baby boys. In fact, of the hundreds of names to show large jumps in popularity, these categories made up a significant proportion. Royal was a huge climber for baby boys last year, along with Kingsley, Duke, and Princeton. The name King is also now so popular it's appeared in the Top 200 for only the second time since the SSA began collecting baby names data in 1880.

Other choices for baby boys include names so grand they can't help but be epic. Legend jumped 185 spots last year as the most epic of epic names, followed by Apollo, Atlas, and Ace. In hot pursuit (pun intended) were names such as Axl, Dash, Ford, and Chevy—perfect for your tiny car enthusiast of the future.

For girls, the name Khaleesi was another big mover last year, which if you're a *Game of Thrones* fan you'll know means "Queen" in the Dothraki language. In fact, it was one of the highest climbers of the year, jumping a whopping 300 places, followed swiftly by Amirah ("princess" in Arabic). Names that haven't had an impact yet include Queenie and

Duchess, but if princess-themed names are moving up then it's only a matter of time . . .

> Obviously the most influential royal baby name of 2015 was that chosen by Prince William and the Duchess of Cambridge for their daughter. Two days after her birth, it was announced that Will and Kate's daughter would be called Charlotte Elizabeth Diana. It's a great choice, with a nod to several important people in the couple's life. First off, Charlotte is the feminine form of Charles (like William's dad, the Prince of Wales and heir to the throne), and the middle name of Kate's sister Pippa. Second, Elizabeth is obviously a fitting tribute to the current Queen of England, Elizabeth II, and Diana . . . well, you just can't go wrong with naming your daughter after William's late mother, Diana Spencer—also known fondly as Princess Di.

Other rising trends for baby girls include geographical names, such as Holland and Meadow, and botanical names such as Oakley, Juniper, and Magnolia. Perfect for your little aspiring explorer or botanist!

The effects of the entertainment industry

Characters in TV shows, movies, and books have been having a huge impact on baby names in the last few years. In 2015 the sequel to *Divergent*, *Insurgent*, was released and the world was re-introduced to Tris (short for Beatrice). While Tris is still working its way into the Top 1,000, Beatrice jumped over 100 places the year the first movie was released—possibly as a direct result of the movie. The third installment in the series, *Allegiant*, is set for release in 2016, so it will be interesting to see if the trend continues.

Also released in 2015 was the fourth installment of *The Hunger Games* series, *Mockingjay—Part 2*. *The Hunger Games* has had an enormous impact on baby names: since the books and movies were first released, the names Peeta and Gale have entered the boys' names lists for the first time ever. In fact, the spelling "Gael" is one of the biggest climbers, moving up an astonishing 350 places in a single year. The name Katniss was given to 38 baby girls last year (doubling since last year), Finnick was also awarded to 38 baby boys, and the name Primrose, or "Prim," has started to climb the charts after over 100 years away from the Top 1,000, which supports the idea that parents are choosing old-fashioned names again. The more unusual names of Rue and Cato have also been adopted by some parents: the name Rue, a small and sympathetic character in the opening installment of the series, was given to 31 baby girls last year, and, rather alarmingly, the name of the cruel, brutal character Cato was given to 18 baby boys. Johanna, an important character later in the series, was given to a whopping 564 girls last year—the most popular *Hunger Games* name so far.

Disney's *Frozen* was about as massive as you can get: one of the highest grossing animated films of all time, and an entire industry of merchandise to boot. Last year saw the launch of an animated short called *Frozen Fever*, and it served the desired purpose of reminding folks why they love Nordic princesses so much . . . oh, and why they should pick Scandinavian names for their babies. The name Elsa moved up a staggering 242 places last year, and Anna even bumped up one place to 34th, which could mean that *Frozen* is helping maintain its place in the charts. Some of the more traditional Scandinavian names have shown less dramatic increases in popularity, although they are definitely being given to babies now: Kristoff was given to 32 little boys last year (a five-fold increase), and Olaf, the goofy-but-lovable snowman, was given to 22—up from nine the year before. Still, with discussions afoot over a full-length *Frozen* sequel, it's really only a matter of time until Kristoff, Olaf, and Sven catch up with their peers.

Other movies don't seem to inspire parents as much. *Cinderella* and *Avengers: Age of Ultron* were both massive box-office hits, but parents didn't seem as keen to choose character names for their babies as usual. It's extremely likely in these two examples that the names are just too "out there" for most of us! Even the more mainstream ones lacked impact: the name Natasha, after Scarlett Johansson's character Natasha Romanoff/The Black Widow, actually dropped 70 places last year, and as for Kermit the Frog . . . well . . .

> An Israeli couple called their baby girl "Like" after the Facebook button. Their other children are called Pie and Vash, which means honey.

The movie *Noah* was a box office success in 2014, and the impact of it continued to be felt in baby names during 2015. Noah topped the boys' charts for the first time in history the year the film was released, and maintained its position last year. It's possible it's no more than a coincidence, but it's also likely that as the name got tossed around in the media, more parents started considering it as a potential candidate, and then their final choice. Other names to have emerged from the film included Ila, Naameh, and Methuselah. Ila seems like the one most likely to become popular in the next few years, as it's so similar to other popular names like Emma, Isabella, and Ella.

> Quvenzhané Wallis, the pint-sized Academy Award nominee and the star of 2015's *Fathers and Daughters*, has had to repeatedly explain how to properly pronounce her name and where it comes from. A hybrid of her mother's and father's names (Qulyndreia and Venjie), with the addition of the Swahili word for fairy (zhané), Quvenzhané was often heard correcting interviewers during the movie's promotional season. There's a lesson in there for all baby namers.

TV inspiration

Game of Thrones, HBO's runaway success of a fantasy-world drama based on the George R. R. Martin series of books, has been held accountable for the increase in popularity of the name Arya. It was a big climber for girls' names last year and jumped nearly 60 places—it's now in position 216, but was unheard of before 2010. The spelling "Aria" also saw an increase in popularity and appeared in 31st place, its highest ever, which is a jump of over 300 places in just five years. As mentioned on page 10, Khaleesi is one of this year's highest climbers, and Daenerys was given to 86 babies in 2015—a name that no one could either pronounce or spell before *Game of Thrones* hit our screens.

Elsewhere on network television, girls' names continue to be directly impacted by the characters on our screens. Violet, for example, from Maggie Smith's acerbic character Violet Crawley, the Dowager Countess of Grantham, from *Downton Abbey*, has proved particularly popular— over 4,000 baby girls were given the name Violet last year, and even nine baby boys. Political thriller *Scandal* may be at least somewhat responsible for the rise in popularity of the name Olivia—after the lead character Olivia Pope, played by Kerry Washington. Shonda Rhimes, the creator of *Scandal*, was also responsible for *Grey's Anatomy* and last year's *How to Get Away With Murder*, starring Viola Davis. The name Viola fits nicely into the 100-year rule, where names tend to come back around in popularity after 100 years or so, and last year 192 babies were given this name—which means it's definitely due a comeback. Annalise, a name popular around 25 years ago, is more popular for the time being, sitting comfortably in the Top 500—will next year push it even further ahead?

The sporting year

Names of sporting heroes are often an inspiration for new parents, particularly those with moving stories. Michael Sam, the first openly gay player to be drafted to the NHL, may have helped keep both the names Michael and Sam in the spotlight in 2015 after his appearance on *Dancing with the Stars*. Tom Brady, the MVP from 2015's Superbowl win by the New England Patriots, caused the name Tom to jump 20 places from the year before and LeBron James, the hugely successful NBA star, inspired dozens of parents to pick his name for their babies last year, and it saw an increase of 5% from the year before.

Broadcast around the world in 2015 were the FIFA Soccer Women's World Cup, held in Canada, the World Athletic Championships, held in Beijing, the US Tennis Open, and the Rugby Union World Cup, held in England. While we're not big on rugby here, the national sports stars participating definitely have an effect on baby names in their home countries—perhaps the results will feed into our charts eventually. Think Quade Cooper (Australia), Richie McCaw (New Zealand), Victor Matfield (South Africa), and Euan Murray (Scotland).

The FIFA Women's World Cup once again proved that female athletes can be hugely influential on baby names. Hope Solo and Abby Wambach of the USA have both had an impact over the last few years since their success during the 2012 London Olympics win, although Hope's run-in with the law did dampen her name's popularity a little more recently. Abby, however, has been steadily climbing up the ranks and now appears in the Top 500, alongside her longer name of Abigail (currently in eighth place).

Celebrity power

After a rather boring few years of celebrities choosing charming-but-dull names for their offspring, 2015 saw the glorious return of more bizarre celebrity-naming trends. Recent deliveries from the celebrity stork have included some really wild baby boy names: Sailor Gene (Liv Tyler and David Gardner), Titan Jewell (Kelly Rowland and Tim Witherspoon), Rocket Zot (Sam Worthington and Lara Bingle), Reign Aston (Kourtney Kardashian and Scott Disick), and Blues Anthony (Jessica Paré and John Kastner).

While the baby-name gods have been slightly kinder to the girls, there are still a handful of unusual ones. How about the trend for giving little girls traditionally male names, like Wyatt Isabelle (Mila Kunis and Ashton Kutcher), James (Ryan Reynolds and Blake Lively), Sidney Aoibheann (Vanessa Carlton and John McCauley), Wilder (CaCee Cobb and Donald Faison), or Ryan (Haylie Duff and Matt Roseberg)? Or perhaps naming your daughter after a famous chapel is more en vogue, like baby Sistine Sabella (Kevin James and Steffiana de la Cruz). Either way, these parents can be sure their girls won't be sharing their names with any other girls in their class—maybe the boys, but not the girls.

Twin babies didn't escape the trend for out-there names either, with twosomes Violet Moon and Knox Blue (Sarah Shahi and Steve Howey), and Cy Aridio and Bowie Ezio (Zoe Saldana and Marco Perego) making appearances on the list. However, there were some blissfully normal names this past year too, including Henry (Amanda Peet and David Benioff), Poppy (Nate Berkus and Jeremiah Brent), Sasha (Shakira and Gerard Piqué), and Scarlett May (Molly Sims and Scott Stuber). Mind you, with the way celebrity baby names tend to go, the babies with the 'normal' names will probably end up being the ones that eventually stand out!

What about Blue?

Beyoncé caused quite the stir when she named her daughter Blue Ivy in 2012, but she's neither the first nor the last celebrity to use the name. Other "blue" parents include Cher, John Travolta, The Edge, Geri Halliwell, Alicia Silverstone, and last year both Sarah Shahi and Jessica Paré used the color too. There were also 35 baby girls and baby boys named Blue last year, and Ivy sprang up another few places in the charts. Incidentally, Beyoncé and Jay Z have applied to trademark their daughter's name—not once, but twice. Recently the couple asked for 'Blue Ivy Carter' to be trademarked exclusively to them, for use with baby products and music.

There are some sweet stories from our favorite stars this year. Take Vin Diesel, for example, who named his daughter Pauline after Paul Walker. The two actors starred in *The Fast and the Furious* movies together, and it's a sweet tribute to the deceased Walker that shows how much friendship there was between them. Likewise, Clark Gable's granddaughter recently named her infant son Ocean Clark Gable after the Hollywood legend, keeping tradition and honor alive in the family.

Recent celebrity babies

Andy Rose (Jack and Lisa Osborne)

Blues Anthony (Jessica Paré and John Kastner)

Charlotte Elizabeth Diana (Prince William and Kate Middleton)

Conrad (Reid Scott and Elspeth Scott)

Dashiel Edan (Milla Jovovich and Paul W.S. Anderson)

Edith Vivian Patricia (Cate Blanchett and Andrew Upton)

Ioni James (Coco Rocha and James Conran)

Isaiah Michael (Carrie Underwood and Mike Fisher)

Kit James (Joanna Page and James Thornton)

Logan Lee (Jason Mewes and Jordan Monsanto)

Montgomery Moses Brian (Isla Fisher and Sacha Baron Cohen)

Pauline (Vin Diesel and Paloma Jiménez)

Poppy (Nate Berkus and Jeremiah Brent)

Rocket Zot (Sam Worthington and Lara Bingle)

Rafael (Alec and Hilaria Baldwin)

Ryan (Haylie Duff and Matt Roseberg)

Scarlett May (Molly Sims and Scott Stuber)

Silas Randall (Jessica Biel and Justin Timberlake)

Sistine Sabella (Kevin James and Steffiana de la Cruz)

Violet Moon and Knox Blue (Sarah Shahi and Steve Howey)

Wilder (CaCee Cobb and Donald Faison)

How's this for coming up with a name for your newborn? *The Late Late Show*'s new host James Corden and his wife Julia had a baby girl recently, giving her the name Carey after Julia's maiden name, and during the press rounds it also came out that the couple's first son, Max, was given the middle name McCartney after Sir Paul McCartney. Corden told the story of groveling to Sir Paul to appear on a charity skit show, and said, "I laid it on very thick, telling him, 'People won't die if you do our sketch.' It makes it very difficult for people to say no. He said, 'Bloody hell, James, I've heard some groveling in my time.' I then said, 'That's nothing—if you'd said no, I was going to say I would name my unborn child after you.' To which he said, 'If you promise to do that, I'll do the sketch.' And that's why my son is called Max McCartney Kimberley Corden."

> The Queen's full name is Elizabeth Alexandra Mary Windsor. Her newest great-grandchild's full name is Charlotte Elizabeth Diana Cambridge.

So what do you do if you're a celebrity and you want to keep your baby's name a secret from the press? Well, you could do what Ryan Reynolds and Blake Lively did and simply tell people the wrong name from the start. Last year reports emerged that the couple had called their daughter Violet, like Ben Affleck and Jennifer Garner, but it was all a ruse. Ryan Reynolds said last year of the event and the revealed name: "It's Butternut Squash. No, it's out there. It's James. Everyone knows, and I told everyone who would listen before it was out there that I didn't want to be the first guy screaming it out to the media because, as we know, little girls turn into teenage girls and little teenage girls sometimes scan through the archives and go, 'Why did you do that?'" Fair enough, Ryan, fair enough.

Bizarre celebrity baby names of recent years

Axl (Fergie and Josh Duhamel)

Bear Blaze (Kate Winslet and Ned Rocknroll)

Bingham Hawn (Kate Hudson and Matthew Bellamy, also parents to Ryder)

Blue Ivy (Beyoncé Knowles and Jay Z)

Cosima Violet (Claudia Schiffer and Matthew Vaughn, also parents to Caspar and Clementine)

Cricket Pearl (Busy Philipps and Marc Silverstein—also parents to Birdie Leigh)

Ever Imre (Alanis Morissette and Mario Treadway)

Harper Seven (Victoria and David Beckham—also parents to Brooklyn, Romeo, and Cruz)

Holiday Grace (Harold and Brittany Perrineau)

Ikhyd (M.I.A. and Ben Brewer)

Jagger Jason Blue (Soleil Moon Frye and Jason Goldberg—also
   parents to Sienna Rose)

Kaius Jagger (Rachel Zoe and Roger Berman)

Kahekili Kali (Evangeline Lilly and Norman Kali)

Rainbow Aurora (Holly Madison and Pasquale Rotella)

Rocket Zot (Sam Worthington and Lara Bingle)

Rosalind Arusha Arkadina Altaluna Florence (Uma Thurman and Arpad
   Busson)

Valor (Emile Hirsch)

Busy Philipps recently explained why she named her daughter Cricket
Pearl: "Everyone likes Cricket, Cricket is just the greatest, happiest kid
on the block . . . she's hot in college. Cricket is the coolest girl in school.
She's like the camp counselor that you have a crush on." While the rest
of us might raise an eyebrow or two, we must keep in mind that this is
coming from a woman with a fairly unusual name herself . . .

> Colin Firth doesn't like his name, apparently. He was quoted as
> saying: "Colin is the sort of name you'd give your goldfish for a
> joke. I once saw an episode of *Blackadder* with a dachshund in it
> called Colin. It seemed his name alone was supposed to reduce
> you to fits of laughter."

State differences

What's interesting about US baby name statistics is that there is such
variety in the popularity of names across different states and territories . . .

- The name Gabriel appears as one of the most popular boys' names
  only in Alaska, while the name Emma appears in every single Top 5
  girls' list in the country for the domestic states.

- While the names William and Liam were popular across the board, only parents in Wyoming and Alaska were likely to name their baby boys Wyatt.

- Baby girls were predominantly given names such as Ava, Olivia, or Sophia, except in Maine, where Lillian made the Top 5.

- Dylan was only a Top 5 contender for baby boys in Puerto Rico, and Zoe was only a Top 5 contender for baby girls in District of Columbia.

   The fifth most popular boys' name in North Dakota is currently Owen, even though it was given to only 48 babies.

It seems as though geography can have a major impact on baby-naming decisions, and population density can certainly change the rankings. States with smaller populations, like Wyoming or Vermont, usually have slightly different names making up their Top 5 each year. Wyoming, for example, has Wyatt listed for baby boys, and Brooklyn for baby girls—and these aren't found in many of the other states listed. The reasoning for this is simple: fewer babies born means each baby name chosen carries greater weight. For Liam to make the number one spot in Alaska it needed only 65 parents to choose it; to have the same impact and overtake Noah in Texas, it would need over 2,100. Likewise, only 44 babies were called Emily in Delaware last year, but it still claimed fifth place.

The name with the most baby girls given it in any state was Sophia in California, with over 3,100 registrations. Likewise, for boys it was Noah in California, with roughly 2,800 registrations. The names with the fewest picks but still able to claim top spots were Emma in Vermont and Olivia in Wyoming with 40 baby girls apiece, and Jackson in Wyoming with a mere 34 picks.

So find your state from the lists below—and make sure your baby won't have another 10 Emmas or Noahs in their class!

Top five baby girl names for each state

State	Rank 1	Rank 2	Rank 3	Rank 4	Rank 5
Alabama	Ava	Emma	Olivia	Isabella	Elizabeth
Alaska	Emma	Olivia	Sophia	Aurora	Isabella
Arizona	Sophia	Emma	Mia	Isabella	Olivia
Arkansas	Emma	Olivia	Ava	Harper	Isabella
California	Sophia	Isabella	Emma	Mia	Olivia
Colorado	Olivia	Emma	Sophia	Isabella	Evelyn
Connecticut	Olivia	Emma	Sophia	Isabella	Ava
Delaware	Sophia	Ava	Emma	Olivia	Emily
Dist. of Columbia	Elizabeth	Olivia	Ava	Emma	Zoe
Florida	Isabella	Sophia	Emma	Olivia	Mia
Georgia	Olivia	Ava	Emma	Madison	Isabella
Hawaii	Emma	Mia	Sophia	Aria	Lily
Idaho	Emma	Olivia	Charlotte	Abigail	Harper
Illinois	Olivia	Emma	Sophia	Isabella	Ava
Indiana	Emma	Olivia	Ava	Sophia	Isabella
Iowa	Emma	Olivia	Harper	Ava	Sophia
Kansas	Olivia	Emma	Harper	Ava	Sophia
Kentucky	Emma	Ava	Olivia	Sophia	Isabella
Louisiana	Emma	Ava	Olivia	Sophia	Aubrey
Maine	Emma	Olivia	Charlotte	Isabella	Lillian
Maryland	Olivia	Ava	Emma	Sophia	Abigail
Massachusetts	Emma	Olivia	Isabella	Sophia	Ava
Michigan	Olivia	Emma	Ava	Sophia	Isabella
Minnesota	Olivia	Emma	Evelyn	Ava	Charlotte
Mississippi	Ava	Emma	Olivia	Madison	Aubrey
Missouri	Emma	Olivia	Ava	Sophia	Harper
Montana	Emma	Harper	Sophia	Ava	Emily
Nebraska	Olivia	Emma	Harper	Ava	Sophia

State	Rank 1	Rank 2	Rank 3	Rank 4	Rank 5
Nevada	Emma	Sophia	Isabella	Mia	Olivia
New Hampshire	Olivia	Charlotte	Sophia	Ava	Emma
New Jersey	Sophia	Olivia	Emma	Isabella	Mia
New Mexico	Mia	Sophia	Isabella	Emma	Olivia
New York	Sophia	Olivia	Emma	Isabella	Mia
North Carolina	Ava	Emma	Olivia	Sophia	Isabella
North Dakota	Harper	Emma	Olivia	Ava	Avery
Ohio	Emma	Olivia	Ava	Sophia	Isabella
Oklahoma	Emma	Olivia	Harper	Isabella	Sophia
Oregon	Emma	Olivia	Sophia	Abigail	Isabella
Pennsylvania	Emma	Olivia	Ava	Sophia	Isabella
Puerto Rico	Mia	Valentina	Amanda	Victoria	Kamila
Rhode Island	Olivia	Ava	Emma	Sophia	Isabella
South Carolina	Emma	Ava	Olivia	Madison	Isabella
South Dakota	Harper	Ava	Olivia	Emma	Sophia
Tennessee	Emma	Olivia	Ava	Sophia	Isabella
Texas	Emma	Sophia	Isabella	Mia	Olivia
Utah	Olivia	Emma	Charlotte	Lucy	Harper
Vermont	Emma	Olivia	Sophia	Ava	Abigail
Virginia	Emma	Olivia	Ava	Sophia	Abigail
Washington	Olivia	Emma	Sophia	Ava	Emily
West Virginia	Sophia	Emma	Olivia	Isabella	Ava
Wisconsin	Olivia	Emma	Ava	Evelyn	Sophia
Wyoming	Olivia	Brooklyn	Emma	Abigail	Elizabeth
Other territories	Olivia	Abigail	Chloe	Claire	Mia

Top five baby boy names for each state

State	Rank 1	Rank 2	Rank 3	Rank 4	Rank 5
Alabama	William	James	John	Mason	Elijah
Alaska	Liam	James	Noah	Wyatt	Gabriel
Arizona	Noah	Liam	Alexander	Daniel	Jacob
Arkansas	Mason	William	Noah	Elijah	James
California	Noah	Jacob	Ethan	Daniel	Alexander
Colorado	Liam	Alexander	Noah	William	Logan
Connecticut	Mason	Noah	Alexander	Jacob	Liam
Delaware	Liam	Michael	Mason	Jacob	Logan
Dist. of Columbia	Alexander	William	John	Benjamin	Charles
Florida	Noah	Liam	Jacob	Michael	Mason
Georgia	William	Mason	Noah	James	Jacob
Hawaii	Noah	Liam	Mason	Aiden	Alexander
Idaho	Liam	William	Mason	Oliver	Samuel
Illinois	Noah	Alexander	William	Michael	Liam
Indiana	Liam	Noah	Elijah	Mason	William
Iowa	Liam	William	Mason	Noah	Owen
Kansas	William	Liam	Noah	Mason	Jackson
Kentucky	William	Elijah	James	Mason	Noah
Louisiana	Mason	Liam	Noah	William	Elijah
Maine	Liam	Mason	Owen	Benjamin	Jackson
Maryland	Noah	Liam	William	Mason	Michael
Massachusetts	Benjamin	William	Jacob	Liam	Michael
Michigan	Liam	Noah	Mason	Carter	Jacob
Minnesota	Henry	William	Liam	Owen	Benjamin
Mississippi	William	James	John	Elijah	Mason
Missouri	Liam	William	Mason	Noah	Elijah
Montana	William	Benjamin	Mason	Liam	Noah

State	Rank 1	Rank 2	Rank 3	Rank 4	Rank 5
Nebraska	Liam	Mason	Noah	William	Henry
Nevada	Noah	Daniel	Ethan	Anthony	Jayden
New Hampshire	Jacob	Mason	Jackson	Benjamin	Owen
New Jersey	Michael	Matthew	Joseph	Liam	Daniel
New Mexico	Noah	Liam	Elijah	Jacob	Daniel
New York	Jacob	Liam	Ethan	Michael	Noah
North Carolina	William	Mason	Noah	Liam	Elijah
North Dakota	Liam	Mason	William	Noah	Owen
Ohio	Liam	Mason	Noah	William	Carter
Oklahoma	William	Mason	Liam	Noah	Elijah
Oregon	Liam	Henry	Noah	Benjamin	Logan
Pennsylvania	Mason	Liam	Noah	Michael	Jacob
Puerto Rico	Sebastian	Ian	Dylan	Jayden	Luis
Rhode Island	Mason	Liam	Benjamin	Logan	Jacob
South Carolina	William	James	Mason	Noah	Jackson
South Dakota	Liam	Lincoln	Logan	Noah	Benjamin
Tennessee	William	Mason	Elijah	James	Noah
Texas	Noah	Jacob	Daniel	Liam	Jayden
Utah	William	Liam	James	Oliver	Lincoln
Vermont	Liam	Mason	Oliver	Carter	William
Virginia	William	Liam	Mason	Noah	James
Washington	Liam	Benjamin	Alexander	Noah	William
West Virginia	Mason	Liam	Hunter	Noah	Colton
Wisconsin	Mason	Liam	William	Logan	Henry
Wyoming	Jackson	Mason	William	Wyatt	Liam
Other territories	Daniel	Noah	David	Liam	Aiden

Baby Names 2016

A .GIF recently made the rounds online, which flashed each state's top pick for baby girls and baby boys for every single year since 1960. A fun new way to look at baby name statistics, it also brought to light a new way for parents to choose their own baby names. These maps, created by the website Deadspin.com, gave parents an opportunity to see how the name they're considering impacts not only the nation, but their own specific state. It also allowed parents to see whether the name they grew up with was as popular as they thought it was—stories of being one of seven Jennifers in a class during the 1970s and 1980s aren't exaggerated. It really was the most popular name for baby girls in each of the 50 states from 1973 to 1978—a fact that is easily traced using the maps provided.

> An Icelandic girl won a 15-year battle in 2013 to keep her birth name after authorities originally deemed "Blaer" too masculine for a girl. As of now she is free to use her real name, which means "light breeze," on her passport and at school.

2 What does 2016 hold for baby names?

Will these trends continue?

Looking forward to 2016, we predict the same trends for choosing either old-fashioned or unique names will continue. The Top 10 names will probably go largely unchanged for both boys and girls if last year is any indication, but we may become even more varied in the names we give our children, and not just stick to the same safe names. There may also be a backlash against very popular names, as parents opt not to give their child the same name as four or five of their potential school friends. As parents grow more globally aware and the demographics of North America change, we may see more culturally and ethnically diverse names appearing in these lists, such as Cosette and Zeik.

The 100-year rule doesn't seem to be failing, and names that were in the 1916 Top 100 will likely appear in 2016 as well. The 50-year rule is also in effect in 2016, and names that were popular 50 years ago are either extremely unpopular with today's parents (think Patricia, Jeffrey, and Susan), or used because they're considered so timeless they've never really gone out of style (William and Michael definitely fit this mold).

Top 10 names from 1916		Top 10 names from 1966	
Boys	**Girls**	**Boys**	**Girls**
1. John	1. Mary	1. Michael	1. Lisa
2. William	2. Helen	2. David	2. Kimberly
3. James	3. Dorothy	3. James	3. Mary
4. Robert	4. Margaret	4. John	4. Michelle
5. Joseph	5. Ruth	5. Robert	5. Karen
6. Charles	6. Mildred	6. William	6. Susan
7. George	7. Anna	7. Mark	7. Patricia
8. Edward	8. Elizabeth	8. Richard	8. Tammy
9. Frank	9. Frances	9. Jeffrey	9. Angela
10. Thomas	10. Virginia	10. Thomas	10. Jennifer

For girls' names, it's certain that those ending in -a will continue to dominate the Top 20 for at least a while longer. There are currently 10 names in that group that end in -a for 2015, constituting exactly half, and of those ten, five moved up places from the year before (Emma, Olivia, Sofia, Amelia, and Victoria); three stayed put (Isabella, Ava, and Mia), and only two moved down (Sophia and Ella). There's also Harper in 11th place, which sounds as though it could easily end in -a too. Other similar-sounding names in the Top 20 include Emily, Avery, Chloe, and Aubrey, which presumably means that names ending in -y or -ie sounds will also stick around for a few more years. To top it all off, two of the Top 20 names are so similar they're essentially the same name with a different spelling: Sophia and Sofia. In fact, there are only five names that don't fit into one of the -a or -y/ie molds—Abigail, Madison, Charlotte, Elizabeth, and Evelyn—and all of those have also grown considerably in popularity over the last 10 years.

With boys' names, trends are a little harder to predict. There are definitely names that sound very similar in the Top 20, such as Mason, Ethan, Logan, Aiden, Jayden, and Jackson, and a few -ah/-er names (Noah, Alexander, and Elijah). Also, names beginning with J are pretty big right now (Jacob, James, Jayden, Jackson, and Joseph), and if you really want to dig deep, a great many of the names in the boys' list are straight from the Bible: Alexander, Benjamin, Daniel, David, Elijah, Ethan, Jacob, James, Joseph, Matthew, Michael, and of course Noah. There is a great deal more shuffling in the ranks going on in the boys' names list, with huge differences over the last 10 years—especially in names listed outside the Top 10. Therefore, it's probable that parents expecting baby boys in 2016 will be following trends like traditional or religious names instead.

Most popular Biblical names of all time

According to data from the Social Security Administration, these are the most popular names taken from the Bible since they began keeping records:

1. Jacob	6. Matthew
2. Ethan	7. Elijah
3. Noah	8. James
4. Michael	9. Benjamin
5. Daniel	10. Joshua

Baby Names 2016

In general, American parents prefer to give their children full-length names rather than shortened versions or nicknames, and this trend doesn't show much sign of stopping. Elizabeth (14th) appears higher up the charts than Ellie (55th), and Robert (61st) is much higher than Bobby (752nd). We see this over and over again: Jacob (ranked fourth) is more popular than Jake (190th), Abigail (8th) is higher up than Abby (389th) or Abbie (791st), and Eve (460th) is much further down the charts than Evelyn (16th). However, it must be said that in some cases picking short versions of traditional names is on the rise. The name Ella (17th last year), for example, is a shortened version of Eleanor (78th), while Leo (97th) is a shortened version of either Leon (321st) or Leonardo (114th); both of these shorter names are clearly more popular than the longer ones. In Europe this is particularly fashionable right now, so perhaps in 2016 we will see much more of this trend, and even a few surprises.

What about the theory that you can tell the political leanings of a family by the name a parent gives their child? Well, in a study conducted at the University of Chicago last year, researchers noticed that parents with more liberal leanings tended to give names that contained softer sounds, like -a and -l. Examples included Ella, Sophia, Liam, and Lena. However, parents with more conservative views chose names with harder or stronger sounds, like -d, -b, -t, and -k. Examples of those names were Kurt, Kim, Donald, and Bryce. However, the researchers also noted that the level of education each parent obtained had as much of an impact as their political viewpoint: well-educated parents chose unusual names, but with traditional spellings (such as Atticus or Finnegan), and less-educated parents chose traditional names with more unusual spellings (such as Andruw instead of Andrew). So, while it's true that politicians and political stances definitely affect baby name trends, it might have quite a lot to do with levels of education as well.

Predicted 2016 Top 10 baby names

Boys		Girls	
1. Noah	6. Ethan	1. Emma	6. Elizabeth
2. Liam	7. Aiden	2. Olivia	7. Mia
3. Jacob	8. Alexander	3. Sophia	8. Ava
4. Mason	9. Jayden	4. Isabella	9. Abigail
5. William	10. Michael	5. Charlotte	10. Madison

2016 events

Other influences on the names parents choose in 2016 may come from the worlds of sport, politics, and celebrity. In 2016 there are a couple of major sporting events, and athletes who perform well at them will no doubt become inspirational for new parents. While there isn't much this year to excite us domestically, other than the usual run of baseball's World Series, college basketball's March Madness, and of course football's Superbowl, the rest of the world (and some keen fans here in the USA) will be watching the international events such as the Summer Olympics and Paralympics, UEFA Euro 2016, the Tour de France, and various tennis competitions such as Wimbledon and the US Open.

> A new law passed in 2014 in Sonora, Mexico, states parents cannot give their babies names that are defined by authorities as "derogatory, pejorative, discriminatory or lacking in meaning." Names on the published list include Twitter, Burger King, Hitler, Facebook, Harry Potter, Escroto (Spanish for scrotum), and Batman.

There is a chance that not only sports stars themselves, but also the names they choose for their own children might prove influential. It wouldn't be the first time: after it was discovered that beach volleyball legend Kerri Walsh-Jennings was pregnant during her 2012 Olympic gold medal-winning run in London, there was much interest in what she would name her baby. It turned out to be Scout Margery, after the character in *To Kill A Mockingbird*, and 137 sets of parents immediately followed Walsh-Jennings's lead and chose that name for their new daughters the same year.

There is a history of successful athletes creating baby name trends: Jackie Robinson, the first African-American baseball player to play professionally and one of the great legends of the sport, increased the popularity of both the name Jack (for boys) and Jackie (for girls) during the peak of his fame in the US. He can be credited, in large part, for the continuous popularity of these names even in the 21st century—particularly after the film based on his life, *42: The True Story of an American Legend*, came out a few years ago and brought new attention to his story.

> When Pope Francis I was elected a few years ago, there was a flurry of parents choosing to honor him. The name Francis jumped nearly 100 places last year alone and Frances (for baby girls) also moved up 70 spots. In fact, Francis is now the most popular name for baby boys in Italy.

2016 is predicted to be a stormy year for politics, with the general election bringing in a new President and Vice President. At the time of writing, Hillary Clinton and Ted Cruz have both thrown their hats into the ring, although this will no doubt change the closer to Election Day we get. Politicians have a hazy history of influencing baby names—it's not true to say that children are frequently named after presidents or prime ministers, but there are exceptions. President Barack Obama's name has yet to enter the Top 1,000 in the US, with fewer than 10 baby boys named that last year, but Vice President Joe Biden has seen his name increase in popularity during his time in office: the name Joseph has popped back up to position 20 after a spell further down the charts, and looks set for a good comeback.

President Barack Obama's daughters are named Malia and Sasha, and the name Malia jumped a whopping 350 places in 2008, the year he was first elected. Sasha, which was already fairly common, also jumped a further 100. Now that the President's term is almost over, his daughters' names are also fading away—Sasha is in its lowest position in a decade, and Malia is also falling fast. When British Prime Minister David Cameron's baby girl was named Florence Rose Endellion in 2010, the media went wild and a flurry of parents in the UK started choosing the name Florence for their baby girls. In fact, it jumped an astonishing 26 places the year she was born, and 144 overall in the last 10 years. The unusual middle name of Endellion is a nod to the village of St Endellion in Cornwall, where she was born during her parents' vacation, three weeks earlier than anticipated.

Bizarre names from the UK

According to parenting website Bounty, parents in the UK are developing extremely unusual tastes in baby names. Last year, website users registered the following names for their children, among others: Prosper, Perseus, Luck, Kassius, Lohan, Bramwell, and Denton for boys; and Tea, Vogue, Tru, Pinky, Phoenix, Purdy, Pepsi, Peppa, and Nirvana for girls.

There's always the outside chance of a regal influence. Queen Elizabeth, who will be 90 in 2016, is now Britain's longest-reigning monarch, since she surpassed Queen Victoria. She has now been on the throne longer than the 63 years and seven months Queen Victoria reigned. It's possible, although unlikely, that she will choose to step down for son Prince Charles, sparking renewed interest in both her name and his. The name Elizabeth is in 10th place in the US right now, and has held firm in the Top 20 for over 50 years. Victoria is in 19th place, and it too has been about the same place for over a decade. Both are considered such classic names that it's hard to imagine them disappearing entirely.

Banned names around the world

@—China

Akuma (meaning "devil")—Japan

Anus—Denmark

Chow Tow (meaning "smelly head")—Malaysia

Dalmata (meaning "Dalmatian")—Italy

Gesher (meaning "bridge")—Norway

Monkey—Denmark

Ovnis (meaning "UFO")—Portugal

Q—Sweden

Sor Chai (meaning "insane")—Malaysia

Stompy—Germany

Significant dates in 2016

So, what else might influence baby names this year? Well, there are a number of significant anniversaries coming up that might alert new parents to some names they haven't come across before. In 2016 it will be Prince William and Kate Middleton's 5th wedding anniversary and 25 years since Tim Berners-Lee first developed the concept of the World Wide Web. It's been 30 years since Andrew Lloyd Webber's musical *Phantom of the Opera* hit the stage, and the 200th anniversary of the writing of the carol *Silent Night* by Josef Mohr and Franz X. Gruber. It will also mark 150 years since the publication of *Crime and Punishment* by

Fyodor Dostoevsky, 200 years since Jane Austen's *Emma* was published, and 500 years since Thomas More's *Utopia* made its first appearance.

2016 will be Charlotte Brontë's 200th birthday, Beatrix Potter's and H.G. Wells's 150th birthdays, 75 years since the death of Virginia Woolf, and sweet little clone Dolly the Sheep's 20th birthday (although she won't be around to eat any birthday cake, bless her).

> Tahra Dactyl, who made headlines for her name after being featured in a local newspaper article recently, must have parents with a sense of humor . . . or a serious interest in paleontology.

What does all of this mean for baby names though? Well, usually when significant anniversaries come around there is a lot of media attention and the people involved in the original event are featured prominently. Don't be surprised, therefore, if names linked to these anniversaries start becoming popular. For example, Will and Kate's wedding anniversary is in April, along with Princess Charlotte's first birthday, and this means their names will appear everywhere at that time. After the surge of baby Georges in 2013, it's assured that these anniversaries will have an influence on baby names chosen around April. Take a look at the anniversary names above and see if any of them will work for your own baby's birth day.

The influence of the entertainment industry

As always, pop culture will probably be the most prominent influence on baby names in the coming year. Celebrities expecting new arrivals from the celebrity stork include Keira Knightley, Jaime King, and sisters Emily and Zooey Deschanel—which must be incredibly exciting if you're lucky enough to be part of the Deschanel clan. If the choices of names these celebrities make are particularly noteworthy, they may well influence the choices made by the general population.

Baby Names 2016

The Huffington Post released an article recently that broke down the names chosen by celebrities into common categories. Of the 50+ names they analyzed, every single one fell into one of 10 fields: authors (e.g. Harper, David Beckham's daughter), cities (Tennessee, Reese Witherspoon's son), colors (Blue Ivy, Beyoncé's daughter), comic book characters (Kal-El, Nicolas Cage's son), countries (Moroccan, Mariah Carey's son), fruits (Clementine, Ethan Hawke's daughter), New York boroughs (Bronx, Ashlee Simpson's son), music icons (Louis, Sandra Bullock's son), old Hollywood (Ava, Jeremy Renner's daughter), and Shakespearean characters (Exton, Robert Downey Jr.'s son). It's quite impressive that *all* the celebrity names they analyzed slotted so neatly into these 10 categories!

Expected new arrivals

Carey Mulligan and Marcus Mumford

Kanye West and Kim Kardashian

Ashlee Simpson and Evan Ross

Lena Headey

Jennifer Love Hewitt and Brian Hallisay

Leighton Meester and Adam Brody

Jaime King and Kyle Newman

Zooey Deschanel and Jacob Pechenik

Lily Cole and Kwame Ferreira

Kristin Cavallari and Jay Cutler

Max Greenfield and Tess Sanchez

Katherine Jenkins and Andrew Levitas

Andy Roddick and Brooklyn Decker

The year 2016 looks set to continue a recent pattern of remakes, reboots and sequels. Upcoming movies in 2016 include *Finding Dory*, a sequel to Disney/Pixar's *Finding Nemo*; a new *Tarzan* film; a sequel to *Alice in Wonderland*; *Ghostbusters III*; and yet another *Resident Evil* movie. There will also be the usual sprinkling of superhero films to wade through, such as *Batman v. Superman: Dawn of Justice*, and *X-Men: Apocalypse*.

Names that are featured in these films stand a good shot of influencing baby names if past years are anything to go by. *Finding Dory*, for example, could spike added interest in the name Dory—already a fairly popular name in some states. *Tarzan* has the potential to influence the name Jane—which hasn't been that popular in recent memory and is due for a comeback. Also, *Alice in Wonderland* and *Resident Evil*'s sequels could help launch Alice into the USA's Top 50, as it's been making a slow but steady climb in recent years to position 97.

Bruce Wayne, the brooding star of the Batman franchise, is an unlikely influence on baby names in 2016, just like his counterpart Clark Kent—a.k.a. Superman—although it's interesting that both characters have two names that could work as either forenames or surnames. Those sneaky masked crime fighters. Both Bruce and Clark have had a small surge in popularity over the last few years, but unfortunately none of the four names listed are anywhere near the top of the charts at the moment. As there has been a run of Batman and Superman-themed flicks in recent years, it's unlikely that this particular sequel will make much of a difference . . . but you never know.

When remakes of old films are released, it's a great chance to analyze baby names over a period of time. You can look back at when the original versions were released and see how trends were affected at the time. For example, when 20th Century Fox and George Lucas released the original *Star Wars* movies in 1977, 1980, and 1983, the name Luke immediately moved up in the charts. In fact, between 1976 and 1980, the name jumped an unprecedented 130 places to end up in the Top 100—something that had never happened before. It has continued to be a popular choice and last year it appeared in position 28 for the first time. After the new version, *Star Wars VII: The Force Awakens*, comes out in late 2015, it may climb higher still. Likewise, the name Leia had never appeared in any Top 1,000 charts before 1977, but suddenly popped up in 1978 and 1980—coinciding with two movie release dates. Last year the name was given to 605 baby girls and is definitely due for a comeback.

Fifty Shades of . . . baby names?

One of the more unusual trends to have emerged from books and movies in recent years was the impact of the *Fifty Shades of Grey* series, by E.L. James. The books, which focused on a highly charged sexual relationship between a young woman and a wealthy businessman, were launched as a movie franchise in 2015, which means the names of characters in the series started popping up again. Between 2011 and 2013, when the books were published in the USA, Anastasia jumped a staggering 120 places. Even the name Grey (normally spelled "Gray" over here), was given to 205 babies last year. With the potential release of the second installment, 2016 looks as though it will pull focus back to the names again, and its impact will reach even further.

TV series set to air in 2016 include a new series of *The Walking Dead*, the popular drama about a zombie apocalypse. The original series starred Brit actor Andrew Lincoln, and his last name's appearance in the charts has been significantly impacted since the first series aired. Lincoln has risen about 400 places in the last ten years, and Maggie, the name of another character, has stayed in the Top 250. Any new series of this program could have the same, or similar, impact from the names of its characters or actors.

Other popular TV programs set to air this year include *Game of Thrones*, *Empire*, *Arrow*, *Nashville*, *The Blacklist*, and further series of *Doctor Who*, *Jane the Virgin*, *Orange is the New Black*, and *How to Get Away with Murder*. As some of you may be heavily pregnant, putting your feet up and watching some TV, you may be influenced by some of these shows. What about Tyrion (Lannister; *Game of Thrones*), Oliver (Queen; *Arrow*), Rayna (James; *Nashville*), Raymond "Red" (Reddington; *The Blacklist*), Clara (Oswin Oswald; *Doctor Who*), Jane (Villanueva; *Jane the Virgin*), Piper (Chapman; *Orange is the New Black*), Wes (Gibbons; *How to Get Away with Murder*) . . . or even Cookie (Lyon; *Empire*)?

> The name Marnie, from the HBO drama *Girls*, is seeing a bit of a comeback. Derived from a Hebrew term meaning "rejoiced," it has been searched for seven times as often since the fifth season came out. It was last seen in the charts in the 1960s, when Hitchcock's film *Marnie* was released, and was chosen by singer Lily Allen for her youngest daughter Marnie Rose in 2013. Also, according to the users of parenting website BabyCenter, Shoshanna has risen by 67% in popularity.

HBO's *Game of Thrones* has had an astonishing influence on baby names since its inception. The most unusual name to have emerged is Khaleesi, which is technically equivalent to Queen or Duchess on the show, and used as a royal title for the character of Daenerys Targaryen. Never used as a baby name prior to 2011, there were 368 baby girls given it last year. Other popular names from the show are Arya, Tyrion, Brienne, and Jon.

Reality series will continue to influence our decisions—especially after Kim Kardashian with singer/rapper Kanye West named their daughter North (also known as Nori, which is a lot cuter) and expect baby number two in late 2015. The name North was only given to 13 babies last year and probably won't trend any higher, but apparently it is now one of the most popular search terms for baby names out there. However, Nori could definitely see a rise in popularity as it's less obscure—although

2016 Rising Stars

Boys	Girls
Clark	Alice
Christian	Clara
Lincoln	Cookie
Oliver	Dory
Red	Jane
Reign	Khaleesi
Tyrion	Marnie
Wes	Piper

it's a shame it doesn't start with a "K"! Sister Kourtney's children are Mason Dash, Penelope Scotland and Reign Aston, and even the SSA has admitted that the astonishing rise of the name Mason can be attributed to her, saying a few years ago after it hit rank number two, "Some may attribute this year's rise to number two to reality TV star Kourtney Kardashian's son." It's quite impressive that a single baby can have that much impact on the baby-naming world, but then we are talking about the Kardashians . . .

Fictional characters with hidden meanings in their names

Bran Stark (*Game of Thrones*)—Bran is an old Irish name from the word for "raven"

Darth Vader (*Star Wars*)—darth is related to "dark" or "death"; vader is Dutch for "father"

Frodo Baggins (*Lord of the Rings*)—from *fród*, meaning "wise by experience" in Old English

Katniss Everdeen (*The Hunger Games*)—from the katniss plant, meaning "archer" in Latin

Nyota Uhura (*Star Trek*)—from the Swahili term for "star freedom"

Remus Lupin (*Harry Potter*)—Remus was an ancient Roman orphan raised by wolves; *lupinus* is the Latin word for "wolfish"

3 How to choose a name

Top tips on choosing a name

- **Fall in love with the name(s) you've chosen.** If you plough through this book and none of them jump off the page at you, then you probably haven't found the right one yet. Pick a name that makes you smile because, if you love it, hopefully your child will too.

- **Don't listen to other people.** Sometimes, grandparents and friends will offer baby-naming "advice" to you, which may not always be welcome. If you've got your heart set on a name, keep it a secret until after the birth. Trust your own instincts and remember: no one will really care once they see your baby. Its name will simply be its name.

- **Find a name with meaning.** Having a name that has a back story helps your child understand their significance in the world, so whether you name them after a religious saint or prophet, an important political figure, or a hero in a Greek tragedy, ensure they know where their name came from. They may just be inspired to be as great as their namesake.

- **Have fun.** Picking out names should be fun. Laughing at the ones you'd never dream of choosing can really help you narrow it down to the ones you would. You can also experiment with different spellings, pronunciations, or variations of names you like, or go to places where you might feel inspired.

- **Expand your mind.** Don't rule out the weird ones just yet! As a teenager I went to school with a girl named Siam. Her parents had conceived her on a honeymoon trip to Thailand and gave her the country's old name as a result. She loved growing up and having an unusual name, as I'm sure Penelope Scotland (Kourtney Kardashian and Scott Disick's daughter) and Milan (Shakira and Gerard Piqué's son) do too. Also, don't be afraid to play around with spellings and pronunciations, even if the results are a little less than conformist. The name Madison, for example, could be spelled Maddison, Madyson, Maddiesun, although you might want to be careful you don't saddle your child with a name that's impossible to spell, pronounce, or fit onto a passport application form.

  > The shortest baby names are only two letters long (Al, Ed,
  > Jo, and Ty), but the longest could be any length imaginable.
  > Popular 11 letter-long names include Bartholomew, Christopher,
  > Constantine, and Maximillian.

- **Try it out.** While you're pregnant, talk to your baby and address it using a variety of your favorite names to see if it responds. There are numerous stories of names being chosen because the baby kicked when it was called Charlie or Aisha, but was suspiciously silent when it was called Dexter or Mildred, so see if it has a preference! Try writing names down and sticking them to your fridge, practicing a few signatures, or saying one out loud enough times to see if you ever get sick of it.

- **Do NOT pick the name of an ex.** No matter how lovely Brad Pitt thought the name "Jennifer" was, it's doubtful Angelina Jolie would have allowed him to use it for one of their daughters. The same is probably true of picking the names of your friends' exes. They are unlikely to thank you if they have to say a name they loathe repeatedly. Just steer clear of any names you know will have problems for other people, paying particular attention to your partner and loved ones.

- **What if you can't agree?** This is probably the trickiest problem in the baby-naming process to solve. It's wise to research a number of names you and your partner are both interested in and make a point of discussing your reasons for liking or disliking them long before the baby is due to be born. The labor and delivery room is probably not the best place to argue as you'll both be tired, emotional, and at least one of you will be in pain. Avoid sticking to your guns on a name one of you really isn't happy with because it might lead to resentment down the road, with your baby caught in the middle. You could try compromising and picking two middle names so you both have a name in there you love, or you could each have five names you're allowed to "veto" but no more. Whichever way you go about it, it is important that you both eventually agree on the name you are giving your baby, even if it means losing out on the one you've had your heart set on for a while.

- **Apps.** With all the new technology literally at our fingertips, how about putting some of it to good use? There are hundreds of new apps for smartphones and tablets that promise to help you narrow down the endless lists of potential names to the one you'll love.

Think to the future

One important aspect of naming your child is thinking ahead to their future. Will the name you've chosen stand the test of time? Will names popular in 2016 remain popular in 2040? Will they be able to confidently enter a room and give a crucial business presentation with an awkward or

> ### Popular names from the past
>
> | Boys | Girls |
> |------|-------|
> | Abraham | Agatha |
> | Arthur | Bertha |
> | Edmund | Clara |
> | Emmett | Edith |
> | Franklin | Gladys |
> | Gilbert | Mabel |
> | Jasper | Pearl |
> | Neville | Theodora |
> | Percival | Wilhelmina |
> | Vincent | Winifred |

unpronounceable name? Will they be able to hand their business card over to a potential client without that client looking bemused every time? Even sooner, can they survive the potential minefields of elementary school and junior high with a name that could easily be shortened to something embarrassing?

Would you want to try catching criminals as Sheriff Apple Blossom or have other politicians take you seriously with a name like Senator Fortune Scarlett? You don't want to give your child a name that they just cannot live with for the rest of their lives, so make your choice based on what's appropriate for an adult as well as a child. To make this easier you might want to choose a longer name that can be shortened or extended as your child desires.

If your child doesn't like the name you've given them because their first and last names make a funny combination, they may choose to use just their first name professionally as an adult. A colleague of mine goes by "Shiney" only—omitting her last name on business cards and emails because it's a euphemism for male genitalia.

> One woman in Ohio legally changed her name last year because she felt her new name lived up to her personality more. Sheila Ranea Crabtree officially became Sexy Crabtree in 2014.

The topical website Buzzfeed.com recently ran an article on funny names of real people whose names were also reflective of their professions.

Examples included Brad Slaughter, who was a meat manager at a supermarket; Les MacBurney, a firefighter; and Sue Yoo, a lawyer. At the same time another article appeared, listing all the reasons why having an unusual name was a hassle—examples given were not ever being able to find your name on novelty souvenirs, coffee shop baristas not knowing how to spell or pronounce your name for your order, and other people giving you "fun, new" nicknames because they can't be bothered with your normal one. Obviously these are just funny articles and not meant to be taken seriously, but they are things to consider when thinking long-term about your baby's name.

Names that should've been banned, but weren't

Anna Banana Baptista

Benson and Hedges (twins)

Ford Mustang

Hairy Berry

Kaos

Laxative Thomas

Masport and Mower (twins)

Midnight Chardonnay

Number 16 Bus Shelter

Spiral Cicada

Superman (changed from 4Real)

Violence

Stereotypes—true or false?

Will the name you choose actually affect your child's life? Will names that seem clever make your child brainier? Will names with positive meanings make your child into a happier person? The answer is . . . possibly.

One thing you should consider is how your child's name will be perceived by the outside world. Typically, judgments are passed on a person before they are met, and made purely based on their name, such as at job interviews or in school. A survey of 3,000 teachers found that 49% of them make assumptions about their pupils based on their names alone. Topping the "naughty" charts were Callum, Connor, and Jack for boys; and Chelsea, Courtney, and Chardonnay for girls. On the other hand, the names in the "clever" category were Alexander, Adam, and Christopher for boys; and Elizabeth, Charlotte, and Emma for girls.

Inspirational names		Aspirational names	
Destiny	Joy	Armani	Ferrari
Happy	Peace	Aston	Jaguar
Heaven	Serenity	Bugatti	Mercedes
Hope	Unique	Chanel	Porsche
Innocence	Unity	Dolce	Prada

Some experts believe that parents who choose inspirational names for their offspring (Destiny, Serenity, Unique) or names of products they would like to own (Armani, Jaguar, Mercedes) are projecting a future onto their child for them to aspire to, and therefore help shape their child's life. However, there's absolutely no evidence that this actually works!

Research has also indicated that there are certain names more likely to provoke strong responses in people than others. A study analyzed the number of stickers given to children as rewards for good behavior. Children named Abigail and Jacob are more likely to be praised for being well behaved than children named Beth and Josh, and children who do not shorten their name or go by nicknames are more likely to be better behaved, too.

Ivy League names	
Alcott	Graydon
Arthur	Katherine
Beatrice	Martha
Caroline	Robert
Charles	Victoria

However, personality and character have a far greater influence than name alone and, after a while, a name becomes just a name.

> Actor Jeremy Sisto took over a month to name his newborn son in 2012, eventually settling on the dubious "Bastian Kick." He claims he and his wife "didn't want to rush into anything."

> A recent university study suggests that names are particularly important for language development in early childhood. Apparently, a child's name is one of the first words they can identify (probably from all that cooing into the cot that goes on when they're born), and they use it to learn how to construct and deconstruct sentences. Their name anchors the sentence spoken to them, enabling them to pick out other familiar words and sounds and put them all together to identify the meaning of the entire thing. Brainy stuff!

Quirky names

There are lots of advantages to having a quirky name. For one thing, your child's name will never be forgotten by other people, and if they do something influential with their life their name could become an inspiration for other parents. On the other hand, a quirky name often requires a quirky personality. If you don't think your genes could stand up to a name like Satchel or Kerensa, perhaps it's time to think of one a little more run-of-the-mill.

A quirky name often says more about the parents than the child, and their own personalities may affect the personality of their child in a significant way. A conventional family that names their baby John will probably find he becomes a conventional child, whereas a quirky family that names their baby Zanzibar will also find he develops a quirky personality. The name itself is not the leading factor; it's the quirky or conventional behavior encouraged by the parents who chose the name that's important.

Children who are told they have inherited an ancestor's name or are named after an influential character from history seem to be more driven and focused than children who are told disappointingly, "We just liked the sound of it." As a parent, therefore, it seems it's okay to pick an unusual name if you have a story or reason behind it. So naming your child Atticus (after Atticus Finch from Harper Lee's *To Kill A Mockingbird*, known for being a strong and moral character), or even Harper (like the Beckhams did), may not be a bad idea. . .

Names that sound "clever"

Abner

Cassidy

Haley

Penelope

Portia

Shanahan

Todd

Ulysses

Washington

Wylie

However, be warned: there is also new research from baby website Bounty which says that as many as one in five parents regrets their choice of baby name. Of the 3,000 parents interviewed, 20% said they no longer thought the unusual choice of spelling or pronunciation was appropriate. Around 8% said they were tired of people mispronouncing their child's name, and 10% thought the novelty of the original pick had worn off. They also said they would now pick a new name which had not occurred to them or been an option before.

One possible way to avoid potential regret or humiliation is to do what website Nameberry recommends, and that's to download the Social Security Administration's hard data on baby names from last year, and scour the names down at the bottom of the lists for inspiration. You are likely to find a wealth of unusual and currently unpopular names there, but it's comforting to know that your child won't be the only one in the world with that name. Suggestions from last year's data include Aneka, Dollie, Lynea, Retta, and Zeya for girls; and Blair, Hernando, Olly, Rolf, and Yogi for boys.

While avoiding any kind of possible connection to a fictional character is nigh on impossible, you can help make things easier for your child by educating them about their namesake and encouraging them to read more about them. Stay up-to-date with new cartoons and children's characters in 2016 to prepare both yourself and your child for preschool and childhood. That way they can be proud of their name and have ammunition if things get rough in the schoolyard.

Controversial names adopted by real people

Adolf Hitler
Beelzebub
Desdemona
Hannibal Lecter
Himmler
Jezebel
Lucifer
Mussolini
Stalin
Voldemort

Cartoon characters named after real people

Yogi Bear (named after baseball player Yogi Berra)

Buzz Lightyear (named after astronaut Buzz Aldrin)

Alvin, Simon, and Theodore Chipmunk (named after record executives)

Garfield (named after creator Jim Davis's grandfather)

Calvin and Hobbes (named after John Calvin [theologian] and Thomas Hobbes [philosopher])

Rock Lee (from *Naruto*, named after Bruce Lee)

Jimmy Neutron (named after the scientist James Chadwick, whose nickname was Jimmy Neutron)

Oscar (from *Cerebus*, named after writer Oscar Wilde)

Homer, Marge, Lisa, and Maggie Simpson (named after creator Matt Groening's family members)

Teenage Mutant Ninja Turtles (all named after Renaissance painters: Raphael, Michelangelo, Donatello, and Leonardo)

Masculine vs feminine

How do we define what makes a name masculine or feminine? Well, it may be to do with the sounds the letters create, either when written down or spoken aloud. Harder-sounding combinations (-ter, -it, -ld) tend to be found in masculine names, and softer-sounding combinations (-ie, -ay, -la) are more associated with feminine names. You therefore end up with Sophia, Joanie, and Bella, and Harold, Walter, David, and Oscar. If you're planning on choosing a feminine-sounding name, approach with caution: recent research suggests that girls who are given particularly "girly" names—think Tiana, Kayla, and Isabella—are much more likely to misbehave when they reach school age. These "feminine" girls were also far less likely to choose subjects at school like math and science, while their sisters with more masculine names—such as Morgan, Alexis, and Ashley—were encouraged to excel in these courses.

Gold digger names

According to a survey by background check website DirtSearch.org, these names are supposedly more likely to belong to "gold diggers":

1. Jennifer
2. Jessica
3. Michelle
4. Lisa
5. Ashley

6. Amanda
7. Melissa
8. Stephanie
9. Nicole
10. Angela

Nowadays, names are becoming more androgynous and loads of names appear in both boys' and girls' lists: Madison, Riley, Hayden, and, of course, Alex—some form of which appears in the Top 100 for both boys and girls every year. Therefore, if you want a more gender-neutral name for your new arrival, you won't be alone.

But what about your own gender? Does the fact you're a man or woman mean you are more likely to pick certain names for your child? Well, it looks like this isn't the case, but there might be an element of truth to it. Apparently, mothers are prone to picking names that are similar to, or exactly the same as, their maiden name, if they got rid of it when they got married. This system allows a mother to pass on a part of their own lineage, as well as the father's. A lot of celebrities do this too, allowing a child to either use their middle name as an additional last name, or ignore it altogether. Either way, it ensures the famous mom's name gets to stick around a bit longer!

Another recent study by baby website Bounty found that mothers tend to win the argument over who gets to pick the final name of a newborn, with four in ten moms ignoring the choices selected by dads, and one in ten dads just simply backing down. However, four in ten couples don't make the final decision until after the baby is born, and a third will argue about it before settling—but hey, at least they're talking about it!

> One soccer-obsessed father decided to name his newborn son after not just one of the players from his local team, but all fourteen of them. UK Burnley fans Stephen and Amanda Preston registered their son's birth in 2011 with the name Jensen Jay Alexander Bikey Carlisle Duff Elliot Fox Iwelumo Marney Mears Paterson Thompson Wallace Preston. Baby Jensen, as he's known, was taken to his first Burnley soccer match at just eight days old.

Nicknames

Nicknames are unavoidable. They can range from the common—Mike from Michael, Sam from Samantha—to the trendy, funny, or downright insulting. Don't be put off though if the name you love has an unfortunate nickname associated with it—if you don't encourage the use of nicknames, chances are that they won't stick. Another way to avoid embarrassing nicknames is to select one for your child that you actually like so that others don't even get a mention. Call your daughter Elizabeth by the name Liz,

Bizarre baby names from around the country

Boys	Girls
Aero	Ace
Burger	Kaixin
Donathan	Leeloo
Espn	Monalisa
Haven'T	Rogue
Kix	Sesame
Pawk	Thinn
Rysk	Yoga
Zaniel	Zealand

Lizzie, or Libby if you don't like Betty or Beth, and no one will even consider the alternatives. You can pre-empt possible nicknames to some extent by saying the name you've chosen out loud and trying to find rhymes for it. This is a clever way to avoid children's chants and nursery rhyme-type insults, such as Dora the Explorer or Georgie Porgie. But don't be too concerned about playground chants—most children are subjected to them at some point and emerge unscathed.

> Pronunciation matters: a Swedish couple
> were once banned from naming their child
> "Brfxxccxxmnpcccclllmmnprxvclmnckssqlbb11116," which
> they claimed was pronounced "Albin."

Your last name

Try to avoid first names that might lead to unfortunate phrases when combined with your last name, to prevent a lifetime of embarrassment for your child. The best way to work out if this might happen is to write down all the names you like alongside your child's last name and have someone else read them out loud. This second pair of eyes and ears might just spot something you didn't. The age of the internet has given parents a wonderful new weapon in their baby-naming arsenal: the search engine. Before you settle on anything final, try searching for any examples of the complete first, middle, and last name of your new baby. You may find out that your baby has an axe-murderer namesake—or, like one of my colleagues, the same name as a well-known porn star.

> In 2004 the Peacock family drew some attention after they
> named their baby Drew. Apparently neither parent had actually
> said their son's name out loud until it was too late . . . and little
> Drew Peacock will have to live with it forever. Make sure you say
> your child's full name out loud before your final decision!

Initials

What last name will your baby have? Will it lend itself easily to amusing acronyms when coupled with certain first and middle names? My brother-in-law was going to be called Andrew Steven Schmitt before he was born, until his parents realized at the last minute what his initials would spell . . .

It's also worth taking the time to think about how credit cards display names or seeing your child's name written out on a form. Nobody should have to go through life known as S. Lugg because their parents didn't think that far ahead.

Using family names

Some families have a strong tradition of using names for babies that come from the family tree. There are instances where naming your son Augustine VIII is simply not an option; it's a rule. Another way families do this is to give children the name of their parent of the same sex and add "Junior" (Jr.) to the end. This could only create a problem if that child then decides to carry on the tradition and name their child after themselves—after all, who wants to be known as Frederick Jr. Jr.?

There are pros and cons with using family names.

- **Pro:** Your child will feel part of a strong tradition, which will create a sense of security for them and help make them feel a complete member of the family.

- **Pro:** If you're having a problem selecting a name you and your partner both agree on, this is a very simple solution and will make your new child's family very happy.

- **Con:** You might not actually like the name that's being passed down. Naming your child the 12th Thumbelina in a row might not actually hold the same attraction for you as for the generation before.

- **Con:** Another drawback could be if the cultural associations with that name have changed in your lifetime and it is no longer appropriate.

One way to include a family name is to compromise. You could use the name as a middle name, or refer to your baby by a nickname instead. Another possible solution is to use monikers—if your family is insisting your daughter be called Jade, maybe you could choose Giada instead. Or if your partner is determined the next child be called Michael after himself and it turns out to be a girl, choose Michaela in its place. In many Jewish families the tradition is to take the name of a deceased relative and give it to a new baby. If this thought fills you with dread, you could opt for a possible solution a lot of families adopt, which is to use the first initial instead. If you're not keen on Solomon, pick Samuel; if you don't like Ruth, choose Rebecca.

> The biggest babies born last year in the USA were called Sammisano Joshua Talai Otuhiva and Andrew Jacob Cervantez. They weighed an astonishing 16lb 7oz and 15lb 2oz, respectively. The UK's biggest kid however, was weighed in at 15lb 7oz, and his parents named him George King. King by name, King by nature!

Spellings and pronunciation

Once you've finally agreed upon a name, it's time to consider how you wish it to be spelled and pronounced. Some parents love experimenting with unusual variations of traditional names, while others prefer for names to be instantly recognizable. Try to avoid making a common name too long or too unusual in its spelling as this will be the first thing your child learns how to write. They will also have to spell it out constantly during their lifetime, as other people misspell or mispronounce their name. Substituting the odd "i" for a "y" isn't too bad, but turning the name Jonathan into Jonnaythanne doesn't do anyone any favors.

> A palindrome name is a name that is spelt the same backwards and forwards, as with Bob, Elle, Eve, and Hannah.

One aspect of spellings and pronunciation to consider when choosing a name is how other people will interpret them. According to a BBC article last year, a greater proportion of names that are more anglicized in the USA, Australia, New Zealand, and the UK get called back for job interviews than names that aren't. Of course this is more of a problem on the side of the employer, whose discriminatory practices should be changed, but it is food for thought. Several people interviewed for the article had legally changed their names to more anglicized versions— Arielle to Ari, Norhidayah to Heidi, and Dickman to Davids—and received more interest when job-hunting as a result.

According to the journal *Scientific American*, participants in a 2014 study were more likely to believe statements from names they could pronounce, and distrust statements from those they could not. The study only used names from countries outside of the USA, to adjust for pre-existing prejudices, and found that the harder-to-pronounce the name, the less trustworthy the statement coming from it seemed to be. Interesting stuff, and worth thinking about if you're debating whether to add that extra "xyz" to your baby's name.

Middle names

Giving your child a middle name is generally acknowledged to be standard practice these days. In fact, it has become fairly uncommon to name a child *without* a middle name, although the use of second and third names only became popular around the turn of the 20th century. Before then, giving a child a middle name was seen as a status symbol; it was only really used when a man married a higher-class woman and they wanted to keep the woman's maiden name as a reminder of the child's heritage. Once the fashion caught on, it became very popular to give more than one middle name to children of status, but it's only been since the 1900s that it has become standard for everyone.

> ## "Text speak" spellings
>
> An
> Camron
> Conna
> Ema
> Esta
> Flicity
> Jayk
> Lora
> Patryk
> Samiul
> Summa
> Wilym

Regardless of your status, a middle name can have just as much of an impact as a first name, so your choice for your own baby should be made as carefully as the decision about their first name. After all, a recent study by the website Netmums.com found that three quarters of parents chose a single middle name for the baby, and one in six parents chose two or more.

Here are some common trends in 2016 to help you choose.

- **Opposite-length names.** It has become very popular to give a child either a long first name and short middle name (e.g. Jennifer Ruth, Nicholas John), or vice versa.

- **Name from the family tree.** Honoring your ancestors is another popular trend for 2016. Parents are frequently looking back to their own lineage for interesting, unusual, or influential names.

- **Unusual names.** Parents who like a quirky name but aren't quite brave enough to give it to their child as a first name are using it as a middle name.

- **Maiden name or parent name.** It is becoming increasingly common to use a parent's first name, or a mother's maiden name, as a middle name for a baby.

You may have already decided what middle name to give your child due to tradition or culture, in which case the following advice may be moot. In Hispanic cultures, for example, middle names are often the mother's surname or other name to promote that matriarchal lineage. Similarly, parents who have not taken each other's surnames or are not married may choose to give their child one surname as a middle name and one as a last name so both parents are represented. Other traditions may use an old family name, passed down to each first-born son or daughter, to encourage a sense of family pride and history. A decision about what middle name to pass on may have therefore already been made for you, even before your own birth.

Of course, there are always the stars who take trends and just run with them, using not only something wacky but also multiple names when one will do; ex-glamour model Holly Madison did that with her daughter: Rainbow Aurora. Holly defended her choice at the time, publicly saying:

> There are a lot of smug haters out there who bag on my choice of a name, but I don't care about what they think. I want my daughter to be proud of who she is and learn to speak up and stand up for herself at a young age

Sweden has a pretty strict naming law, enacted in 1982, which says: "First names shall not be approved if they can cause offense or can be supposed to cause discomfort for the one using it, or names which for some obvious reason are not suitable as a first name." However, they did recently approve the use of "Google" as a middle name.

Many people actually choose to go by their middle name instead of their forename, so it could be seen as a safety net if you're worried your child won't like their name. Some famous examples of multiple middle names include Canadian actor Kiefer Sutherland, who has shortened his name considerably from Kiefer William Frederick Dempsey George Rufus Sutherland. Even the British royal family likes to give many middle names: Prince Charles's full name is Charles Philip Arthur George Mountbatten-Windsor, and Prince William is William Arthur Philip Louis Mountbatten-Windsor. The newest heir to the throne, born in 2015, is of course Princess Charlotte Elizabeth Diana, named after the current queen and her late grandmother, Diana Spencer. Then there's her brother, born in 2013, Prince George Alexander Louis, named after King George VI and Lord Louis Mountbatten.

Celebrities who go by middle names

Antonio Banderas (José Antonio Domínguez Banderas)

Ashton Kutcher (Christopher Ashton Kutcher)

Bob Marley (Nesta Robert Marley)

Brad Pitt (William Bradley Pitt)

Brooke Shields (Christa Brooke Camille Shields)

Dakota Fanning (Hannah Dakota Fanning)

Evangeline Lilly (Nicole Evangeline Lilly)

Hugh Laurie (James Hugh Calum Laurie)

Kelsey Grammer (Allen Kelsey Grammer)

Reese Witherspoon (Laura Jeanne Reese Witherspoon)

Rihanna (Robyn Rihanna Fenty)

Will Ferrell (John William Ferrell)

Naming twins, triplets, and more

Twin names with the same meaning

Bernard and Brian (strong)

Daphne and Laura (laurel)

Deborah and Melissa (bee)

Dorcas and Tabitha (gazelle)

Elijah and Joel (God)

Eve and Zoe (life)

Irene and Salome (peace)

Lucius and Uri (light)

Lucy and Helen (light)

Sarah and Almira (princess)

If you have discovered you are expecting multiples, congratulations! Naming multiples needn't be any different to naming a single child . . . unless you want it to be. You could stick to the same process everyone else does, by picking an individual name for each individual child. Even "Octomom" Nadya Suleman chose eight different names for her octuplets, although they do all sound reasonably similar: Isaiah, Jeremiah, Jonah, Josiah, Maliyah, Makai, Nariyah, and Noah.

A Texan woman gave birth to two sets of identical twin boys on the same day in 2013. Conceived naturally, the chances of which are one in 70 million, Tressa and Manuel Montalvo named their miracles Ace, Blaine, Cash, and Dylan (ABCD).

Mariah Carey and Nick Cannon chose to use names starting with the same letter when naming their girl/boy twins: Monroe and Moroccan Scott. "Scott" is the same middle name as Nick Cannon's and is his grandmother's maiden name, and as Mariah Carey doesn't have a middle name, they skipped one for Monroe too.

Of course, when all's said and done you can just stick to giving each child a name unique to them. For triplets, quads, and more, this is probably an easier choice than twisting your head around three names with the same meaning, or trying to create four anagrams you like for all of your babies. Some parents do like to use a theme though, such as going down the alphabet (think Alastair, Benjamin, Christopher, and David), or doing what the famous acting Phoenix clan did and giving each child a name to do with nature: River, Rain, Joaquin (Leaf), Liberty, and Summer.

> ## Popular twin names
>
> Brandon and Brian
> Daniel and David
> Ella and Emma
> Faith and Hope
> Gabriella and Isabella
> Isaac and Isaiah
> Jacob and Joshua
> Madison and Morgan
> Matthew and Michael
> Taylor and Tyler

One mother in Mississippi got the surprise of her life in 2014, when she gave birth not to the triplets she was expecting—but to identical quads! Rushing to come up with another name in a hurry, the family settled on Kenleigh Rose, Kristen Sue, Kayleigh Pearl, and Kelsey Roxanne. The four baby girls are now known as the "Fugate Four" and join big sister Katelyn.

> ## Celebrity twin names of the past few years
>
> Cy Aridio and Bowie Ezio (Zoe Saldana and Marco Perego)
> Darby and Sullivan (Patrick Dempsey and Jillian Fink)
> Dolly Rebecca Rose and Charlie Tamara Tulip (Rebecca Romijn and
>   Jerry O'Connell)

Gideon and Harper (Neil Patrick Harris and David Burtka)

Hazel and Phinnaeus (Julia Roberts and Danny Moder)

John and Gus (Julie Bowen and Scott Phillips)

Kane and Kaia (Kim Zolciak and Kroy Biermann)

Max and Emme (Jennifer Lopez and Marc Anthony)

Monroe and Moroccan Scott (Mariah Carey and Nick Cannon)

Poppy and Charlie (Anna Paquin and Stephen Moyer)

Tristan and Sasha (Chris Hemsworth and Elsa Pataky)

Victoria and Ysabel (Michael Jordan and Yvette Jordan)

Violet Moon and Knox Blue (Sarah Shahi and Steve Howey)

Vivienne Marcheline and Knox Léon (Angelina Jolie and Brad Pitt)

Names for triplets

Abel, Bela, and Elba (anagrams)

Aidan, Diana, and Nadia (anagrams)

Amber, Jade, and Ruby (jewels)

Amy, May, and Mya (anagrams)

April, May, and June (months)

Ava, Eva, and Iva (similar)

Daisy, Lily, and Rose (flowers)

Jay, Raven, and Robin (birds)

Leah, Lianne, and Liam (similar)

Olive, Violet, and Sage (colors)

River, Rain, and Summer (nature)

Things to avoid

There are a few tricks to keep in mind when naming twins or multiples, but they are pretty simple ones:

- Don't use very long names. You will often find yourself needing to write both names down, or calling both children for dinner, and very long names might get so bothersome you end up not using them. Instead, use shorter versions of the names you like (such as Max for Maximilian, or Eve for Evangeline) as either their registered first name or just as a common nickname you like.

- Don't get too complicated. Again, having to remember the spellings of all the names and middle names you've given your multiples can be made a lot easier if you keep things simple. Use traditional spellings if possible.

- Don't forget that your babies are still individuals. If you use names that sound so similar you often mix them up, your children may get frustrated as they get older and other people confuse them. Instead, keep those nearly identical names you love as middle names, and use this opportunity to explore more individual forenames to match your babies' unique personalities.

  > The first quintuplets (and perhaps the most famous, still) ever known to have survived infancy were the Dionne family, from Canada. Born in 1934, their names were Yvonne, Annette, Cécile, Émilie, and Marie.

part two

Boys' Names

A Boys' names

Aaron

Hebrew, meaning "mountain of strength." In the Bible, Aaron was the older brother of Moses and the first high priest of Israel.

Abasi

Egyptian Arabic, meaning "male"; Swahili, meaning "stern."

Abdiel

Hebrew, meaning "servant of God." Also the name of an important seraph in Milton's *Paradise Lost*.

Abdul

(alt. Abdullah)

Arabic, meaning "servant of God." Often followed with a suffix indicating who Abdul is the servant of (e.g. Abdul-Basit, servant of the creator).

Abel

Hebrew, meaning "breath" or "breathing spirit." The biblical son of Adam and Eve who was killed by his brother Cain.

Abelard

German, meaning "resolute."

Aberforth

Gaelic, meaning "mouth of the river Forth." Name of Dumbledore's brother in the "Harry Potter" series.

Abner

Hebrew, meaning "father of light." Abner was the commander of Saul's army in the Bible.

Abraham

(alt. Abram; abbrev. Abe)

Hebrew, meaning "exalted father." Famous Abrahams include President Abraham Lincoln and Abraham Van Helsing—the vampire hunter and doctor in Bram Stoker's *Dracula*.

Absalom

(alt. Absalon)

Hebrew, meaning "father/leader of peace." The name of King David's favorite son in the Bible, and one of Chaucer's curly-haired characters in *The Canterbury Tales*.

Acacio

Greek origin, meaning "thorny tree." Now widely used in Spain.

Ace

Latin, meaning "unit." Also used to mean "number one" or "the best."

Achebe

Nigerian, meaning "may the earth protect us."

Achilles

Greek, mythological hero of the Trojan War, whose heel was his only weak spot.

Achim

Hebrew, meaning "God will establish"; Polish, meaning "The Lord exalts." Also a shortened form of Joachim.

Ackerley

Old English, meaning "oak meadow."

Adam

(alt. Adome, Admon)

Hebrew, meaning "man" or "earth." The biblical creation story names Adam as the first man on Earth.

Adão

Portuguese variant of Adam, meaning "earth."

Addison

Old English, meaning "son of Adam." Also used as a female name.

Ade

Yoruba, meaning "peak" or "royal." A common name in Nigeria.

Adelard

French or German, meaning "brave" or "noble." Became popular in Canada during the nineteenth century.

Adin

Hebrew, meaning "slender" or "voluptuous"; Swahili, meaning "ornamental."

Aditya

Sanskrit, meaning "belonging to the sun." Refers to the offspring of Aditi—the mother of the gods.

Adlai

Hebrew, meaning "God is just," or sometimes "ornamental." Four generations of Adlai Stevensons went into politics.

Adler

Old German, meaning "eagle."

Adley

English, meaning "son of Adam."
Also used as a girls' name.

Adolf

(alt. Adolfo, Adolph)

Old German, meaning "noble
majestic wolf." Popularity of the
name plummeted after World War II,
for obvious reasons.

Adonis

Phoenician, meaning "Lord." Adonis
was the god of beauty and desire in
ancient Greek mythology.

Adrian

(abbrev. Ade)

Latin origin, meaning "from Hadria,"
a town in northern Italy.

Adriel

Hebrew, meaning "of God's flock."
Adriel was one of Saul's sons-in-law
in the Bible.

Aeneas

Greek/Latin origin, meaning "to
praise." Name of the hero who
founded Rome in Virgil's *Aeneid*.

Aero

Greek, meaning "air."

Aeson

Greek, after the father of Jason in
ancient Greek mythology.

Afonso

Portuguese, meaning "eager noble
warrior." King Afonso of Portugal was
nicknamed "The Conqueror" during
the Middle Ages.

Agamemnon

Greek, meaning "leader of the
assembly." Figure in mythology,
commanded the Greeks at the siege
of Troy.

Agathon

Greek, meaning "good" or
"superior." The name of a tragic poet
in ancient Greece.

Agustin

Latin/Spanish, meaning "venerated."

Ahab

Hebrew, meaning "father's brother."
Name of the obsessed captain in
Herman Melville's *Moby-Dick*.

Ahijah

Hebrew, meaning "brother of God"
or "friend of God." Common name
in the Bible.

Ahmed

Arabic/Turkish, meaning "worthy
of praise." Also one of the prophet
Muhammad's many given names.

Aidan

(alt. Aden, Aiden)

Gaelic, meaning "little fire." Derives
from Aodh, the name of a Celtic sun
god.

Aidric

Old English, meaning "oaken."

Airyck

Old Norse, from Eric, meaning "eternal ruler."

Ajani

Nigerian, meaning "he fights for what he is"; Sanskrit, meaning "of noble birth."

Ajax

Greek, meaning "mourner of the Earth." A Greek hero from the siege of Troy.

Ajay

Hindi, meaning "unconquerable." One of the most popular names in India.

Ajit

Sanskrit, meaning "invincible." Another name for Shiva or Vishnu in Hindu mythology.

Akeem

Arabic, meaning "wise or insightful." Popular name in Nigeria.

Akio

Japanese, meaning "bright man." Akio Morita was one of the founders of Sony.

Akira

Japanese, meaning "intelligent." Also the name of one of the most successful Japanese anime films of all time.

Akiva

Hebrew, meaning "to protect" or "to shelter." Rabbi Akiva is an important figure in the Jewish faith.

Akon

American, meaning "flower." Made popular after rapper Akon.

Aksel

Hebrew/Danish, meaning "father of peace."

Aladdin

Arabic, meaning "servant of Allah." Character in *The Arabian Nights*, made popular by Disney.

Alan
(alt. Allan, Allen, Allyn, Alun)

Gaelic or Old French, meaning "rock." One of the oldest names still widely used in Western countries, dating back to the eleventh century.

Alaric

Old German, meaning "noble regal ruler." Also the name of a king who helped bring about the fall of the Roman Empire.

Alastair
(alt. Alasdair, Alastor, Allister; abbrev. Al, Ali)

Greek/Gaelic, meaning "defending men." Also the name of a demon in *Supernatural*.

Alban

Latin, meaning "from Alba"; Welsh and Scottish Gaelic word for "Scotland."

Alberic

Germanic, meaning "Elfin king."

Albert

(alt. Adalberto, Adelbert, Alberto, Elbert)

Old German, meaning "noble, bright, famous." Prince Albert was the husband of Queen Victoria.

Albus

(alt. Albin)

Latin, meaning "white." Albus Dumbledore is headmaster of Hogwarts School in the "Harry Potter" series.

Alcaeus

Greek, meaning "strength." The name of an ancient Greek poet.

Alden

Old English, meaning "old friend."

Aldis

Latvian, meaning "from the old house."

Aldo

Latin, meaning "the tall one." Also the name of the main gorilla character in *Planet of the Apes*.

Aldric

English, meaning "old king."

Aled

Welsh, meaning "child" or "offspring."

Aleph

Hebrew, meaning "first letter of the alphabet," or "leader." The aleph is the first character of many Middle Eastern alphabets.

Alessio

Italian, meaning "defender."

Alexander

(alt. Alexandro, Alessandro, Alejandro; abbrev. Al, Alec, Alek, Alex, Alexei, Sandro, Sandy, Xander, Zander)

Greek, meaning "defending men." Alexander the Great was an undefeated fourth-century king whose empire stretched from Greece to modern Pakistan. The abbreviation Alexei is enduringly popular in Russia.

Alfonso

Germanic/Spanish, meaning "noble and prompt, ready to struggle." Alfonso Cuarón Orozco is the director of *Gravity*. Alfonso Ribeiro is known for *Fresh Prince of Bel Air* and *Dancing With The Stars*.

Alford

Old English, meaning "old river/ ford."

Alfred

(alt. Alfredo; abbrev. Alf, Alfi, Alfie)

English, meaning "elf" or "magical counsel." Name of legendary English king Alfred the Great.

Algernon

(abbrev. Algie)

French, meaning "with a moustache." A popular name for the nobility in eighteenth- and nineteenth-century England. *Flowers for Algernon* is a novel by Daniel Keyes.

Ali

(alt. Allie)

Arabic, meaning "noble, sublime."

Alijah

Hebrew, meaning "the Lord is my God."

Alois

German, meaning "famous warrior." Also the name of Adolf Hitler's father.

Alok

Sanskrit, meaning "cry of triumph."

Alon

Hebrew, meaning "oak tree." A popular name in Jewish communities.

Alonso

(alt. Alonzo)

Germanic, meaning "noble and ready."

Aloysius

Italian saint's name, meaning "fame and war."

Alpha

First letter of the Greek alphabet and synonymous with "beginning."

Alphaeus

Hebrew, meaning "changing." Father of two of the Apostles in the Bible.

Alpin

Gaelic, meaning "related to the Alps." The House of Alpin was a dynasty of Scottish kings.

Altair

Arabic, meaning "flying" or "bird." Altair is one of the brightest stars seen in the night sky.

Alter

Yiddish, meaning "old man."

Alton

Old English, meaning "old town."

Alvin

(alt. Alvie)

English, meaning "friend of elves." Often associated with *Alvin and the Chipmunks*.

Alwyn
(alt. Alwen)
Welsh, meaning "wise friend."

Amachi
African, meaning "who knows what God has brought us through this child." Used for both boys and girls.

Amadeus
Latin, meaning "God's love." One of composer Wolfgang Amadeus Mozart's many given names.

Amadi
Igbo, meaning "appeared destined to die at birth." Often given to babies who survive against the odds.

Amado
Spanish, meaning "God's love."

Amador
Spanish, meaning "one who loves." Two towns in California were named after rancher José María Amador.

Amari
Hebrew, meaning "given by God." Used for both boys and girls.

Amarion
Arabic, meaning "populous, flushing." Made popular after R&B singer Omarion.

Amasa
Hebrew, meaning "burden." Found in the Bible.

Ambrose
Greek, meaning "undying, immortal." St. Ambrose of Milan was one of the four original doctors of the Church.

Americo
Germanic, meaning "ever powerful in battle."

Amias
Latin, meaning "loved."

Amir
Arabic, meaning "chieftain" or "commander." Amir or Emir is a title for a high-ranking sheikh in many Muslim communities.

Amit
Hindi, meaning "infinite." One of the many name of the Hindu god Shri Ganesha.

Ammon
Hebrew, meaning "the hidden one." The Ammonites were an ancient group of people named in the Bible.

Amory
German/English, meaning "work" and "power."

Amos

Hebrew, meaning "encumbered" or "burdened."

Anacletus

Latin, meaning "called back" or "invoked." Also the name of the third Pope.

Anakin

American, meaning "warrior." Made famous by Anakin Skywalker in the *Star Wars* films.

Ananias

Greek/Italian, meaning "answered by the Lord." Ananias Dare was the first baby born to English parents in the New World, making him the first ever "modern" American.

Anastasius

(alt. Anastasios)

Greek, meaning "resurrection." A very popular name for popes, emperors, and saints.

Anatole

French, meaning "sunrise."

Anders

Greek, meaning "lion man." A very popular name in Sweden.

Anderson

English, meaning "male." Anderson Cooper is a TV host.

Andrew

(alt. Andreas, Andre, Andy)

Greek, meaning "man" or "warrior." Andrew Lincoln is known for his role in *The Walking Dead*.

Androcles

Greek, meaning "glory of a warrior." *Androcles and the Lion* was a well-known folktale in the second century, and influenced Aesop's *Fables*.

Angel

Greek, meaning "messenger." A very popular name in Hispanic communities. Used for both boys and girls.

Angelo

Italian, meaning "angel."

Angus

(abbrev. Gus)

Scottish, meaning "one choice." Name of Merida's horse in *Brave*.

Anil

Sanskrit, meaning "air" or "wind."

Anselm

German, meaning "helmet of God." St. Anselm was an influential figure in the formation of Christianity.

Anson

English, meaning "son of Agnes." Anson Jones was the last independent President of Texas, before it became incorporated into the USA.

Anthony
(alt. Antony; abbrev. Ant, Tony)
English, from the old Roman family name. *Antony and Cleopatra* is a Shakespearean play about the romance between Roman general Mark Antony and Cleopatra of Egypt.

Antipas
Hebrew, meaning "for all or against all." Herod Antipas is acknowledged as being responsible for the executions of John the Baptist and Jesus Christ in the Bible.

Antwan
(alt. Antoine.)
Old English, meaning "flower."

Apollo
Greek, meaning "to destroy." Greek god of poetry, music, and the sun.

Apostolos
Greek, meaning "apostle." The Apostolos is a text believed to have been written by one of the Apostles.

Ara
Armenian, from the legendary king of the same name.

Aragorn
Literary, used by Tolkien in "The Lord of the Rings" trilogy.

Aram
Hebrew, meaning "Royal Highness." Also the name of an ancient region in modern-day Syria.

Aramis
Latin, meaning "swordsman." One of the Three Musketeers in Alexandre Dumas's novel.

Arcadio
Greek/Spanish, meaning "paradise."

Archibald
(alt. Archie)
Old German, meaning "genuine/bold/brave." The middle name of Reverend William Spooner.

Ardell
Latin, meaning "eager, burning with enthusiasm."

Arden
Celtic, meaning "high."

Ares
Greek, meaning "ruin." Son of Zeus and Hera, and the Greek god of war.

Ari
Hebrew, meaning "lion" or "eagle." Also used to refer to an important man in Hebrew.

Arias
Germanic, meaning "lion." Sometimes used as a spelling variation of Eric.

Ariel

Hebrew, meaning "lion of God."
One of the archangels, the angel of
healing and new beginnings.

Arild

Old Norse, meaning "battle
commander."

Aris

Greek, meaning "best figure."
Popular name in Greece.

Ariston

Greek, meaning "the best." Also the
name of Plato's father.

Aristotle

Greek, meaning "best." Also an
ancient Greek philosopher.

Arjun

Sanskrit, meaning "bright and
shining." Taken from Arjuna, an
ancient and legendary archer.

Arkady

Greek, region of central Greece.
Popular throughout eastern
Europe.

Arlan

Gaelic, meaning "pledge" or "oath."

Arlie

Old English place name, meaning
"eagle wood."

Arliss

(alt. Arlis)

Hebrew, meaning "pledge." A 1990s
sitcom.

Arlo

Spanish, meaning "barberry
tree."

Armani

(alt. Armand)

Old German, meaning "soldier." A
well-known Italian designer.

Arnaldo

Spanish, meaning "eagle power."

Arnav

Indian, meaning "the sea."

Arnold

(abbrev. Arnie)

Old German, meaning "eagle ruler."
Arnold Schwarzenegger is an actor,
former bodybuilder, and former
Governor of California.

Arrow

English, from the common word
denoting weaponry.

Art

Irish, from the name of a warrior in
Irish mythology, Art Oenfer (Art the
Lonely). Also used as a shortened
form of Arthur.

Arthur
(alt. Artie, Artis)

Celtic, probably from "artos," meaning "bear." Made famous by the tales of King Arthur and the Knights of the Round Table.

Arturo

Celtic or Italian, meaning "strong as a bear."

Arvel

From the Welsh "Arwel," meaning "wept over." Arvel Crynyd appears in *Star Wars*, and Arvel the Swift in *The Elder Scrolls V: Skyrim*.

Arvid

English, meaning "eagle in the woods." Popular name in Scandinavia.

Arvind

Sanskrit, meaning "red lotus." Also derived from the word for "white lotus," upon which the Hindu goddess Lakshmit sits.

Arvo

Finnish, meaning "value" or "worth."

Asa

Hebrew, meaning "doctor" or "healer." Popular with Puritans in the seventeenth century.

Asante

African, meaning "thank you." Also the language of the Ashanti people.

Asher

Hebrew, meaning "fortunate" or "lucky." One of the twelve sons of Jacob in the Bible.

Ashley

Old English, meaning "ash meadow." Used for both boys and girls.

Ashok

Sanskrit, meaning "not causing sorrow." Popular in India and Sri Lanka.

Ashton

English, meaning "settlement in the ash-tree grove." The middle name of actor Ashton Kutcher (see page 61).

Aslan

Turkish, meaning "lion." The name of the lion from C. S. Lewis's *The Lion, The Witch, and The Wardrobe*.

Asriel
alt. Azriel

Hebrew, meaning "God is my help." Lord Asriel is an important character in the "His Dark Materials" trilogy. Azriel is the name of the angel of death in Christianity and Judaism.

Astrophel

Latin, meaning "star lover."

Athanasios

Greek, meaning "eternal life." Extremely popular in ancient and modern Greece.

Atílio

Portuguese, meaning "father."

Atlas

Greek, meaning "to carry." In ancient Greek mythology Atlas was a Titan forced to carry the weight of the heavens.

Atlee

Hebrew, meaning "God is just."

Atticus

Latin, meaning "from Athens." Atticus Finch is a central character in Harper Lee's *To Kill A Mockingbird*.

Auberon

Old German, meaning "royal bear." Also the name of a Shakespearean fairy king.

Aubrey

Old German, meaning "power." Used for both boys and girls.

Auden

Old English, meaning "old friend." W. H. Auden is considered to be one of the most influential twentieth-century poets.

Audie

Old English, meaning "noble strength." Audie L. Murphy was one of the most decorated US soldiers during World War II.

August

Latin, meaning "magnificent."

Augustus

(alt. Augustas; abbrev. Gus)

Latin, meaning "venerated." Also the name of a spoiled child in *Charlie and the Chocolate Factory*.

Aurelien

French, meaning "golden." An ancient Roman emperor.

Austin

Latin, meaning "venerated." Also the city in Texas.

Avi

Hebrew, meaning "father of a multitude of nations."

Awnan

Irish, meaning "little Adam."

Axel

Hebrew, meaning "father is peace." Made famous by Guns 'n' Roses frontman Axl Rose.

Azarel

(alt. Azaryah)

Hebrew, meaning "helped by God." Also the name of an evil spirit in the Bible.

Azuko

African, meaning "past glory." Popular in Japan.

B Boys' names

Babe

American, meaning "baby."
George Herman "Babe" Ruth was a legendary baseball player.

Baden

German, meaning "battle." Also the name of a city in Switzerland known for its hot springs.

Bailey

English, meaning "bailiff." A popular Irish crème liqueur.

Baird

Scottish, meaning "poet" or "one who sings ballads."

Bakari

Swahili, meaning "hope" or "promise."

Baker

English, from the word "baker."

Baldwin

Old French, meaning "bold, brave friend."

Balin

Old English, meaning "powerful and strong." Balin was one of the Knights of the Round Table.

Balthazar

Babylonian, meaning "protect the king." Also the name of one of the Three Wise Men in the Nativity.

Balwinder

(alt. Balvinder)

Hindi, meaning "merciful, compassionate."

Bannon

Irish, meaning "descendant of O'Banain."

Barack

African, meaning "blessed." Made popular by the 44th President of the United States Barack Obama.

Barclay

Old English, meaning "birch tree meadow," and Persian, meaning "messenger."

Barker

Old English, meaning "shepherd."

Barnaby
(abbrev. Barney)

Greek, meaning "son of consolation." *Barnaby Rudge* is one of Charles Dickens's less well-known novels.

Barnard

English, meaning "strong as a bear."

Baron

Old English, meaning "young warrior." A title given to certain men of nobility in Europe.

Barrett

English, meaning "strong as a bear."

Barron

Old German, meaning "old clearing."

Barry
(abbrev. Baz)

Irish Gaelic, meaning "fair haired." *Great Gatsby* film director Baz Luhrman's real name is Mark.

Bartholomew
(abbrev. Bart, Barty)

Hebrew, meaning "son of the farmer." Bartholomew "Bart" Simpson is the character from the *The Simpsons*.

Barton

Old English, meaning "barley settlement." A popular name for towns in the UK.

Baruch

Hebrew, meaning "blessed." Also the name of a Jewish blessing ceremony.

Bascom

Old English, meaning "from Bascombe."

Bashir

Arabic, meaning "well educated" and "wise." Journalist Martin Bashir is known for his infamous interviews with Diana, Princess of Wales, and Michael Jackson.

Basil

Greek, meaning "royal, kingly." Also the name of the herb.

Basim

Arabic, meaning "smile." Popular in Arabic-speaking communities.

Bastien

Greek, meaning "revered."

Baxter

Old English, meaning "baker." One of the most popular names for towns across the USA.

Bayard

French, meaning "auburn haired." Bayard Rustin was one of Martin Luther King Jr.'s mentors and advisors during the Civil Rights Movement.

Bayo

Nigerian, meaning "to find joy."

Beau

French, meaning "handsome." Actor Beau Bridges' real name is Lloyd Vernet Bridges.

Beck

Old Norse, meaning "stream." Singer Beck Hansen is usually known as just "Beck."

Beckett

Old English, meaning "beehive" or "bee cottage."

Beckham

English, meaning "homestead by the stream." Finding popularity as a given name due to English soccer star David Beckham.

Belarius

Shakespearean, meaning "a banished lord." From Shakespeare's play *Cymbeline*.

Benedict

Latin, meaning "blessed." Made popular after actor Benedict Cumberbatch.

Benjamin

(abbrev. Ben, Benny)

Hebrew, meaning "son of the south." Benjamin Franklin was one of the Founding Fathers of the USA.

Bennett

French/Latin vernacular form of Benedict, meaning "blessed."

Benoit

French form of Benedict, meaning "blessed."

Benson

English, meaning "son of Ben." The title of the 1980s sitcom *Benson*.

Bentley

Old English, meaning "bent grass meadow." Popularity has increased since the shows *16 and Pregnant* and *Teen Mom* first aired.

Benton

Old English, meaning "town in the bent grass."

Beriah

Hebrew, meaning "in fellowship" or "in envy." The son of Asher in the Bible.

Bernard
(abbrev. Bernie)
Germanic, meaning "strong, brave bear."

Berry
Old English, meaning "berry." Also used as a shortened form of Bernard or Barry.

Berton
Old English, meaning "bright settlement." Berton Averre is the guitarist from The Knack.

Bertrand
(alt. Bertram; abbrev. Bert, Bertie)
Old English, meaning "illustrious." The name of a *Sesame Street* muppet. Bertram (Bertie) Wooster was one of P.G. Wodehouse's most beloved characters. Bert is also a shortened form of Albert.

Bevan
Welsh, meaning "son of Evan."

Bicknell
Old English, meaning "from Bicknell."

Bilal
Arabic, meaning "wetting, refreshing." Popular in many Muslim communities.

Birch
Old English, meaning "bright" or "shining." Also a type of tree.

Birger
Norwegian, meaning "rescue."

Bishop
Old English, meaning "bishop." Bishops are members of the Church who oversee several parishes and jurisdictions.

Bjorn
Old Norse, meaning "bear." Bjorn Ulvaeus was one of the founding members of ABBA.

Bladen
Hebrew, meaning "hero."

Blaine
Irish Gaelic, meaning "yellow." Has risen in profile due to David Blaine, known for his magic, illusions, and extreme stunts.

Blair
English, meaning "plain."

Blaise
French, meaning "lisp" or "stutter."

Blake
Old English, meaning "dark, black."

Blas
(alt. Blaze)
German, meaning "firebrand." Also the name of a mountain in the Alps.

Bo

Scandinavian, from Robert, meaning "bright fame." Also the name of the Obamas' pet dog.

Boaz

Hebrew, meaning "swiftness" or "strength." The name of an influential character in the Bible.

Boden
(alt. Bodie)

Scandinavian, meaning "shelter" or "messenger."

Bogumil

Slavic, meaning "God's favor."

Bond

Old English, meaning "peasant farmer." Usually associated with the fictional character James Bond.

Boris

Slavic, meaning "battle glory." Boris Yeltsin was the President of Russia during the 1990s.

Boston
(alt. Bosten)

English, meaning "town by the woods."

Bowen

Welsh, meaning "son of Owen." The Bowen knot is a common sight in heraldic symbolism.

Boyd

Scottish Gaelic, meaning "yellow."

Bradley
(abbrev. Brad)

Old English, meaning "broad" or "wide." Actor Brad Pitt's full name is William Bradley Pitt.

Brady

Irish, meaning "large-chested." Name of the family in *The Brady Bunch*.

Bradyn
(alt. Braden, Bradan)

Gaelic, meaning "descendant of Bradan."

Bram

Gaelic, meaning "raven." Bram Stoker was the author of *Dracula*.

Brando

Old Norse, meaning "sword" or "flaming torch." Name of the movie star Marlon Brando.

Brandon
(abbrev. Bran)

Old English, meaning "gorse." Brandon "Bran" Stark is a main character in *Game of Thrones*.

Brandt

Old English, meaning "beacon."

Brannon

Gaelic, meaning "raven."

Branson

English, meaning "son of Brand." Sir Richard Branson is a famous entrepreneur.

Brant

Old English, meaning "hill."

Braulio

Greek, meaning "shining."

Brayden

Irish, meaning "broad meadow."

Brendan

Gaelic, meaning "prince." Actor Brendan Fraser is known for his role in the "Mummy" series.

Brennan

Gaelic, meaning "teardrop."

Brent

English, meaning "hill." Brent Seabrook currently plays for the Chicago Blackhawks.

Brenton

English, meaning "hill town."

Brett
(alt. Bret)

English, meaning "a Breton." Made popular by Poison lead vocalist Bret Michaels.

Brian

Gaelic, meaning "high" or "noble." Singer songwriter Brian Wilson was a founding member of The Beach Boys.

Brice

Latin, meaning "speckled."

Brier

French, meaning "heather." Also the name of a type of thorny plant.

Brock

Old English, meaning "badger." One of the more popular characters in the Pokémon franchise.

Broderick

English, meaning "ruler." Last name of the actor Matthew Broderick.

Brody

Gaelic, meaning both "ditch" and "brother." Brody Jenner is known for being part of the Jenner/Kardashian clan.

Brogan

Irish, meaning "sturdy shoe."

Brooklyn

American, from the New York City borough of the same name. Brooklyn Beckham is the eldest son of soccer star David and singer turned fashion designer Victoria Beckham.

Bruce

Scottish, meaning "high" or "noble." Bruce Jenner was a decathlete during the 1976 Olympics, and a member of the Jenner/Kardashian clan.

Bruno

Germanic, meaning "brown." Bruno Tonioli is a judge on *Dancing With The Stars*.

Bryant

English variant of Brian, meaning "high" or "noble." Associated with basketball legend Kobe Bryant.

Bryce

Scottish, meaning "of Britain."

Bryden

Irish, meaning "strong one."

Bryson

(alt. Brycen)

Welsh, meaning "descendant of Brice." Bryson was the name of an ancient Greek philosopher and also a mathematician from the same time.

Bubba

American, meaning "boy." The restaurant chain Bubba Gump Shrimp Co. takes its name from the characters of Benjamin Buford "Bubba" Blue and Forrest Gump in the movie *Forrest Gump*.

Buck

American, meaning "goat" or "deer," specifically a male deer.

Bud

(alt. Buddy)

American, meaning "friend." Buddy has been used as a stage name by a number of musicians including Buddy Holly and Buddy Guy.

Burdett

Middle English, meaning "bird."

Burke

French, meaning "fortified settlement."

Burl

French, meaning "knotty wood."

Buzz

American, from Busby, meaning "village in the thicket." Buzz Aldrin was the second man on the moon and Buzz Lightyear is a Disney hero character.

Byron

Old English, meaning "barn." Famour Byrons include the poet Lord Byron.

C

Boys' names

Cabot
Old English, meaning "to sail."

Cade
(alt. Caden, Caiden, Kayden)
English, meaning "round, lumpy." A character in the novel *Gone With The Wind*.

Cadence
Latin, meaning "with rhythm." Poetry, music, and marching all have some type of cadence.

Cadogan
Welsh, meaning "battle glory and honor." Sir Cadogan is a knight in a painting in the "Harry Potter" series.

Caedmon
Celtic, meaning "wise warrior." An early English poet.

Caelan
Gaelic, meaning "slender."

Caerwyn
(alt. Carwyn, Gerwyn)
Welsh, meaning "white fort" or "settlement."

Caesar
(alt. Cesar)
Latin, meaning "head of hair." Made famous by the first Roman emperor, Julius Caesar.

Caetano
Portuguese, meaning "from Gaeta, Italy."

Caillou
French, meaning "pebble." Name of a children's cartoon character.

Cain
Hebrew, meaning "full of beauty." Brother of Abel in the Bible.

Cainan

Hebrew, meaning "possessor" or "purchaser."

Cairo

Egyptian city near Giza. Also home of the Great Pyramids.

Calder

Scottish, meaning "rough waters."

Caleb
(alt. Cal, Calen)

Hebrew, meaning "dog." A character in the Bible.

Calix

Greek, meaning "very handsome."

Callahan

Irish, meaning "contention" or "strife."

Callum
(alt. Calum)

Gaelic, meaning "dove." Very popular name in Ireland.

Calvin
(alt. Kalvin)

French, meaning "little bald one." Associated with the comic strip *Calvin and Hobbes*.

Camden
(alt. Kamden)

Gaelic, meaning "winding valley." A district in north London, UK, known for its market.

Cameron

Scottish Gaelic, meaning "crooked nose." Also the name of Ferris Bueller's best friend in *Ferris Bueller's Day Off*. Used for boys and girls.

Camillo

Latin, meaning "free born" or "noble."

Campbell

Scottish Gaelic, meaning "crooked mouth." The name of a famous brand of soup.

Canaan

Hebrew, meaning "to be humbled." A region heavily referenced in the Bible.

Candido

Latin, meaning "candid" or "honest." Candido Jacuzzi was the inventor of the Jacuzzi tub.

Canon
(alt. Cannon)

French, meaning "of the church." Originally given to members of a certain order in the Church.

Canton

French, meaning "dweller of corner." Also the name given to provinces of Switzerland.

Cappy

Italian, meaning "lucky." Can also be a nickname for Captain.

Carden

Old English, meaning "wool carder"—which refers to someone who would "card" wool to remove impurities from it.

Carey

Gaelic, meaning "love." Used for both boys and girls.

Carl

(alt. Carlo, Carlos, Karl)

Old Norse, meaning "free man." Carl Jung was a famous psychologist.

Carlton

Old English, meaning "free peasant settlement." Carlton is a character in the sitcom *The Fresh Prince of Bel Air*.

Carmelo

Latin, meaning "garden" or "orchard."

Carmen

Latin/Spanish, meaning "song." The title of an opera by French composer Georges Bizet. Used for boys and girls.

Carmine

Latin, meaning "song." Also the name of a bright-red pigment used in the production of red fruit juices.

Carnell

English, meaning "defender of the castle."

Carson

(alt. Carsten)

Scottish, meaning "marshdwellers." Carson Daly is a late night TV host.

Carter

Old English, meaning "transporter of goods." Jimmy Carter was the 39th President of the United States and Carter Camper is an American professional ice hockey player.

Cary

Celtic, meaning "love." Old Celtic river name. Cary Elwes is a current actor and Cary Grant was the stage name of the dashing English-American actor of the 1930s–1950s awarded an honorary Oscar in 1970.

Case

(alt. Casey, Kacey, Kasey)

Irish Gaelic, meaning "alert" or "watchful."

Cash

Latin, shortened form of Cassius, meaning "empty, hollow." Associated with musician Johnny Cash.

Casimer

Slavic, meaning "famous destroyer of peace."

Cason

Latin, from Cassius, meaning "empty, hollow."

Casper
(alt. Kasper)
Persian, meaning "treasurer." The ghost character in *Casper the Friendly Ghost*.

Caspian
English, meaning "of the Caspy people." Taken from the children's novel *Prince Caspian*.

Cassidy
Gaelic, meaning "curly haired." Originated from the last name Caiside.

Cassius
(alt. Cassio)
Latin, meaning "empty, hollow." Legendary boxer Muhammad Ali's birth name was Cassius Clay.

Cathal
Celtic, meaning "battle rule." Variation of Charles.

Cato
Latin, meaning "all-knowing." Also the name of a character in *The Hunger Games*.

Cecil
Latin, meaning "blind." Cecil B. DeMille was a legendary film director.

Cedar
English, name of an evergreen tree.

Cedric
Welsh, meaning "spectacular bounty." Taken from Sir Walter Scott's novel *Ivanhoe*.

Celestino
Spanish/Italian meaning "heavenly."

Chad
(alt. Chadrick)
Old English, meaning "warlike, warrior." Also the name of an African country.

Chaim
(alt. Chayyim)
Hebrew, meaning "life."

Champion
English, from the word "warrior."

Chance
English, from the word "chance," meaning "good fortune."

Chandler
Old English, meaning "candle maker and seller." Made famous by Chandler Bing from 1990s sitcom *Friends*.

Charles
(alt. Charley, Charlie; abbrev. Chas)
Old German, meaning "free man." Charles, Prince of Wales, is heir to the British throne.

Chase

(alt. Chace)

Old French, meaning "huntermen." Actor Chace Crawford is known for his role on *Gossip Girl*.

Chaska

Native American name usually given to first son.

Che

Spanish, shortened form of José. Made famous by Che Guevara.

Chesley

Old English, meaning "camp on the meadow."

Chesney

English, meaning "place to camp." Also used as a girls' name.

Chester

Latin, meaning "camp of soldiers." Chester Arthur was the 21st President of the United States and Chester Bennington is the lead singer of rock band Linkin Park.

Chima

Old English, meaning "hilly land."

Christian

(abbrev. Chris)

English, from the word "Christian." Actor Christian Slater is known for his roles in *Heathers* and *Breaking In*.

Christopher

(alt. Christophe, Kristopher; abbrev. Chris, Kris)

Greek, meaning "bearing Christ inside." Christopher Columbus is credited with discovering America.

Cian

Irish, meaning "ancient." Father of Lug in Gaelic mythology.

Ciaran

Irish, meaning "black." Actor Ciaran Hinds is known for his recent voice work as Gree in *Rio 2*, and the Troll King in *Frozen*.

Cicero

Latin, meaning "chickpea." Also the Roman philosopher and orator.

Cimarron

City in western Kansas.

Ciprian

Latin, meaning "from Cyprus." Popular in ancient Rome.

Ciro

Spanish, meaning "sun." Also the title of a seventeenth-century opera.

Clancy

Old Irish, meaning "red warrior." Clancy has been a popular name for US actors, writers and sports stars. Also a character in *The Simpsons*.

Clarence

Latin, meaning "one who lives near the river Clare." Clarence Thomas is one of the current Associate Justices of the Supreme Court.

Clark

Latin, meaning "clerk." Superman's human name is Clark Kent.

Claude
(alt. Claudie, Claudio, Claudius)

Latin, meaning "lame."

Claus

Variant of Nicholas, meaning "people of victory." Associated with Santa Claus.

Clay

English, from the word "clay." Singer Clay Aiken is known for his appearances on *American Idol*.

Clement
(alt. Clem)

Latin, meaning "merciful." Also the taken name for 14 different popes.

Cletus

Greek, meaning "illustrious." Cletus Spuckler is a hillbilly character in *The Simpsons*.

Clifford
(alt. Clifton; abbrev. Cliff)

English, meaning "ford by a cliff." Associated with Bill Cosby's character Cliff Huxtable on *The Cosby Show*.

Clinton
(alt. Clint)

Old English, meaning "fenced settlement." Actor Clint Eastwood is known for dozens of movie roles, both as an actor and as a director.

Clive

Old English, meaning "cliff" or "slope." Clive Owen is an actor and Clive Davis is a record producer and record label executive.

Clyde

Scottish, from the river that passes through Glasgow. Also the name of one half of the bank robber duo Bonnie and Clyde.

Coby
(alt. Koby, Kobe)

Diminutive of Jacob, meaning "he who supplants." Also used as a girls' name.

Colden

Old English, meaning "dark valley."

Cole
(alt. Coley)

Old French, meaning "coal black." Composer Cole Porter is known for dozens of popular songs and musicals.

Colin

Gaelic, meaning "young creature." Actor Colin Firth is known for his roles in *Pride and Prejudice* and *Love Actually*. Colin Powell was a US Secretary of State and is a retired army general.

Colson

Old English, meaning "coal black."

Colton

English, meaning "swarthy." Actor Colton Haynes is known for his role in *Arrow*.

Columbus

Latin, meaning "dove."

Colwyn

Welsh, from the river in Wales.

Conan

Gaelic, meaning "wolf." Comedian Conan O'Brien is known for his work as a late-night TV host.

Conley

Gaelic, meaning "sensible."

Connell

(alt. Connolly)

Irish, meaning "high" or "mighty."

Connor

(alt. Conrad, Conroy)

Irish, meaning "lover of hounds." Very popular name in Ireland.

Constant

(alt. Constantine)

English, from the word "constant." Popular with Puritans during the seventeenth century.

Cooper

Old English, meaning "barrel maker."

Corban

Hebrew, meaning "dedicated and belonging to God." Corban Knight currently plays for the Florida Panthers.

Corbett

(alt. Corbin, Corby)

Norman French, meaning "young crow."

Cordell

Old English, meaning "cord maker." An old term for people who made or sold cords.

Corey

Gaelic, meaning "hill hollow." Corey Hart currently plays for the Pittsburgh Pirates.

Corin

Latin, meaning "spear."

Cormac

Gaelic, meaning "impure son." American writer Cormac McCarthy is the author of modern classics *No Country for Old Men* and *The Road*.

Cornelius

(alt. Cornell)

Latin, meaning "horn." Cornelius Fudge is the Minister for Magic in the "Harry Potter" series.

Cortez

Spanish, meaning "courteous."

Corwin

Old English, meaning "heart's friend" or "companion."

Cosimo

(alt. Cosme, Cosmo)

Italian, meaning "order" or "beauty." Masculine form of Cosima.

Coty

French, meaning "riverbank." Refers to people who live on the French coast.

Coulter

English, meaning "young horse."

Courtney

Old English, meaning "domain of Curtis." Used for both boys and girls.

Covey

English, meaning "flock of birds."

Cowan

Gaelic, meaning "hollow in the hill."

Craig

Welsh, meaning "rock." Comedian Craig Ferguson is known for his work as a late night TV host.

Crispin

Latin, meaning "curly haired." A patron saint of shoemakers.

Croix

French, meaning "cross."

Cruz

Spanish, meaning "cross." Made famous after David and Victoria Beckham chose it for their third son.

Curran

Gaelic, meaning "dagger" or "hero."

Curtis

(alt. Curt)

Old French, meaning "courteous." Most popular in the US. Curtis Mayfield was a soul and RnB singer and Curtis LeMay was a General in the US Air Force during World War II.

Cutler

Old English, meaning "knife maker."

Cyprian

English, meaning "from Cyprus." Also the name of an early Christian bishop and writer.

Cyril

Greek, meaning "master" or "Lord." Associated with St. Cyril.

Cyrus

Persian, meaning "Lord." Cyrus the Great was a ruler of Persia in ancient times.

Boys' names

Dai

Welsh, meaning "darling."
Sometimes used as a girls' name.

Daichi

Japanese, meaning "great wisdom."

Daisuke

Japanese, meaning "lionhearted."
Daisuke Matsuzaka currently plays
for Fukuoka SoftBank Hawks.

Dakari

African, meaning "happy."

Dakota

Native American, meaning "friend" or
"ally." Both North and South Dakota
take their names from the Native
American tribe of the same name.

Dale

Old English, meaning "valley." Dale
Earnhardt Jr. is one of the best-known
NASCAR drivers.

Dallin

English, meaning "dweller in the
valley."

Dalton

English, meaning "town in the
valley."

Daly

Gaelic, meaning "assembly."

Damarion

Greek, meaning "gentle."

Damian

(alt. Damon)

Greek, meaning "to tame, subdue."
Actor Damian Lewis is known for his
role in *Homeland*.

Dane

Old English, meaning "from
Denmark." Dane Cook is known for
his stand-up comedy.

Daniel

(abbrev. Dan, Danny)

Hebrew, meaning "God is my judge." Daniel is mentioned several times in the Bible.

Dante

Latin, meaning "lasting." Name of the Italian 13th-century poet Dante Alighieri.

Darby

Irish, meaning "without envy." Name of the main character in Disney's *Darby O'Gill and The Little People*.

Darcy

Gaelic, meaning "dark." Mr. Darcy is a main character in Jane Austen's *Pride and Prejudice*.

Dario

(alt. Darius)

Greek, meaning "kingly." Dario Argento is an Italian film director known for his horror fims.

Darnell

Old English, meaning "the hidden spot." Darnell Dockett currently plays for the Arizona Cardinals.

Darragh

Irish, meaning "dark oak."

Darren

(alt. Darrian)

Gaelic, meaning "great." Darren Aronofsky is a Harvard-educated film director and producer.

Darrick

Old German, meaning "power of the tribe."

Darryl

(alt. Darrell, Daryl)

Old English, meaning "open." Comedian Darrell Hammond was known for his roles on *Saturday Night Live*. The spelling Daryl is more commonly used as a girls' name.

Darshan

Hindi, meaning "vision."

Darwin

Old English, meaning "dear friend." Often associated with naturalist and author Charles Darwin.

Dash

(alt. Dashawn)

American, meaning "enlightened one." Dash is a character in Disney Pixar's *The Incredibles*.

Dashiell

French, meaning "page boy." Author Dashiell Hammett was known for his detective novels.

David
(alt. Daffyd, Davian; abbrev. Dave, Davey, Davie)
Hebrew, meaning "beloved." David was a king of Israel who killed the giant Goliath in the Bible.

Davis
Old English, meaning "son of David."

Dawson
Old English, meaning "son of David." Associated with 1990s drama *Dawson's Creek.*

Dax
(alt. Daxton)
French, from the town in southwestern France. Actor Dax Shepard is known for his role in *Parenthood.*

Dayal
Indian, meaning "kind."

Dayton
Old English, meaning "David's place." Also the name of a city in Ohio.

Dean
(alt. Dino)
Old English, meaning "valley." Actor Dean McDermott is known for his marriage to Tori Spelling.

Declan
Irish, meaning "full of goodness." Declan Porter is a character on *Revenge.*

Dedric
Old English, meaning "gifted ruler."

Deegan
(alt. Deagon, Daegan)
Irish, meaning "black-haired."

Deepak
(alt. Deepan)
Indian, meaning "illumination." Deepak Chopra is known for his work as a doctor and author.

Del
(alt. Delano, Delbert, Dell)
Old English, meaning "bright shining one."

Demetrius
Greek, meaning "harvest lover." One of the star-crossed lovers in Shakespeare's *A Midsummer Night's Dream.*

Dempsey
Irish, meaning "proud."

Denham
(alt. Denholm)
Old English, meaning "valley settlement."

Dennis
(alt. Denny, Denton)
English, meaning "follower of Dionysius." The main character in comic strip *Dennis the Menace.*

Denver

Old English, meaning "green valley." City in Colorado.

Denzel

(alt. Denzil)

English, meaning "fort." Actor Denzel Washington is known for his roles in Malcolm X and Philadelphia.

Deon

Greek, meaning "of Zeus." The male version of Dionne.

Derek

English, meaning "power of the tribe." Dancer and choreographer Derek Hough is known for his work on Dancing With The Stars.

Dermot

Irish, meaning "free man." Actor Dermot Mulroney is known for his roles in My Best Friend's Wedding and New Girl.

Desmond

(abbrev. Des)

Irish, meaning "from south Munster." Former Archbishop Desmond Tutu is a high profile South African social activist.

Destin

French, meaning "destiny."

Devyn

(alt. Devin, Devon)

Irish, meaning "poet."

Dewey

(alt. Dewi)

Welsh, meaning "beloved." One of Donald Duck's three nephews.

Dexter

(alt. Dex)

Latin, meaning "right-handed." Has become more popular since the massive success of TV drama Dexter.

Didier

French, meaning "much desired."

Diego

Spanish, meaning "supplanter." A character in children's cartoon Dora the Explorer.

Dietrich

Old German, meaning "power of the tribe."

Diggory

English, meaning "dyke." Cedric Diggory is a character in the "Harry Potter" series.

Dilbert

English, meaning "day-bright." Main character in the comic strip of the same name.

Dimitri

(alt. Dimitrios, Dimitris)

Greek, meaning "prince." Popular name for boys in Russia.

Dion

Greek, short form of Dionysius.

Dirk

Variant of Derek, meaning "power of the tribe." Famous Dirks include actors Dirk Bogarde and Dirk Benedict. Infamous Dirks include fictional porn star Dirk Diggler, from the film *Boogie Nights*.

Dominic

Latin, meaning "Lord." Actor Dominic Monaghan is known for his roles in *Lost* and *Lord of the Rings*.

Donald

(alt. Donal, Donaldo; abbrev. Don, Donnie)

Gaelic, meaning "great chief." Famous Donalds include actor Donald Sutherland, businessman Donald Trump and, of course, Donald Duck.

Donato

Italian, meaning "gift." Given name of the Italian sculptor Donatello.

Donnell

(alt. Donnie, Donny)

Gaelic, meaning "world fighter."

Donovan

Gaelic, meaning "dark-haired chief."

Doran

Gaelic, meaning "exile."

Dorian

Greek, meaning "descendant of Doris." The title character of Oscar Wilde's *The Picture of Dorian Gray*.

Douglas

(alt. Dougal, Dougie)

Scottish, meaning "black river." Author Douglas Adams is known for his novel *The Hitchhiker's Guide to the Galaxy*.

Draco

Latin, meaning "dragon." Draco Malfoy is a main character in the "Harry Potter" series.

Drake

Greek, meaning "dragon." Drake Bell is an American actor, TV personality, and musician.

Drew

Greek, from Andrew, meaning "man" or "warrior." Drew Carey is known for his work in comedy and as a TV host.

Dudley

Old English, meaning "people's field." The name of Harry's cousin in the "Harry Potter" series.

Duff

Gaelic, meaning "swarthy."

Duke

Latin, meaning "leader." Became popular as a first name after the birth of Giuliana and Bill Rancic's son Duke.

Duncan

Scottish, meaning "dark warrior." King Duncan is a character in Shakespeare's *Macbeth*.

Dustin
(alt. Dusty)

French, meaning "brave warrior." Actor Dustin Hoffman is known for his roles in *Rain Man* and *Tootsie*.

Dwayne

Irish Gaelic, meaning "swarthy." Actor Dwayne Johnson was known as "The Rock" during his professional wrestling career.

Dwight

Flemish, meaning "blond." Dwight D. Eisenhower was the 34th President of the United States.

Dwyer

Gaelic, meaning "dark wise one."

Dylan
(alt. Delyn, Dillon)

Welsh, meaning "son of the sea." Dylan Thomas was a famous Welsh poet.

Long names

Alexander	Bartholomew
Christopher	Demetrius
Giovanni	Maximillian
Montgomery	Nathaniel
Sebastian	Zachariah

Short names

Al	Ben
Dai	Ed
Jay	Jon
Max	Rio
Sam	Ty

E

Boys' names

Eamon
(alt. Eames, Eamonn)

Irish, meaning "wealthy protector." Eamonn Walker is known for his role in *Oz*.

Earl
(alt. Earle, Errol)

English, meaning "nobleman, warrior." Became popular after the sitcom *My Name is Earl*.

Ebenezer
(abbrev. Ebb)

Hebrew, meaning "stone of help." The main character in Charles Dickens's *A Christmas Carol* is Ebenezer Scrooge.

Edgar
(alt. Elgar)

Old English, meaning "wealthy spear." Gothic author Edgar Allen Poe wrote "The Raven," amongst other poems.

Edison

English, meaning "son of Edward." Thomas Edison was one of the most influential American inventors.

Edmund

English, meaning "wealthy protector." Sir Edmund Hillary became the first Westerner to reach the summit of Mount Everest, in 1953.

Edric

Old English, meaning "rich and powerful."

Edsel

Old German, meaning "noble." Car pioneer Henry Ford named his son Edsel.

Edward
(alt. Eduard; abbrev. Ed, Eddie, Eddy, Ned, Ted)

Old English, meaning "wealthy guard." A character in the "Twilight" series.

Edwin

English, meaning "wealthy friend."

Efrain

Hebrew, meaning "fruitful."

Egan

Irish, meaning "fire."

Einar

Old Norse, meaning "battle leader." A popular name for boys in Iceland.

Eladio

Greek, meaning "Greek."

Elam

Hebrew, meaning "eternal." The son of Shem and of Noah in the Bible.

Eldon

Old English, meaning "Ella's hill."

Eldred

(alt. Eldridge)

Old English, meaning "old venerable counsel."

Elgin

Old English, meaning "high minded." Also the name of a town in Scotland.

Eli

(alt. Eliah)

Hebrew, meaning "high." Eli Whitney is credited with inventing the cotton gin.

Elijah

(alt. Elias, Elio, Ellis; abbrev. Eli)

Hebrew, meaning "the Lord is my God." Elias is the Greek form of the same name, Elio is the Spanish version and Ellis the Welsh version. Actor Elijah Wood played Frodo in *The Lord of the Rings*. Elias Disney was Walt Disney's father.

Ellery

Old English, meaning "elder tree."

Elliott

Variant of Elio, meaning "the Lord is my God." Elliot was the little boy in the classic film *E.T.*

Ellison

English, meaning "son of Ellis."

Elmer

(alt. Elmo)

Old English, meaning "noble"; Arabic, meaning "aristocratic." Associated with the children's characters Elmer the Elephant and Elmo from *Sesame Street*.

Elon

Hebrew, meaning "oak tree."

Elroy

French, meaning "king." A cartoon character in *The Jetsons*.

Elton

Old English, meaning "Ella's town." A famous Elton is legendary singer and songwriter Elton John.

Elvin

English, meaning "elf-like." Elvin Bale was a huge circus performer known for cannonball stunts.

Elvis

Figure in Norse mythology. Made famous by the singer Elvis Presley.

Emanuel
(alt. Immanuel, Imanol)

Hebrew, meaning "God is with us."

Emeric

German, meaning "work rule." St. Emeric was known for living a pure and pious life.

Emile
(alt. Emiliano, Emilio)

Latin, meaning "eager." Emile is Remy the rat's older brother in Disney's *Ratatouille*.

Emlyn

Welsh, from the UK town of the same name.

Emmett

English, meaning "universal." Emmett Kelly was known for his role as Weary Willie, the Depression-era clown.

Emrys

Welsh, meaning "immortal." Said to be the birth name of the magician Merlin.

Enoch

Hebrew, meaning "dedicated." Enoch is an ancestor of Noah in the Bible.

Enrico
(alt. Enrique)

Italian form of Henry, meaning "home ruler."

Enzo

Italian, short for Lorenzo, meaning "laurel." Enzo Ferrari was the founder of the Ferrari car company.

Ephron
(alt. Effron, Efron)

Hebrew, meaning "dust."

Erasmo
(alt. Erasmus)

Greek, meaning "to love."

Eric

Old Norse, meaning "ruler." Famous Erics include legendary guitarist Eric Clapton.

Ernest
(alt. Ernesto, Ernie, Ernst)

Old German, meaning "serious." Author Ernest Hemingway wrote the novel *The Old Man and the Sea*, amongst others.

Erskine

Scottish, meaning "high cliff."

Erwin

Old English, meaning "boar friend."

Ethan
(alt. Etienne)

Hebrew, meaning "long lived." Ethan Hawke is an actor. Ethan Coen and his brother Joel are award winning film producers and directors.

Eugene

Greek, meaning "well born." Eugene Allen was a butler at the White House for 34 years and the inspiration for the film *The Butler*.

Evan

Welsh, meaning "God is good." Evan Williams founded Twitter.

Everard

Old English, meaning "strong boar."

Everett

English, meaning "strong boar."

Ewan
(alt. Ewald, Ewell)

Old English, from Owen, meaning "well born" or "noble." Actor Ewan McGregor is known for his roles in *Moulin Rouge* and the "Star Wars" series.

Exton

English, meaning "on the river Exe."

Ezra

Hebrew, meaning "helper." Name of the poet Ezra Pound.

Boys' names

Fabian
(alt. *Fabien, Fabio*)
Latin, meaning "one who grows beans."

Fabrice
(alt. *Fabrizio*)
Latin, meaning "works with his hands."

Faisal
(alt. *Faison*)
Arabic, meaning "resolute."

Faron
Spanish, meaning "pharaoh," and Gaelic for "thunder."

Farrell
Gaelic, meaning "hero."

Faulkner
Latin, from "falcon."

Faustino
Latin, meaning "fortunate."

Felipe
(alt. *Filippo*)
Spanish, meaning "lover of horses."

Felix
(alt. *Felice*)
Italian/Latin, meaning "happy." Felix the Cat was first developed as a cartoon during the silent movie era.

Fennel
Latin, name of a herb.

Ferdinand
(alt. *Fernando*)
Old German, meaning "bold voyager." Ferdinand was a popular name for Roman emperors and kings of Spain, as well as Disney princes.

Fergus

(alt. Ferguson)

Gaelic, meaning "supreme man." King Fergus is Merida's father in Disney's *Brave*.

Ferris

Gaelic, meaning "rock." The lead character from *Ferris Bueller's Day Off*.

Fidel

Latin, meaning "faithful." Fidel Castro was President of Cuba from 1976 to 2008.

Finbarr

Gaelic, meaning "fair head."

Finian

Gaelic, meaning "fair." St. Finnian is an important Irish saint.

Finlay

(alt. Finley, Finn)

Gaelic, meaning "fair-haired courageous one." Actor Finlay Robertson is known for his role in *Doctor Who*. Finn is a character in *Glee* and is also a name in its own right meaning "from Finland."

Finnegan

Gaelic, meaning "fair." *Finnegans Wake* is a work by James Joyce.

Fintan

Gaelic, meaning "little fair one." Fintan supposedly saved one of Noah's granddaughters from the flood.

Flavio

Latin, meaning "yellow hair." *Flavio* is the name of an opera by Handel.

Florencio

(alt. Florentino)

Latin, meaning "from Florence."

Florian

(alt. Florin)

Slavic/Latin, meaning "flower," though it is a masculine name. Popular in Germany and Switzerland and the name of the patron saint of Poland.

Floyd

Welsh, meaning "gray haired." Floyd is the given name of two title-winning American professional boxers.

Flynn

Gaelic, meaning "with a ruddy complexion." Flynn Rider is Rapunzel's unlikely love interest in Disney's *Tangled*.

Fortunato

Italian, meaning "lucky."

Forrest

(alt. Forest)

Old French, meaning "woodsman." Made popular by the movie *Forrest Gump*.

Foster

Old English, meaning "woodsman."

Fotini

(alt. Fotis)

Greek, meaning "light."

Famous male guitarists

Brian (May)

Carlos (Santana)

Chuck (Berry)

Eddie (Van Halen)

Eric (Clapton)

Frank (Zappa)

Jeff (Beck)

Jimi/Jimmy (Hendrix/Page)

Joe (Satriani)

Keith (Richards)

Prince (Rogers Nelson)

Francesco

(alt. Francis, Francisco, Franco, François)

Latin, meaning "from France." After the election of Pope Francis, Francesco has become the most popular name for baby boys in Italy.

Frank

(alt. Frankie, Franklin, Franz)

Middle English, meaning "free landholder." Famous Franks include singers Frank Sinatra and Frank Zappa, and 32nd US President Franklin D. Roosevelt.

Fraser

(alt. Frasier)

Scottish, meaning "of the forest men." *Frasier* was a 1990s sitcom revolving around main character, Dr. Frasier Crane.

Frederick

(alt. Fred, Freddie, Freddy)

Old German, meaning "peaceful ruler." There is a spelling or pronunciation variation of Frederick in virtually every Western language.

Furman

Old German, meaning "ferryman."

G

Boys' names

Gabino

Latin, meaning "God is my strength."

Gabriel
(alt. Gale)

Hebrew, meaning "hero of God." An archangel of God.

Gael
(alt. Gale)

English, old reference to the Celts. Gale has increased in popularity since "The Hunger Games" series.

Gage
(alt. Gaige)

Old French, meaning "pledge."

Galen

Greek, meaning "healer." Name of an ancient Roman philosopher.

Galileo

Italian, meaning "from Galilee." Galileo Galilei was an important physicist during the Scientific Revolution.

Ganesh

Hindi, meaning "Lord of the throngs." One of the Hindu deities.

Gannon

Irish, meaning "fair skinned."

Gareth
(alt. Garth)

Welsh, meaning "gentle." Also the name of one of the Knights of the Round Table.

Garfield

Old English, meaning "spear field." Also the name of the cartoon cat.

Garland

English, as in "garland of flowers."

Garrett
(alt. Garet, Gared, Garratt, Garrod)

Derived in the Middle Ages from Gerald or Gerard. Garret the Great was a political powerhouse in fifteenth-century Ireland. Now most popular as a given name in the US and Ireland.

Gary
(alt. Garry, Geary)

Germanic, meaning "spear." The name peaked in popularity in the 1950s, when actor Gary Cooper won an Oscar. Modern Garys include actor Gary Oldman.

Gaspar
(alt. Gaspard)

Persian, meaning "treasurer." A children's cartoon character from *Gaspar and Lisa*.

Gaston

From the region in the south of France.

Gavin
(alt. Gawain)

Scottish/Welsh, meaning "little falcon." Gavin DeGraw and Gavin Christopher are both singers.

Gene

Greek, shortened form of Eugene, meaning "well born." Made popular by actor and dancer Gene Kelly.

Gennaro

Italian, meaning "of Janus."

Geoffrey
(abbrev. Geoff)

Old German, meaning "peace." Actor Geoffrey Rush appeared in *Shine* and the "Pirates of the Caribbean" series.

George
(alt. Giorgio)

Greek, meaning "farmer." Recently chosen for Queen Elizabeth's great grandson, by William and Kate, the Duke and Duchess of Cambridge. Prince George is now third in line to the throne.

Gerald
(alt. Geraldo, Gerard, Gerardo, Gerhard)

Old German, meaning "spear ruler." Former President of the United States Gerald Ford is the only person to have served as both President and Vice President without being elected to either position, thanks to two infamous resignations before him.

Geronimo

Italian, meaning "sacred name." Geronimo lead the Apache Indians against the Spanish in the 19th century.

Gerry

English, meaning "independent." Famous Gerrys include singer Gerry Rafferty.

Gert

Old German, meaning "strong spear."

Gervase

Old German, meaning "with honor." Gervase Peterson is a long-time *Survivor* contestant.

Giacomo

Italian, meaning "God's son." Legendary womanizer Casanova's full name was actually Giacomo Girolame Casanova.

Gibson

English, meaning "son of Gilbert." The name of a legendary guitar company.

Gideon

Hebrew, meaning "tree cutter." A figure in the Bible.

Gilbert
(alt. Gilberto)

French, meaning "bright promise." One half of the famous comedy opera duo Gilbert and Sullivan.

Giles

Greek, meaning "small goat."

Gino

Italian, meaning "well born."

Giovanni

Italian form of John, meaning "God is gracious." Actor Giovanni Ribisi is known for his roles in *Friends* and *Avatar*.

Giulio

Italian, meaning "youthful."

Giuseppe

Italian form of Joseph, meaning "Jehovah increases."

Glen
(alt. Glenn, Glyn)

English, from the word "glen." Glenn Miller was a world-renowned big band director and composer.

Godfrey

German, meaning "peace of God." Associated with comedian Godfrey.

Gordon

Gaelic, meaning "large fortification." Gordon Ramsay is a chef and reality TV star.

Gottlieb

German, meaning "good love." One of composer Mozart's birth names was Gottlieb.

Graeme
(alt. Graham)
English, meaning "gravelled area."

Grant
English, from the word "grant."

Granville
English, meaning "gravelly town." Granville Woods was the first African-American electrical engineer after the Civil War.

Gray
(alt. Grey)
English, from the word "gray."

Grayson
English, meaning "son of gray."

Green
English, from the word "green." The Green Lantern is a superhero from DC Comics.

Gregory
(alt. Gregorio, Grieg; abbrev. Greg)
English, meaning "watcher." Actor Gregory Peck was known for his role in *To Kill A Mockingbird*.

Griffin
English, from the word "griffin." A mythological creature.

Guido
Italian, meaning "guide." Popularized after the show *Jersey Shore*.

Guillaume
French form of William, meaning "strong protector."

Gulliver
English, meaning "glutton." Made popular after the publication of *Gulliver's Travels* by Jonathan Swift.

Gunther
German, meaning "warrior." Gunther von Hagans is the *Body Works* artist.

Gurpreet
Indian, meaning "love of the teacher."

Gustave
(abbrev. Gus)
Scandinavian, meaning "royal staff."

Guy
English, from the word "guy." Chef Guy Fieri regularly appears on the Food Network.

Boys' names

Habib

Arabic, meaning "beloved one."

Haden

(alt. Haiden, Hayden, Haydn)
English, meaning "hedged valley."

Hades

Greek, meaning "sightless." Name of the underworld in Greek mythology.

Hadrian

From Hadria, a north Italian city. The name of an influential Roman emperor.

Hadwin

Old English, meaning "friend in war."

Hakeem

Arabic, meaning "wise and insightful." Actor Hakeem Kae-Kazim is known for his role in *Hotel Rwanda*.

Hamid

Arabic, meaning "praiseworthy." Hamid Karzai was the President of Afghanistan 2004–14.

Hamilton

Old English, meaning "flat topped hill." Alexander Hamilton was one of the nation's Founding Fathers.

Hamish

Scottish form of James, meaning "he who supplants."

Hampus

Swedish form of Homer, meaning "pledge." Hampus Lindholm currently plays for the Anaheim Ducks.

Hamza

Arabic, meaning "lamb." Also a letter in the Arabic alphabet.

Han

(alt. Hannes, Hans)

Scandinavian, meaning "the Lord is gracious." Han Solo was a central character in the "Star Wars" films.

Hank

German, form of Henry, meaning "home ruler." Singer Hank Williams was a country superstar.

Hansel

German, meaning "the Lord is gracious." *Hansel and Gretel* is a children's fairy tale by the Brothers Grimm.

Hardy

English, meaning "tough."

Harlan

English, meaning "dweller by the boundary wood."

Harland

Old English, meaning "army land." KFC was founded by Colonel Harland David Sanders.

Harley

Old English, meaning "hare meadow." Associated with the Harley Davidson motorcycle company.

Harmon

Old German, meaning "soldier."

Harold

Scandinavian, meaning "army ruler." Actor Harold Ramis was known for his roles in *Ghostbusters* and *Stripes*.

Harrison

Old English, meaning "son of Harry." Famous Harrisons include actor Harrison Ford.

Harry

Old German, form of Henry, meaning "home ruler." Famous Harrys include fictional character Harry Potter and singer Harry Styles.

Hart

Old English, meaning "stag."

Harvey

Old English, meaning "strong and worthy." The title character of the film *Harvey*, starring James Stewart.

Haskell

Hebrew, meaning "intellect."

Hassan

Arabic, meaning "handsome." Hassan Rouhani is the current president of Iran.

Heart

English, from the word "heart."

Heath

English, meaning "heath" or "moor."
Actor Heath Ledger was known for
his roles in *Brokeback Mountain* and
The Dark Knight.

Heathcliff

English, meaning "cliff near a heath."
Also the main male character in
Emily Bronte's novel *Wuthering
Heights*.

Heber

Hebrew, meaning "partner."

Hector

Greek, meaning "steadfast."

Henry

*(alt. Hal, Hale, Henri, Hendrik,
Hendrix)*

Old German, meaning "home ruler."
Eight kings of England were called
Henry. Harry is often used as a name
by boys given the name Henry, as
with Prince Harry, who is officially
Prince Henry of Wales.

Henson

English, meaning "son of Henry."

Herbert

*(alt., Herb, Heriberto; abbrev. Bert,
Herbie)*

Old German, meaning "illustrious
warrior." Herbert Hoover was the
31st President of the United States.

Herman

(alt. Herminio, Hermon)

Old German, meaning "soldier."
Herman Melville was the author of
Moby-Dick.

Hermes

Greek, meaning "messenger."
Hermes was the messenger of the
gods in Greek mythology.

Herschel

Yiddish, meaning "deer."

Hezekiah

Hebrew, meaning "God gives
strength."

Hideki

Japanese, meaning "excellent trees."
The Prime Minister of Japan during
World War II was Hideki Tojo.

Hideo

Japanese, meaning "excellent name."

Hilario

Latin, meaning "cheerful, happy."

Hilary

(alt. Hillary)

English, meaning "cheerful." Sir
Edmund Hillary became the first
Westerner to reach the summit of
Mount Everest, in 1953.

Hillel

Hebrew, meaning "greatly praised."

Hilliard

Old German, meaning "battle guard."

Hilton

Old English, meaning "hill settlement." The name of a large hotel chain.

Hiram
(alt. *Hyrum*)

Hebrew, meaning "exalted brother."

Hiro

Spanish, meaning "sacred name." Hiro is a character on *Heroes*.

Hiroshi

Japanese, meaning "generous."

Hirsch

Yiddish, meaning "deer."

Hobart

English, meaning "bright and shining intellect."

Hodge

English, meaning "son of Roger."

Hogan

Gaelic, meaning "youth." Became well known after the success of sitcom *Hogan's Heroes* in the 1960s. Also made famous by wrestler Hulk Hogan.

Holden

English, meaning "deep valley." Holden Caulfield is the teenage protagonist of *The Catcher in the Rye*.

Hollis

Old English, meaning "holly tree."

Homer

Greek, meaning "pledge." Famous Homers include the ancient Greek poet, and Homer Simpson from *The Simpsons*.

Honorius

Latin, meaning "honorable."

Horace

Latin, common name of the Roman poet Quintus Horatius Flaccus.

Houston

Old English, meaning "Hugh's town."

Howard

Old English, meaning "noble watchman." Famous Howards include Howard Carter, who discovered the tomb of King Tut, and Howard Hughes, the aviator and movie maker.

Howell

Welsh, meaning "eminent and remarkable."

Hoyt

Norse, meaning "spirit" or "soul," or Old English meaning "hill inhabitant." Hoyt Fortenberry is a character in *True Blood*

Hristo

From Christo, meaning "follower of Christ."

Hubert

German, meaning "bright and shining intellect." Givenchy's founder was Count Hubert de Givenchy.

Hudson

Old English, meaning "son of Hugh." Associated with the Hudson River.

Hugh

(alt. Hugo, Huw, Ugo)

Old German, meaning "soul, mind and intellect." Famous Hughs include actors Hugh Jackman, Hugh Laurie, and Hugh Grant.

Humbert

Old German, meaning "famous giant." Made famous by the paedophile protagonist of Vladimir Nabokov's *Lolita*.

Humphrey

Old German, meaning "peaceful warrior." Actor Humphrey Bogart is best known for his role in *Casablanca*.

Hunter

English, from the word "hunter." Name of singer Hunter Hayes.

Hurley

Gaelic, meaning "sea tide."

Huxley

Old English, meaning "Hugh's meadow."

I Boys' names

Iago

Spanish, meaning "he who supplants." Also the name of the villain in Shakespeare's *Othello*.

Ian
(alt. Iain, Ion)

Gaelic, variant of John, meaning "God is gracious." Novelist Ian Fleming wrote the "James Bond" novels.

Ianto

Welsh, meaning "gift of God."

Ibrahim

Arabic, meaning "father of many." An Arabic name for the father of Islam, Abraham.

Ichabod

Hebrew, meaning "glory is good." Also the name of the protagonist in *The Legend of Sleepy Hollow*.

Ichiro

Japanese, meaning "firstborn son."

Idris

Welsh, meaning "fiery leader." Actor Idris Elba is known for his roles in *Luther* and *Mandela: Long Walk to Freedom*.

Ifan

Welsh variant of John, meaning "God is gracious."

Ignacio

Latin, meaning "ardent" or "burning."

Ignatz

German, meaning "fiery."

Igor

Russian, meaning "Ing's soldier."

Ikaika

Hawaiian, meaning "strong."

Ike

Hebrew, short for Isaac, meaning "laughter." Famous Ikes include singer Ike Turner and former US President Dwight D. Eisenhower (known as Ike).

Ilan

Hebrew, meaning "tree."

Ilias

Greek variant of Elijah, Hebrew, meaning "the Lord is my God."

Indiana

Latin, meaning "from India." Also the name of a US state.

Indigo

English, describing a deep blue color derived from a plant.

Indio

Spanish, meaning "indigenous people."

Ingo

Danish, meaning "meadow."

Inigo

Spanish, meaning "fiery." Inigo Montoya is a character in *The Princess Bride*.

Ioannis

Greek, meaning "the Lord is gracious."

Ira

Hebrew, meaning "full grown and watchful."

Irvin
(alt. Irving, Irwin)

Gaelic, meaning "green and fresh water." Composer Irving Berlin is known for songs such as "White Christmas."

Isaac
(alt. Isaak)

Hebrew, meaning "laughter." Isaac was the son of Abraham and Sarah in the Bible and the Qu'ran.

Isadore
(alt. Isidore, Isidro)

Greek, meaning "gift of Isis."

Isai
(alt. Isaiah, Isaias, Izaiah)

Arabic, meaning "protection and security."

Iser

Yiddish, meaning "God wrestler."

Ishmael
(alt. Ismael)

Hebrew, meaning "God listens." The narrator and protagonist of *Moby-Dick*, by Herman Melville.

Israel

Hebrew, meaning "God perseveres."
Also the name of the country.

Istvan

Hungarian variant of Stephen,
meaning "crowned."

Itai

Hebrew, meaning "the Lord is with
me."

Ivan

A Slavic version of John, meaning
"God is gracious." Several Russian
tsars bore the name, including the
infamous Ivan the Terrible. Ivan
Rodriguez was a Major League
Baseball player for many years.

Ivanhoe

Russian, meaning "God is gracious."
Also title of the novel by Walter
Scott.

Ivey

English, variant of Ivy.

Ivo

French, from the word "yves,"
meaning "yew tree."

Ivor

Scandinavian, meaning "yew."
Associated with the Ivor Novello
songwriting awards.

Ivory

English, from the word "ivory."

Boys' names

Jabari
Swahili, meaning "valiant."

Jabez
Hebrew, meaning "borne in pain."

Jace
(alt. Jaece, Jase, Jayce)
Hebrew, meaning "healer."

Jacek
(alt. Jacirto)
Polish, meaning "hyacinth." Derived from the Greek name Hyakinthos, which comes from a myth about a beautiful boy.

Jack
(alt. Jackie, Jacky, Jacques, Jaquez)
From the Hebrew John, meaning "God is gracious." Famous Jacks include actors Jack Black, Jack Nicholson, and Jack Lemon.

Jackson
(alt. Jaxon)
English, meaning "son of Jack." Artist Jackson Pollock is known for his large, paint-splashed paintings.

Jacob
(alt. Jaco, Jacobo, Jago)
Hebrew, meaning "he who supplants." A main character in the "Twilight" series.

Jaden
(alt. Jadyn, Jaeden, Jaiden, Jaidyn, Jayden, Jaydin)
Hebrew, meaning "Jehovah has heard." Will Smith's son is Jaden Smith.

Jafar
Arabic, meaning "stream." The name of the villain in Disney's *Aladdin*.

Jagger

Old English, meaning "one who cuts." Made famous by Rolling Stones singer Mick Jagger.

Jaheem
(alt. Jaheim)

Hebrew, meaning "raised up."

Jahir

Hindi, meaning "jewel."

Jaime

Variant for James, meaning "he who supplants." "J'aime" is also French for "I love."

Jair
(alt. Jairo)

Hebrew, meaning "God enlightens."

Jake

Shortened form of Jacob, meaning "he who supplants." Famous Jakes include actor Jake Gyllenhaal and pitcher Jake Peavy.

Jalen

American, meaning "healer" or "tranquil." Derives from the Greek spelling of Galen.

Jali

Gujarati, meaning "latticed screen."

Jalon

Greek, meaning "healer" or "tranquil."

Jamaal
(alt. Jamal, Jamar, Jamarcus, Jamari, Jamarion, Jamir)

Arabic, meaning "handsome." Jamar is a modern variant of the name.

James
(abbrev. Jamie, Jaimie, Jim, Jimmy)

English, meaning "he who supplants." Famous Jameses include actors James Franco, James Coburn, and Jim Carey and fictional characters James Bond and James T. Kirk.

Jameson
(alt. Jamison)

English, meaning "son of James." Associated with Jameson Irish Whiskey.

Jamil

Arabic, meaning "handsome."

Jamin

Hebrew, meaning "son of the right hand."

Jan
(alt. Janko, János)

Slavic, from John, meaning "the Lord is gracious." Also a term of endearment in Arabic, meaning "dear."

Janus

Latin, meaning "gateway." Roman god of doors, beginnings and endings.

Japheth
(alt. Japhet)

Hebrew, meaning "comely." One of the sons of Noah.

Jared
(alt. Jarem, Jaren, Jaret, Jarod, Jarrod)

Hebrew, meaning "descending." Actor Jared Leto appeared in *Dallas Buyers' Club*.

Jarlath

Gaelic, from Iarlaith, from Saint Iarlaithe mac Loga.

Jarom

Greek, meaning "to raise and exalt." One of the prophets in the Book of Mormon.

Jarrell

Variant of Gerald, meaning "spear ruler."

Jarrett

Old English, meaning "spearbrave."

Jarvis

Old German, meaning "with honor."

Jason
(alt. Jayce)

Greek, meaning "healer." Famous Jasons include actors Jason Sudeikis and Jason Bateman, and singer Jason Derulo.

Jasper

Greek, meaning "treasure holder" or "speckled stone." Jasper as a stone has been used for jewelry for thousands of years.

Javen

Arabic, meaning "youth." One of Noah's grandsons in the Bible.

Javier

Spanish, meaning "bright." Actor Javier Bardem appeared in *Skyfall*.

Jay

Latin, meaning "jaybird." Associated with rapper Jay-Z.

Jaylan
(alt. Jaylen, Jalon)

Greek, meaning "healer."

Jeevan

Indian, meaning "life."

Jefferson

English, meaning "son of Jeffrey." Thomas Jefferson was the third President of the United States.

Jeffrey
(abbrev. Jeff)

Old German, meaning "peace." Famous Jeffs include actors Jeff Bridges and Jeff Daniels.

Jensen
(alt. Jenson)

Scandinavian, meaning "son of Jan." Famous Jensens include actor Jensen Ackles and Formula 1 driver Jenson Button.

Jeremy
(alt. Jem)

Hebrew, meaning "the Lord exalts." Famous Jeremys include Jeremy Renner and Jeremy Irons.

Jeriah

Hebrew, meaning "Jehovah has seen."

Jericho

Arabic, meaning "city of the moon." Site of the epic biblical Battle of Jericho.

Jermaine

Latin, meaning "brotherly." Jermaine Jackson was one of the original members of the Jackson Five.

Jerome

Greek, meaning "sacred name."

Jerry

English, from Gerald, meaning "spear ruler." Famous Jerrys include presenter Jerry Singer, comedian Jerry Seinfeld, and the film *Jerry Maguire*.

Jesse

Hebrew, meaning "the Lord exists." Famous Jesses include outlaw Jesse James.

Jesus

Hebrew, meaning "the Lord is Salvation" and the Son of God.

Jet
(alt. Jett)

English, meaning "black gemstone."

Jethro

Hebrew, meaning "eminent." Famous Jethros include the band Jethro Tull, and the father-in-law of Moses in the Bible.

Jiri
(alt. Jiro)

Czech, meaning "farmer."

Joachim

Hebrew, meaning "established by God." The name of the Virgin Mary's father in the Bible.

Joah
(alt. João)

Hebrew, meaning "God is gracious."

Joaquin

Hebrew, meaning "established by God." Academy Award winner Joaquin Phoenix changed his name to "Leaf" as a child to match his siblings River and Rain.

Joel

Hebrew, meaning "Jehovah is the Lord." Famous Joels include comedian Joel McHale and singer Joel Madden.

John
(alt. Jon, Johnny)

Hebrew, meaning "God is gracious." Famous Johns include musicians John Lennon and John Legend, and *Daily Show* host Jon Stewart. Actor Johnny Depp and singer Johnny Cash are both also Johns by birth.

Jolyon

English, meaning "young."

Jonah
(alt. Jonas)

Hebrew, meaning "dove." A character in the Bible who was swallowed by a whale.

Jonathan
(alt. Johnathan, Johnathon, Jonathon; abbrev. Jon, Johnny, Jonny, Jonty)

Hebrew, meaning "God is gracious." Famous Jonathans include actors Jonathan Taylor Thomas and Jonathan Rhys Meyers, and author Jonathan Swift.

Jordan
(alt. Jory, Judd)

Hebrew, meaning "downflowing." Michael Jordan is a legendary basketball player.

Jorge

From George, meaning "farmer." Actor Jorge Garcia is known for his role as Hurley in *Lost*.

José

Spanish variant of Joseph, meaning "God increases." Associated with Jose Cuervo tequila.

Joseph
(abbrev. Joe, Joey, Joss)

Hebrew, meaning "Jehovah increases." Famous Josephs include actor Joseph Gordon-Levitt and baseball legend Joe DiMaggio.

Joshua
(alt. Joshué; abbrev. Josh)

Hebrew, meaning "Jehovah is salvation." The leader of the Israelites after Moses's death in the Bible. Actor Josh Hutcherson is known for his role in the "Hunger Games" trilogy.

Josiah

Hebrew, meaning "God helps." One of the kings of Judah in the Bible.

Jovan

Latin, meaning "the supreme God."

Joweese

Native American, meaning "chirping bird." More commonly used for girls originally, it has now become a boys' name.

Joyce

Latin, meaning "joy." Used for boys and girls.

Juan

Spanish variant of John, meaning "God is gracious." Juan Pablo Galavis was a notorious contestant on *The Bachelor*.

Jubal

Hebrew, meaning "ram's horn."

Jude

Hebrew, meaning "praise" or "thanks." Associated with the Beatles' song "Hey Jude."

Judson

Variant of Jude, meaning "praise" or "thanks."

Julian

(alt. Julien, Julio; abbrev. Jules)

Greek, meaning "belonging to Julius." The original calendar in the Roman Empire was the Julian calendar.

Julius

Latin, meaning "youthful." Julius Caesar was a Roman emperor.

Junior

Latin, meaning "the younger one." Can also be used as a suffix to names to denote a name that has been passed down generations—for example James Earl Carter, Sr. was the father of US President James Earl Carter, Jr.

Junius

Latin, meaning "young."

Jupiter

Latin, meaning "the supreme God." Jupiter was king of the Roman gods and the god of thunder.

Juraj

Hebrew, meaning "God is my judge."

Jurgen

German form of George, meaning "farmer."

Justice

English, from the word "justice," meaning a set of moral values, ethics, and law.

Justin

(alt. Justus)

Latin, meaning "just and upright." Famous Justins include singers Justin Timberlake and Justin Bieber.

Juwan

Hebrew, meaning "the Lord is gracious."

 **Boys' names**

Kabelo
African, meaning "gift."

Kade
Scottish, meaning "from the wetlands."

Kadeem
Arabic, meaning "one who serves." Actor Kadeem Hardison is known for his role on *A Different World*.

Kaden
(alt. Kadin, Kaeden, Kaedin, Kaiden)
Arabic, meaning "companion."

Kadir
Arabic, meaning "capable and competent."

Kafka
Czech, meaning "bird-like." Name of the influential author Franz Kafka.

Kahekili
Hawaiian, meaning "the thunder." Also the name of several kings of Maui.

Kai
Greek, meaning "keeper of the keys." Kai also means "dog" in Cornish, "ocean water" in Hawaiian, and "food" in Maori.

Kaito
Japanese, meaning "ocean and sake dipper." One of the most popular names for boys in Japan.

Kalani
Hawaiian, meaning "sky."

Kale
German, meaning "free man."

Kaleb
Hebrew, meaning "dog" or "aggressive." Also an alternate spelling for Caleb.

Kalen
(alt. *Kaelen, Kalan*)
Gaelic, meaning "uncertain."

Kaleo
Hawaiian, meaning "the voice."
Kaleo Kanahele is a silver medal-winning paralympian in volleyball.

Kamari
Indian, meaning "the enemy of desire."

Kamil
Arabic, meaning "perfection." Also a Polish and Slovakian name meaning "religious service attender."

Kane
Gaelic, meaning "little battler." The title character of the film *Citizen Kane.*

Kani
Hawaiian, meaning "sound."

Kanye
Town in Botswana. Made popular by rapper Kanye West.

Kareem
(alt. *Karim*)
Arabic, meaning "generous." Kareem Abdul-Jabur is a legendary basketball player.

Karl
(alt. *Karlson*)
Old German, meaning "free man." Actor Karl Urban is known for his roles in *Lord of the Rings* and *Star Trek.*

Kavon
Gaelic, meaning "handsome."

Kayden
Arabic, meaning "companion."

Kazimierz
Polish, meaning "declares peace."

Kazuki
Japanese, meaning "radiant hope."

Kazuo
Japanese, meaning "harmonious man." Depending on the characters/spellings used, Kazuo can also mean "first son" or "first in leadership."

Keagan
(alt. *Keegan, Kegan*)
Gaelic, meaning "small flame."

Keane
Gaelic, meaning "fighter."

Keanu
Hawaiian, meaning "breeze." Actor Keanu Reeves is known for his roles in *Speed* and "The Matrix" trilogy.

Keary

Gaelic, meaning "black-haired."

Keaton

English, meaning "place of hawks." Can be used for boys and girls.

Keeler

Gaelic, meaning "beautiful and graceful." Can be used for boys and girls.

Keenan

(alt. Kenan, Keenen)

Gaelic, meaning "little ancient one." Keenen Ivory Wayans is one of the Wayan comedy brothers.

Keiji

Japanese, meaning "govern with discretion."

Keir

Gaelic, meaning "dark-haired" or "dark-skinned."

Keith

Gaelic, meaning "woodland." Keith Richards is one of the legendary members of the Rolling Stones.

Kekoa

Hawaiian, meaning "brave one" or "soldier."

Kelby

Old English, meaning "farmhouse near the stream."

Kell

(alt. Kellan, Kellen, Kelley, Kelly, Kiel)

Norse, meaning "spring." Associated with the ancient Book of Kells.

Kelsey

Old English, meaning "victorious ship." Actor Kelsey Grammer is known for his roles in Cheers and Frasier.

Kelton

Old English, meaning "town of the keels."

Kelvin

Old English, meaning "friend of ships." A kelvin is a unit of temperature measurement.

Kendal

Old English, meaning "the Kent river valley."

Kendon

Old English, meaning "brave guard."

Kendrick

Gaelic, meaning "royal ruler."

Kenelm

Old English, meaning "bold."

Kenji

Japanese, meaning "intelligent second son." Also the name of a period in Japanese history in the 13th century.

Kennedy

Gaelic, meaning "helmet head." The Kennedy family is a prominent American Catholic dynasty, whose members included the 35th President of the United States, John F. Kennedy.

Kenneth

(alt. Kenne; abbrev. Ken)

Gaelic, meaning "born of fire." Kenneth Branagh is an actor of stage and screen, including in the "Harry Potter" films.

Kennison

English, meaning "son of Kenneth."

Kent

English, meaning "rim or border." Associated with Clark Kent, aka Superman.

Kenton

English, meaning "town of Ken."

Kenya

(alt. Kenyatta, Kenyon)

From the country and mountain in Africa.

Kenzo

Japanese, meaning "wise." Kenzo is the name of a fashion brand.

Keola

Hawaiian, meaning "life."

Keon

(alt. Keoni)

Persian, meaning "King of Kings." In Hawaiian, the name also means "God is gracious."

Kepler

German, meaning "hat maker."

Kermit

(alt. Kerwin)

Gaelic, meaning "without envy." Associated with Kermit the Frog.

Kerr

English, meaning "wetland." Kerr Smith is an American actor.

Keshav

Indian, meaning "beautiful haired." One of the names for Vishnu in the Hindu religion.

Kevin

Gaelic, meaning "handsome beloved." Famous Kevins include actors Kevin Bacon and Kevin Kline.

Khalid

(alt. Khalif)

Arabic, meaning "immortal." Actor Khalid Abdalla is known for his roles in *United 93* and *The Kite Runner*.

Khalil

Arabic, meaning "friend." Khalil Gibran is an influential poet, writer and philosopher, frequently quoted at weddings.

Kian

(alt. Keyon, Kyan)

Persian, meaning "king or realm." In Ireland, the same spelling also means "ancient."

Kiefer

German, meaning "barrel maker." 24 star Kiefer Sutherland's full name is Kiefer William Frederick Dempsey George Rufus Sutherland.

Kieran

(alt. Kieron, Kyron)

Gaelic, meaning "black." Actor Kieran Culkin is known for his role in Scott Pilgrim vs. the World.

Kijana

Swahili, meaning "youth."

Kilby

English, from the town of the same name.

Kilian

Irish, meaning "bright-headed."

Kimani

African, meaning "beautiful and sweet."

King

English, meaning "male ruler of state."

Kingsley

English, meaning "the king's meadow." Kingsley Shacklebolt is a character in the "Harry Potter" series.

Kirby

German, meaning "settlement by a church." Also the name of a small, pink, bubble-like video game character.

Kirk

Old German, meaning "church." Famous Kirks include Kirk Douglas and Captain James T. Kirk from Star Trek.

Klaus

German, meaning "victorious."

Kobe

(alt. Koda, Kody)

Japanese, meaning "a Japanese city." Kobe Bryant plays for the LA Lakers.

Kofi

Ghanaian, meaning "born on Friday." Kofi Annan was the Secretary General of the UN until 2006.

Kohana

Japanese, meaning "little flower."

Kojo
Ghanaian, meaning "Monday."

Korben
(alt. *Korbin*)

Gaelic, meaning "a steep hill." Korben Dallas is a character in *The Fifth Element*.

Kramer
German, meaning "shopkeeper." Kramer is a character from *Seinfeld*.

Kurt
German, meaning "courageous advice." Famous Kurts include *Glee* character Kurt, actor Kurt Russell, and the late Nirvana singer Kurt Cobain.

Kurtis
French, meaning "courtier."

Kwame
Ghanaian, meaning "born on Saturday."

Kyden
English, meaning "narrow little fire."

Kyle
(alt. *Kylan, Kyleb, Kyler*)

Gaelic, meaning "narrow and straight." Actor Kyle Massey is known for his roles on The Disney Channel.

Kyllion
Irish, meaning "war."

Kyree
From Cree, a Canadian tribe.

Kyros
Greek, meaning "legitimate power."

Names of poets

Alfred (Lord Tennyson)

Allen (Ginsberg)

Dylan (Thomas)

Geoffrey (Chaucer)

Langston (Hughes)

Ralph (Waldo Emerson)

Robert (Burns)

Seamus (Heaney)

Walt (Whitman)

William (Wordsworth)

L Boys' names

Laban

Hebrew, meaning "white." Laban is the brother of Rebekah in the Bible.

Lachlan

Gaelic, meaning "from the land of lakes."

Lacy

Old French, after the place in France. Masculine form of Lacey.

Lalit

Hindi, meaning "beautiful."

Lamar
(alt. Lemar)

Old German, meaning "water." Lamar Odom is known for his marriage to Khloe Kardashian and his skills as a basketball player.

Lambert

Scandinavian, meaning "land brilliant."

Lambros

Greek, meaning "brilliant and radiant."

Lamont

Old Norse, meaning "law man."

Lance

French, meaning "land." Lance Armstrong is a disgraced former racing cyclist.

Lancelot

Variant of Lance, meaning "land." The name of one of the Knights of the Round Table.

Landen
(alt. Lando, Landon, Landyn, Langdon)

English, meaning "long hill."

Lane
(alt. Layne)

English, from the word "lane."

Lannie
(alt. Lanny)

German, meaning "precious." Also a nickname for Rowland or Orlando.

Larkin

Gaelic, meaning "rough" or "fierce." Philip Larkin was a famous poet.

Laron

French, meaning "thief."

Lasse

Finnish, meaning "girl." (Still, ironically, a boy's name.) Lasse Holstrom is a film director and Lasse Viren one of the all-time great long distance runners.

Laszlo

Hungarian, meaning "glorious rule."

Lathyn

Latin, meaning "fighter."

Latif

Arabic, meaning "gentle."

Laurel

Latin, meaning "bay." One of the founders of Jamaican ska music was Laurel Aitken. Used for both boys and, more commonly, girls.

Laurent

French, from Lawrence, meaning "man from Laurentum." The founder of YSL was Yves Saint Laurent.

Lawrence
(alt. Lars, Laurence; abbrev. Larry)

Latin, meaning "man from Laurentum." Actor Laurence Olivier is a stage legend also known for his roles in dozens of Hollywood movies. Larry King was a longstanding live TV presenter.

Lawson

Old English, meaning "son of Lawrence."

Lazarus

Hebrew, meaning "God is my help."

Leandro

Latin, meaning "lion man."

Lear

German, meaning "of the meadow." The title character in Shakespeare's play King Lear.

Lee
(alt. Leigh)

Old English, meaning "meadow" or "valley." Famous Lees include actor Lee Marvin and JFK assassin Lee Harvey Oswald.

Leib

Yiddish, meaning "lion."

Leif
(alt. Leiv, Lief, Liev)

Scandinavian, meaning "heir." Actor Liev Schreiber is known for his roles in X-Men Origins: Wolverine, and the "Scream" trilogy.

Leith

From the Scottish town of the same name.

Lennox
(alt. Lenny)

Gaelic, meaning "with many elm trees." Famous Lennoxes include boxer Lennox Lewis.

Leo

Latin, meaning "lion." Also the name of the star sign.

Leon

Latin, meaning "lion." Associated with the band Kings of Leon.

Leonard

Old German, meaning "lion strength." Actor Leonard Nimoy was known for his role in *Star Trek*.

Leonardo

Italian, meaning "bold lion." Artist Leonardo da Vinci painted the *Mona Lisa*.

Leopold

German, meaning "brave people."

Leroy

French, meaning "king." The title character of the song "Bad Bad Leroy Brown."

Lesley
(alt. Leslie; abbrev. Les)

Scottish, meaning "holly garden." Used for both boys and girls.

Lester

English, meaning "from Leicester."

Lewis

French, meaning "renowned fighter." Famous Lewises include comedian Lewis Black and author Lewis Carroll.

Lexar
(alt. Lex, Lexer)

Shortened form of Alexander, meaning "man's defender."

Liam

German, meaning "helmet." Famous Liams include actor Liam Neeson and One Direction member Liam Payne.

Lincoln

English, meaning "lake colony." Abraham Lincoln was the 16th President of the United States.

Lindsay
(alt. Lindsey)

Scottish, meaning "linden tree." Singer Lindsey Buckingham is a founding member of Fleetwood Mac. Can be used for boys and girls.

Linus

Latin, meaning "lion." A character in the *Peanuts* cartoon.

Lionel

English, meaning "lion." Famous Lionels include singer Lionel Richie, and composer Lionel Bart.

Llewellyn

Welsh, meaning "like a lion."

Lloyd

Welsh, meaning "gray-haired and sacred." Andrew Lloyd Webber is the composer of *Cats* and other musicals.

Logan

Gaelic, meaning "hollow." Associated with sci-fi novel *Logan's Run*.

Lonnie

English, meaning "lion strength."

Lorcan

Gaelic, meaning "little fierce one."

Louis
(alt. Lou, Louie, Luigi, Luis)

French, meaning "famous warrior." Famous Louises include One Direction singer Louis Tomlinson and designer Louis Vuitton.

Lucas
(alt. Lukas, Luca)

English, meaning "man from Luciana." George Lucas is the legendary *Star Wars* producer.

Lucian
(alt. Lucio)

Latin, meaning "light."

Ludwig

German, meaning "famous fighter." Ludwig van Beethoven was a hugely influential composer.

Luke
(alt. Luc, Luka)

Latin, meaning "from Lucanus" (in southern Italy). Famous Lukes include the Gospel of Luke from the Bible, *Star Wars* character Luke Skywalker, and actor Luke Perry.

Lupe

Latin, meaning "wolf." Lupe Fiasco is a rapper.

Luther

German, meaning "soldier of the people." Superman's arch enemy is supervillain Lex Luther.

Lyle

French, meaning "the island." Lyle Lovett is a country singer songwriter and actor.

Lyn
(alt. Lyndon)

Spanish, meaning "pretty." Used for both boys and girls.

M Boys' names

Mac
(alt. Mack, Mackie)
Scottish, meaning "son of."

Macaulay
Scottish, meaning "son of the phantom." Name of the actor Macaulay Culkin.

Mace
English, meaning "heavy staff" or "club." Also a shortened form of Mason.

Mackenzie
Scottish, meaning "the fair one." Actor Mackenzie Crook is known for his roles in *Pirates of the Caribbean* and *Game of Thrones*.

Mackland
Scottish, meaning "land of Mac."

Macon
French, from the name of towns in France and Georgia.

Macsen
Scottish, meaning "son of Mac."

Madden
(alt. Mads)
Irish, meaning "descendant of the hound." Associated with the Madden NFL gaming series.

Maddox
(alt. Maddux)
English, meaning "good" or "generous." Derived from Madoc, who was a legendary Welsh prince. Name chosen by Angelina Jolie for her first adopted child, now Maddox Jolie-Pitt.

Madison
(alt. Madsen)

Irish, meaning "son of Madden." James Madison was the fourth President of the United States.

Magnus
(alt. Manus)

Latin, meaning "great." Popular name in Scandinavia.

Maguire

Gaelic, meaning "son of the beige one." The title character of the movie Jerry Maguire.

Mahesh

Hindi, meaning "great ruler." One of the names for Lord Shiva in the Hindu faith.

Mahir

Arabic, meaning "skillful."

Mahlon

Hebrew, meaning "sickness."

Mahmoud

Arabic, meaning "praiseworthy." Mahmoud Ahmadinejad was the President of Iran until 2013.

Mahoney

Irish, meaning "bear."

Major

English, from the word "major." Reported as one of the fastest climbing boys' names.

Makal

From Michael, meaning "close to God."

Makani

Hawaiian, meaning "wind."

Makis

Hebrew, meaning "gift from God."

Mako

Hebrew, meaning "God is with us."

Malachi
(alt. Malachy)

Irish, meaning "messenger of God." The name of a Jewish prophet in the Bible.

Malcolm

English, meaning "Columba's servant." Well-known Malcolms include activist Malcolm X, and sitcom Malcolm in the Middle.

Mali

Arabic, meaning "full and rich." Also the name of a West African republic.

Manfred

Old German, meaning "man of peace." Associated with the band Manfred Mann.

Manish
(alt. Manesh)

English, meaning "manly."

Manley

English, meaning "manly and brave."

Mannix

Gaelic, meaning "little monk." Associated with the show *Mannix*.

Manoi
(alt. Manos)

Japanese, meaning "love springing from intellect."

Manuel

Hebrew, meaning "God is with us."

Manus

Gaelic, meaning "great." Popular during the Viking period.

Manzi

Italian, meaning "steer."

Marcel
(alt. Marcelino, Marcello)

French, meaning "little warrior." Marcel Marceau was perhaps the most famous mime of all time.

Mariano

Latin, meaning "from the god Mars." Also a tribute to the Virgin Mary.

Mario
(alt. Marius)

Latin, meaning "manly." Famous Marios include presenter Mario Lopez, and Nintendo character Mario.

Mark
(alt. Marc, Marco, Marcus, Marek, Markus)

English, meaning "from the god Mars." Famous Marks include the Gospel of Mark in the Bible, and actors Mark Hamill and Mark Wahlberg.

Marley
(alt. Marlin, Marlow)

Old English, meaning "meadow near the lake." Famous Marleys include singer Bob Marley, and the infamous Labrador dog Marley.

Marlon

English origin, meaning "little hawk." Aactor Marlon Brando is a famous bearer of this name.

Marshall

Old French, meaning "caretaker of horses."

Martin
(alt. Marty)

Latin, meaning "dedicated to Mars." Famous Martins include actors Martin Freeman and Martin Sheen, and director Martin Scorsese.

Marvel

English, from the word "marvel." Associated with Marvel comic books.

Marvin

Welsh, meaning "sea friend."
Famous Marvins include singer
Marvin Gaye, composer Marvin
Hamlish, and character Marvin
the Martian.

Mason

English, from the word for someone
who works with either stone or
brick.

Mathias

(alt. Matthias)

Hebrew, meaning "gift of God."
Matthias was the apostle chosen to
replace Judas in the Bible.

Matthew

(alt. Mathieu; abbrev. Matt)

Hebrew, meaning "gift of the Lord."
Famous Matthews include the Gospel
of Matthew from the Bible, and
actors Matthew McConaughey and
Matthew Perry.

Maurice

(alt. Mauricio)

Latin, meaning "dark skinned" or
"Moorish." Famous Maurices
includ children's author Maurice
Sendak.

Maverick

American, meaning "nonconformist
leader." Made popular by the movie
Top Gun.

Maximillian

(alt. Max, Maxie, Maxim, Maximilian)

Latin, meaning "greatest." Also the
name of several Roman emperors.
More common now in the
abbreviated form Max, as with actor
Max Greenfield.

Maximino

Latin, meaning "little Max."

Maxwell

Latin, meaning "Maccus' stream."
Actor Maxwell Caulfield is known for
his role in Dynasty.

Maynard

Old German, meaning "brave." A
character from Desperate Housewives.

McArthur

Scottish, meaning "son of Arthur."
Associated with General Douglas
MacArthur.

McCoy

Scottish, meaning "son of Coy."

Mckenna

(alt. Mackenna)

Irish Gaelic, meaning "son of the
handsome one." Also used as a girls'
name.

Mearl

English, meaning "my earl."

Mederic

French, meaning "doctor."

Mekhi

African, meaning "who is God?" Actor Mekhi Phifer is known for his roles in *ER* and *8 Mile*.

Mel

Gaelic, meaning "smooth brow." Famous Mels include actor Mel Gibson. Also an abbreviation for Melvin.

Melbourne

From the city in Victoria, Australia.

Melchior

Persian, meaning "king of the city." The name of one of the Three Kings in the Bible.

Melton

English, meaning "town of Mel."

Melva

Hawaiian, meaning "plumeria."

Melville

Scottish, meaning "town of Mel." Herman Melville is the author of *Moby-Dick*.

Melvin

(alt. Melvyn; abbrev. Mel)

English, meaning "smooth brow." Actor Melvyn Douglas was known for his roles in *Hud* and *Being There*.

Memphis

Greek, meaning "established and beautiful." Also the name of the Tennessee city.

Mercer

English, from the word "mercer."

Merl

French, meaning "blackbird."

Merlin

Welsh, meaning "sea fortress." Merlin is perhaps the most famous wizard of all, appearing in stories from the medieval era.

Merrick

Welsh, meaning "Moorish."

Merrill

Gaelic, meaning "shining sea."

Merritt

English, from the word "merit."

Merton

Old English, meaning "town by the lake."

Meyer

Hebrew, meaning "bright farmer."

Michael

(alt. Michel, Michele, Migeul; abbrev. Mick, Mickey, Mike, Mikey)

Hebrew, meaning "resembles God." Famous Michaels include the archangel, singers Michael Jackson and Michael Bublé, and legendary basketball player Michael Jordan.

Michalis
(alt. Miklos)
Greek form of Michael, meaning "resembles God."

Michelangelo
Italian, meaning "Michael's angel." Name of the famous Italian artist who painted the Sistine Chapel.

Milan
From the name of the Italian city. Also the name of Shakira's oldest son.

Miles
(alt. Milo, Milos, Myles)
English, from the word "miles." Famous Mileses include trumpeter Miles Davies, singer Miles Kane, and *Star Trek: Next Generation* character Miles O'Brien.

Milton
English, meaning "miller's town." Poet John Milton was the author of *Paradise Lost*.

Miro
Slavic, meaning "peace."

Misha
Russian, meaning "who is like God."

Mitchell
(abbrev. Mitch)
English, meaning "who is like God."

Modesto
Italian, meaning "modest." Also the name of a Californian town.

Moe
Hebrew, meaning "God's helmet." Moe is a character from *The Simpsons*.

Mohamed
(alt. Mohammad, Mohamet, Mohammed, Muhammad)
Arabic, meaning "praiseworthy." Acknowledged as the prophet and founder of Islam.

Monroe
Gaelic, meaning "mouth of the river Rotha." Marylin Monroe was a screen legend.

Monserrate
Latin, meaning "jagged mountain."

Montague
(abbrev. Monty)
French, meaning "pointed hill."

Montana
Latin, meaning "mountain." Also the name of the state.

Monte
Italian, meaning "mountain."

Montgomery
(abbrev. Monty)

Variant of Montague, meaning "pointed hill." Actor Montgomery Clift was known for his roles in *From Here to Eternity* and *A Place in the Sun*.

Moody

English, from the word "moody."

Mordecai

Hebrew, meaning "little man."

Morgan

Welsh, meaning "circling sea." Famous Morgans include actor Morgan Freeman and filmmaker Morgan Spurlock. Can be both a boys' and girls' name.

Moritz

Latin, meaning "dark skinned and Moorish." Also a German variation of Maurice.

Moroccan

Arabic, meaning "from Morocco." Popularized by Mariah Carey's choice for her son.

Morpheus

Greek, meaning "shape." The Roman god of dreams in the epic poem *Metamorphoses*.

Morris

Welsh, meaning "dark-skinned and Moorish."

Morrison

English, meaning "son of Morris." Associated with singer and guitarist Jim Morrison.

Mortimer

French, meaning "dead sea."

Morton

Old English, meaning "moor town."

Moses
(alt. Moshe, Moshon)

Hebrew, meaning "savior." A key figure in the Bible.

Moss

English, from the word "moss."

Mungo

Gaelic, meaning "most dear." Lake Mungo is in Australia.

Murphy

Irish, meaning "sea warrior." Murphy's Law states if something can go wrong, it will.

Murray

Gaelic, meaning "lord and master."

Mustafa

Arabic, meaning "chosen." Also a name for the prophet Muhammad in Islam.

Myron

Greek, meaning "myrrh."

N

Boys' names

Najee

Arabic, meaning "dear companion." Also the name of an influential jazz musician.

Nakia

Arabic, meaning "pure."

Nakul

Indian, meaning "mongoose." Choreographer Nakul Dev Mahajan has made a name for himself as a mainstream Bollywood choreographer.

Naphtali

Hebrew, meaning "wrestling." One of Joseph's brothers in the Bible.

Napoleon

Italian origin, meaning "man from Naples." Name of the French general who became Emperor of France.

Narciso

Latin, from the myth of Narcissus, who drowned after gazing at his own reflection.

Nash

English, meaning "at the ash tree." Singer songwriter Graham Nash is known for his involvement with Crosby, Stills & Nash.

Nasir

Arabic, meaning "helper."

Nathan

(alt. Nathaniel; abbrev. Nate)

Hebrew, meaning "God has given." The name of several characters in the Bible.

Naveen

Indian, meaning "new." Actor Naveen Andrews is known for his roles in *Lost* and *The English Patient*.

Ned

Originally a nickname for Edward, meaning "wealthy guard." Now used frequently in its own right. Ned Flanders is a character from *The Simpsons*.

Neftali

Hebrew, meaning "struggling."

Nehemiah

Hebrew, meaning "comforter."

Neil

(alt. Neal, Niall)

Irish, meaning "champion." Famous Neils include astrophysicist Neil deGrasse Tyson, actor Neil Patrick Harris, and singer Neil Young.

Neilson

Irish, meaning "son of Neil."

Nelson

Variant of Neil, meaning "champion." Famous Nelsons include Nelson Mandela and Lord Horatio Nelson.

Nemo

Latin, meaning "nobody." Made popular after the Disney/Pixar film *Finding Nemo*.

Neo

Latin, meaning "new." Neo is a character in "The Matrix" trilogy.

Nephi

Greek, meaning "cloud."

Nessim

Arabic, meaning "breeze."

Nestor

Greek, meaning "traveler." Also the name of a king in ancient Greek mythology.

Neville

Old French, meaning "new village." Neville Longbottom is a character in the "Harry Potter" series.

Newton

English, meaning "new town." Scientist Sir Isaac Newton is celebrated as the discoverer of gravity.

Nicholas

(alt. Nicklas, Nicolas, Niklas, Nikola; abbrev. Nick, Nicky, Nicoi)

Greek, meaning "victorious." Famous Nicholases include Saint Nicholas (the original Santa Claus), actor Nicolas Cage, and alchemist Nicholas Flamel.

Nigel

Gaelic, meaning "champion." Producer Nigel Lythgoe is known for his work on *So You Think You Can Dance*.

Nikhil

Sanskrit, meaning "whole" or "entire."

Nikita

Greek, meaning "unconquered." Used for both boys and girls.

Nimrod

Hebrew, meaning "we will rebel." A prominent character in the Bible.

Nissim

Hebrew, meaning "wonderful things."

Noah

Hebrew, meaning "peaceful." A prominent character in the Bible, the subject of the movie *Noah*.

Noel

French, meaning "Christmas." Famous Noels include comedian and actor Noel Coward.

Nolan

Gaelic, meaning "champion."

Norbert

Old German, meaning "northern brightness." Norbert is the pet dragon in the "Harry Potter" series.

Norman

(abbrev. Norm)

Old German, meaning "northerner." The Norman people of the Middle Ages originated from Normandy in France.

Normand

French, meaning "from Normandy."

Norris

Old French, meaning "northerner."

Norton

English, meaning "northern town."

Norval

French, meaning "northern town."

Norwood

English, meaning "northern forest."

Nova

Latin, meaning "new." Also the name of a vast nuclear explosion in a white dwarf star.

Nuno

Latin, meaning "ninth."

Nunzio

Italian, meaning "messenger."

Boys' names

Oakley

English, meaning "from the oak meadow." The name of a brand of clothing.

Obadiah

Hebrew, meaning "God's worker." Used throughout the Bible to indicate a servant of God.

Obama

African, meaning "crooked." Last name of the current President of the United States.

Obed

Hebrew, meaning "servant of God."

Oberon

(abbrev. Obi, Obie)

Old German, meaning "royal bear." The Fairy King in Shakespeare's *A Midsummer Night's Dream*.

Octave

(alt. Octavian, Octavio)

Latin, meaning "eight." An octave is a series of eight notes in a musical scale.

Oda

(alt. Odell, Odie, Odis)

Hebrew, meaning "praise God."

Ogden

Old English, meaning "oak valley."

Oisin

Celtic, meaning "fawn." From an ancient Irish poet.

Ola

Norse, meaning "precious." Ola Nordmann is a personification of Norway, in the same way Uncle Sam represents the USA.

Olaf
(alt. Olan)

Old Norse, meaning "ancestor." The name of the animated snowman in Disney's Frozen.

Oleander
Hawaiian, meaning "joyous."

Oleg
(alt. Olen)

Russian, meaning "holy."

Olin
Russian, meaning "rock."

Oliver
(alt. Olivier; abbrev. Ollie, Olly)

Latin, meaning "olive tree." Associated with the musical Oliver! and Disney's Oliver and Company.

Omar
(alt. Omari, Omarion)

Arabic, meaning "speaker." Actor Omar Epps is known for his roles in House and Resurrection.

Ora
Latin, meaning "hour."

Oran
(alt. Oren, Orrin)

Gaelic, meaning "light and pale."

Orange
English, from the word "orange," applied to both the fruit and the color.

Orion
From the ancient Greek legend of a massive hunter.

Orlando
(alt. Orlo)

Old German, meaning "old land." Famous Orlandos include actor Orlando Bloom, the Shakespearean character Orlando from As You Like It, and the city of Orlando in Florida.

Orpheus
Greek, meaning "beautiful voice." A legendary ancient Greek musician, poet and prophet.

Orson
Latin, meaning "bear." Film director Orson Welles was known for the movies Citizen Kane and Touch of Evil.

Orville
Old French, meaning "gold town." Associated with popcorn brand Orville Redenbacher.

Osaka
From the Japanese city.

Osborne
(alt. Osbourne)

Norse, meaning "bear god." Associated with Sharon and Ozzy Osbourne's family.

Oscar

Old English, meaning "spear of the gods." The Oscars is the nickname for the Academy Awards.

Oswald

German, meaning "God's power." Oswald the Lucky Rabbit was Walt Disney's first creation.

Otha
(alt. Otho)

German, meaning "wealth."

Othello

Old German, meaning "wealth." From the Shakespearean character and play.

Otis

German, meaning "wealth." Otis Redding was a legendary singer and several US sports stars share the same given name.

Otten

German, meaning "son of Otto."

Otto

German, meaning "wealthy." Anne Frank's father was called Otto Frank.

Owain

Welsh, meaning "youth."

Owen
(alt. Eoghan, Eoin)

Welsh, meaning "well born and noble" or "little warrior." Famous Owens include actor Owen Wilson. Eoghan and Eoin are the Irish variants.

Oz

Hebrew, meaning "strength." Associated with *The Wizard of Oz*.

P

Boys' names

Pablo
Spanish, meaning "little." Famous Pablos include artist Pablo Picasso.

Paco
Native American, meaning "eagle." Paco Rabanne is a Spanish fashion designer and brand name. His real first name is Francisco.

Padma
Sanskrit, meaning "lotus."

Padraig
Irish, meaning "noble."

Panos
Greek, meaning "all holy."

Paolo
Italian, meaning "little."

Paresh
Sanskrit, meaning "supreme standard."

Parker
Old English, meaning "park keeper."

Pascal
Latin, meaning "Easter child." The more common female equivalent is Pascale.

Patrick
(alt. Patrice; abbrev. Paddy, Pat)
Irish, meaning "noble." St. Patrick is the patron saint of Ireland.

Patten
(alt. Patton)
English, meaning "noble." Patton Oswalt is a comedian.

Paul
Hebrew, meaning "small." Paul was one of Jesus's main disciples.

Pavel
Latin, meaning "small."

Pax

Latin, meaning "peace."

Paxton

English, meaning "town of peace."

Payne

Latin, meaning "peasant."

Payton

Latin, meaning "peasant's town."

Pedro

Spanish form of Peter, meaning "rock."

Penn

English, meaning "hill." Penn Jillette is a magician and one half of Penn and Teller.

Percival
(alt. Percy)

French, meaning "pierce the valley." The name of one of the Knights of the Round Table.

Perez

Hebrew, meaning "breach." Famous Perezes include Perez Morton, the lawyer and revolutionary Boston patriot, and professional gossiper Perez Hilton.

Pericles

Greek, meaning "far-famed." Pericles was an influential ancient Greek general and statesman.

Perrin

Greek, meaning "rock."

Perry

English, meaning "rock." Associated with the series *Perry Mason*.

Pervis

English, meaning "purveyor."

Peter
(alt. Pedro, Petros, Pierre, Piers; abbrev. Pete)

Greek, meaning "rock." St. Peter was one of Jesus's disciples in the Bible.

Peyton

Old English, meaning "fighting man's estate." Peyton Manning plays for the Denver Broncos.

Philip
(alt. Phillip; abbrev. Phil, Pip)

Greek, meaning "lover of horses." Famous Philips include husband of the Queen, Prince Philip, Philip the Apostle, and author Philip Pullman.

Philo

Greek, meaning "love."

Phineas
(alt. Pinchas)

Hebrew, meaning "oracle." A character in the cartoon *Phineas and Ferb*.

Phoenix

Greek, meaning "dark red." In ancient Greek mythology, a phoenix is a bird that has the power to regenerate itself from its ashes.

Pierce
(alt. Pierson)

Meaning "son of Piers."

Placido

Latin, meaning "placid." Placido Domingo is a famous tenor opera singer.

Pradeep

Hindi, meaning "light."

Pranav

Sanskrit, meaning "spiritual leader."

Presley

Old English, meaning "priest's meadow." Made famous by legendary singer Elvis Presley.

Preston

Old English, meaning "priest's town." Preston Burke is a character from *Grey's Anatomy*.

Primo

Italian, meaning "first." Also a slang term for "excellent."

Primus

Latin, meaning "first." Often used as a name for villains in Marvel comic books.

Prince

English, from the word "prince." Associated with singer and guitarist Prince.

Prospero

Latin, meaning "prosperous." Prospero is the protagonist in Shakespeare's play *The Tempest*.

Pryce
(alt. Prize)

Old French, meaning "prize."

Pryor

English, meaning "first." Famous Pryors include legendary comedian Richard Pryor.

Ptolemy

Greek, meaning "aggressive" or "warlike."

Boys' names

Qabil
(alt. Quabil, Quadim)
Arabic, meaning "able."

Quadir
Arabic, meaning "powerful."

Quaid
Irish, meaning "fourth."

Quemby
Norse, meaning "from the woman's estate."

Quentin
(alt. Quinten, Quintin, Quinton, Quintus)
Latin, meaning "fifth." Director Quentin Tarantino is known for his movies including *Kill Bill* and *Django Unchained*.

Quillan
Gaelic, meaning "sword."

Quillon
Gaelic, meaning "club."

Quincy
Old French, meaning "estate of the fifth son." Quincy Jones is a music mogul.

Quinlan
Gaelic, meaning "fit, shapely and strong."

Quinn
Gaelic, meaning "counsel." Quinn is a character from *Glee*.

R

R Boys' names

Radames

Slavic, meaning "famous joy." A character in the Verdi opera *Aida*.

Raekwon

Hebrew, meaning "God has healed." Associated with Raekwon of Wu-Tang Clan.

Rafael
(alt. Rafe, Rafer, Raffi, Raphael)

Hebrew, meaning "God has healed." One of the archangels in the Bible.

Ragnar

Old Norse, meaning "judgment warrior." Ragnar Lodbrok was a legendary Norse ruler from the Viking era.

Raheem
(alt. Rahim)

Arabic, meaning "merciful and kind."

Rahm

Hebrew, meaning "mercy."

Rahul
(alt. Raoul, Raul)

Indian, meaning "efficient." Rahul was the Buddha's son.

Raiden
(alt. Rainen)

From the Japanese god of thunder.

Rainer

Old German, meaning "deciding warrior."

Raj

Sanskrit, meaning "kingdom," and Polish, meaning "heaven."

Rajesh
(alt. Ramesh)

Indian, meaning "ruler of kings."

Raleigh

Old English, meaning "deer's meadow." Made famous by the explorer Sir Walter Raleigh.

Ralph

Old English, meaning "wolf." Famous Ralphs include actor Ralph Fiennes, fashion brand Ralph Lauren, and character Ralph from *The Simpsons*.

Ram

English, from the word for a male sheep.

Ramiro

Germanic, meaning "powerful in battle." Popular name for baby boys in Argentina.

Ramsey
(alt. Ramsay)

Old English, meaning "wild garlic island." Gordon Ramsay is a celebrity chef.

Randall
(alt. Randal, Randolph, Randy)

Old German, meaning "wolf shield." Can be traced back to the poem "Lord Randall" in 1882.

Raniel

English, meaning "God is my happiness."

Ranjit

Indian, meaning "influenced by charm."

Rannoch

Gaelic, meaning "fern." Also the name of an area in the Scottish Highlands.

Rashad

Arabic, meaning "good judgment."

Rashid
(alt. Rasheed)

Indian, meaning "rightly guided." Ar-Rashid, meaning "The Guide," is one of Allah's names in the Islamic tradition.

Rasmus

Greek, meaning "beloved."

Raven

English, from the word for the large, black bird.

Ravi

Hindi, meaning "sun."

Ray

English, from the word "ray." Famous Rays include singer Ray Charles. Other well-known Rays were actually given the name Raymond.

Raymond
(alt. Rayner; abbrev. Ray)

English, meaning "advisor." Title character of the sitcom *Everybody Loves Raymond*. Actors Ray Winstone and Ray Liotta are both Raymonds.

Raz

Israeli, meaning "secret" or "mystery."

Reagan

(abbrev. Reggie)

Irish, meaning "little king." Ronald Reagan was the 40th President of the United States.

Reginald

(abbrev. Reg, Reggie)

Latin, meaning "regal." Singer Sir Elton John's birth name was Reginald Kenneth Dwight.

Regis

Latin, meaning "of the king."

Reid

Old English, meaning "by the reeds."

Reilly

(alt. Riley)

Irish, meaning "courageous."

Remus

Latin, meaning "swift." Famous Remuses include Romulus and Remus of the ancient Roman myth, and the "Harry Potter" character Remus Lupin.

Rémy

French, meaning "from Rheims."

Renatus

(alt. Renat, Renate, Renato, Rene)

Latin, meaning "rebirth."

Reno

Latin, meaning "renewed." Also the name of the city in Nevada.

Reuben

Spanish, meaning "a son." The name of a sandwich containing corned beef, Swiss cheese, and sauerkraut.

Reuel

Hebrew, meaning "friend of God."

Rex

Latin, meaning "king." The kings of ancient Rome were called Rex, before it became a republic.

Rey

Spanish, meaning "king," and Telugu, meaning "friend."

Reynold

Latin, meaning "king's advisor."

Rhodes

German, meaning "where the roses grow." Also the name of the Greek island.

Rhodri

Welsh, meaning "ruler of the circle."

Rhys

(alt. Reece, Riece)

Welsh, meaning "enthusiasm."
Famous Rhyses include actors
Jonathan Rhys Meyers and Rhys Ifans.

Richard

*(alt. Ricardo, Rikardo; abbrev. Dick,
Dickie, Richie, Rick, Ricki, Ricky,
Ritchie)*

Old German, meaning "powerful
leader." Famous Richards include
37th President of the United States
Richard Nixon, comedian Richard
Pryor, and actor Richard Gere.

Ridley

English, meaning "cleared wood."
Director Sir Ridley Scott is known
for the films *Gladiator* and *Thelma &
Louise*.

Rigby

English, from the place in Lancashire.
Often associated with the Beatles'
song "Eleanor Rigby."

Riky

Irish Gaelic, meaning "courageous."

Ringo

English, meaning "ring." Ringo Starr
was the drummer with the Beatles.

Rio

Spanish, meaning "river." *Rio* is a
song by Duran Duran and the title
of a computer-animated adventure
comedy film.

Riordan

Gaelic, meaning "bard."

Rishi

Sanskrit, meaning "scribe."

Roald

Scandinavian, meaning "ruler."
Roald Dahl is the author of *Charlie
and the Chocolate Factory* and other
children's books.

Robert

*(alt. Roberto; abbrev. Bob, Bobby,
Dobby, Rob, Robbie)*

Old German, meaning "bright fame."
Famous Roberts include actors
Robert de Niro and Robert Pattinson,
and legendary singers Bob Dylan and
Bob Marley.

Robin

English, from the word for the small,
flame-breasted bird. Famous Robins
include comedian Robin Williams,
singer Robin Thicke, and outlaw
legend Robin Hood.

Robinson

English, meaning "son of Robin."
The eponymous hero of the novel
Robinson Crusoe.

Rocco

(alt. Rocky)

Italian, meaning "rest." Also the
name of Madonna's son.

Roderick
(abbrev. Rod, Roddy)

German, meaning "famous power."
A character from *The Following*.

Rodney
(abbrev. Rod, Roddy)

Old German, meaning "island near the clearing."

Rodrigo

Spanish form of Roderick, meaning "famous power." Famous Rodrigos include Spanish composer Joaquin Rodrigo.

Roger

Old German, meaning "spear man." Famous Rogers include athlete Roger Bannister, The Who singer Roger Daltrey, and tennis pro Roger Federer.

Roland

Old German, meaning "renowned land."

Rolf

Old German, meaning "wolf."

Rollie
(alt. Rollo)

Old German, meaning "renowned land."

Roman

Latin, meaning "from Rome." Associated with the Roman people.

Romeo

Latin, meaning "pilgrim to Rome." Made famous by Shakespeare's play *Romeo and Juliet*. Also the name of David and Victoria Beckham's second son.

Ronald
(alt. Ron, Ronnie)

Norse, meaning "mountain of strength." Ron Weasley is a character in the "Harry Potter" series.

Ronan

Gaelic, meaning "little seal."

Rory

English, meaning "red king." Rory Calhoun was an actor. Golfer Rory McIlroy has won the US Open.

Ross
(alt. Russ)

Scottish, meaning "cape."

Rowan
(alt. Roan)

Gaelic, meaning "little red one." Rowan Atkinson is a comedian and comic actor, and also the voice of Zazu in *The Lion King*.

Roy

Gaelic, meaning "red." Famous Roys include singer Roy Orbison.

Ruben

Hebrew, meaning "son."

Rudolph

(alt. Rudy)

Old German, meaning "famous wolf." The name of Santa's legendary reindeer.

Rufus

Latin, meaning "red-haired." Actor Rufus Sewell is known for his role in *A Knight's Tale*.

Rupert

Variant of Robert, meaning "bright fame." Actor Rupert Grint is known for his role in the "Harry Potter" series.

Russell

Old French, meaning "little red one." Comedian Russell Brand is known for his role in *Arthur*.

Rusty

English, meaning "ruddy."

Ryan

Gaelic, meaning "little king." Famous Ryans include actor Ryan Gosling and comedian Ryan Stiles.

Ryder

English, meaning "horseman."

Rye

English, from the word "rye."

Ryker

From Richard, meaning "powerful leader." *Ryker's Islands* is a fictional prison facility in Marvel Comics stories.

Rylan

English, meaning "land where rye is grown."

Ryley

Old English, meaning "rye clearing."

S

Boys' names

Saber
(alt. Sabre)
French, meaning "sword."

Sagar
African, meaning "ruler of the water."

Sage
English, meaning "wise." Can also refer to the herb.

Sakari
Native American, meaning "sweet."

Salim
(alt. Saleem)
Arabic, meaning "secure." The Salim Khan family are a Bollywood dynasty.

Salvador
Spanish, meaning "savior." Famous Salvadors include artist Salvador Dali.

Salvatore
Italian, meaning "savior." There have been dozens of the Italian, Sicilian, or New York mafia called Salvatore.

Samir
Arabic, meaning "pleasant companion."

Samson
Hebrew, meaning "son of Sam." The character Samson from the Bible had extraordinary strength.

Samuel
(alt. Sam, Sama, Sammie, Sammy)
Hebrew, meaning "God is heard." Famous Samuels include a prophet from the Bible, actor Samuel L. Jackson, and author Samuel Langhorne Clemens (known as Mark Twain).

Sandeep
(alt. Sundeep)
Hindi, meaning "lighting the way."

Sanjay
Hindi, meaning "victory." Sanjay Gupta is a well-known TV doctor.

Santana
Spanish, meaning "saint." Associated with guitarist Carlos Santana.

Santiago
Spanish, meaning "Saint James." Also the name of the capital city of Chile.

Santino
Spanish, meaning "little Saint James."

Santo
(alt. Santos)
Latin, meaning "saint."

Sasha
(alt. Sacha, Sascha)
Russian, derived from Alexander, meaning "defending men." Sasha can be used for boys or girls. In the US, female Sashas are significantly more common.

Sawyer
English, meaning "one who saws wood." Associated with the novel *Tom Sawyer*.

Scott
(alt. Scottie)
English, meaning "from Scotland." Scott Dixon is an IndyCar champion, and cartoonist Scott Adams created *Dilbert*.

Seamus
Irish variant of James, meaning "he who supplants." Seamus Heaney is a Nobel prize-winning poet.

Sean
(alt. Shaun, Shawn)
Variant of John, meaning "God is gracious." Famous Seans include actors Sean Penn and Sean Connery.

Sebastian
(alt. Sébastien; abbrev. Seb)
Greek, meaning "revered." The name of the crab character in Disney's *The Little Mermaid*.

Sergio
(alt. Serge)
Latin, meaning "servant."

Seth
Hebrew, meaning "appointed." Famous Seths include actors Seth MacFarlane and Seth Greene.

Severus
Latin, meaning "severe." Severus Snape is a character in the "Harry Potter" series.

Seymour

English, from the place name in northern France. Famous Seymours include Principal Seymour Skinner of *The Simpsons*, and actor Philip Seymour Hoffman.

Shane

Variant of Sean, meaning "God is gracious." Famous Shanes include actors Shane West and Shane Harper.

Sharif

Arabic, meaning "honored." Also a name for descendants of one of Muhammad's grandchildren.

Shea

Gaelic, meaning "admirable."

Shelby

Norse, meaning "willow." Associated with the Mustang car.

Sherlock

English, meaning "fair-haired." The name of the lead character in Sir Arthur Conan Doyle's "Sherlock Holmes" novels.

Sherman

Old English, meaning "shear man."

Shmuel

Hebrew, meaning "his name is God."

Shola

Arabic, meaning "energetic."

Sidney
(alt. Sid, Sydney)

English, meaning "wide meadow." Actor Sidney Poitier is known for his roles in *Guess Who's Coming to Dinner* and *In The Heat of the Night*.

Sigmund

Old German, meaning "victorious hand." Associated with neurologist Sigmund Freud.

Silvanus
(alt. Silvio)

Latin, meaning "woods." An ancient Roman deity of woods and fields.

Simba
(alt. Sim)

Swahili, meaning "lion." Associated with the character from Disney's *The Lion King*.

Simon
(alt. Simeon)

Hebrew, meaning "to hear." Famous Simons include music producer Simon Cowell and actor Simon Pegg.

Sinbad

Persian, meaning "Lord of Sages." Literary merchant adventurer.

Sindri

Norse, meaning "dwarf."

Sipho
African, meaning "the unknown one."

Sire
English, from the word used to address reigning kings or nobility.

Sirius
Hebrew, meaning "brightest star." Sirius Black is a character from the "Harry Potter" series.

Skipper
English, meaning "ship captain."

Skyler
Dutch, meaning "guarded" or "scholar."

Solomon
Hebrew, meaning "peace." One of the most important kings in the Bible and the Torah.

Sonny
American English, meaning "son." Singer Sonny Bono was half of Sonny and Cher.

Soren
Scandinavian, meaning "brightest star."

Spencer
English, meaning "guardian." Famous Spencers include actor Spencer Tracy and reality TV star Spencer Pratt.

Spike
English, from the word "spike." Director Spike Lee is known for *Do the Right Thing* and *4 Little Girls*.

Stanford
English, meaning "stone ford." Made famous by Stanford University.

Stanley
(alt. Stan)

English, meaning "stony meadow." Famous Stanleys include director Stanley Kubrick, actor Stanley Tucci, and comic book writer Stan Lee.

Stavros
Greek, meaning "cross."

Stellan
Latin, meaning "starred."

Steno
German, meaning "stone."

Stephen
(alt. Stefan, Stefano, Steffan, Steven; abbrev. Steve, Stevie)

English, meaning "crowned." Famous Stephens include author Stephen King, physicist Stephen Hawking, and actor Stephen Fry.

Stewart
(alt. Stuart)

English, meaning "steward." Stewart Copeland was the American drummer in The Police.

Stoney

English, meaning "stone like."

Storm

English, from the word "storm."

Sven

Norse, meaning "boy." The name of the reindeer character in Disney's *Frozen*.

Syed

(alt. Sayyid)

Arabic, meaning "lucky." Associated with the character from *Lost*.

Sylvester

Latin, meaning "wooded." The name of the cartoon cat.

Old name, new fashion

Augustus	Norris
Bertrand	Percival
Edgar	Reginald
Felix	Sebastian
Gilbert	Theodore
Hector	Winston
Jasper	

Boys' names

Tacitus

Latin, meaning "silent, calm." Also the name of an ancient Roman historian.

Tad

English, from the word "tadpole."

Taj

Indian, meaning "crown." Made famous by the Indian palace the Taj Mahal.

Takashi

Japanese, meaning "praiseworthy."

Takoda

Sioux, meaning "friend to everyone."

Talbot
(alt. Tal)

English, meaning "command of the valley." Aristocratic name.

Tamir

Arabic, meaning "tall and wealthy."

Tanner

Old English, meaning "leather-maker."

Taras
(alt. Tarez)

Scottish, meaning "crag." Taras was the son of Poseidon in ancient Greek mythology.

Tarek
(alt. Tarik)

Arabic, meaning "to strike."

Tarian

Welsh, meaning "shield."

Tariq

Arabic, meaning "morning star."

Tarquin

Latin, from the Roman clan name. Tarquin Hall is a poet.

Tarun

Hindi, meaning "young."

Tatanka

Hebrew, meaning "bull." Legendary Native American leader Sitting Bull's Western name was Tatanka Lyotake.

Tate

English, meaning "cheerful." Actor Tate Donovan is known for his role in *Damages*.

Taurean

English, meaning "bull-like." Also used to describe people born under the Taurus star sign.

Tavares

English, meaning "descendant of the hermit."

Tave

(alt. Tavian, Tavis, Tavish)

French, from Gustave, meaning "royal staff," and in Nordic cultures it can mean "guarantor."

Taylor

(alt. Tay)

English, meaning "tailor." Famous Taylors include actor Taylor Lautner and singer Taylor Hanson.

Tennessee

Native American, meaning "river town." Also the name of the state.

Terence

(alt. Terrill, Terry)

English, meaning "tender." Actor Terence Stamp is known for his roles in *Billy Budd* and *The Collector*.

Tex

English, meaning "Texan."

Thane

(alt. Thayer)

Scottish, meaning "landholder." Actor Thane Bettany is the father of actor Paul Bettany.

Thatcher

(alt. Thaxter)

Old English, meaning "roof thatcher."

Thelonious

Latin, meaning "ruler of the people." Thelonious Monk was an influential jazz pianist and composer.

Theodore

(abbrev. Theo)

Greek, meaning "God's gift." Theodore Roosevelt was the 26th President of the United States.

Theophile

Latin, meaning "beloved of God," also "one who loves God."

Theron

Greek, meaning "hunter."

Thierry

French variant of Terence, meaning "tender." Made famous by soccer star Thierry Henry.

Thomas

(alt. Thom, Tom, Tomlin, Tommy)

Aramaic, meaning "twin." Famous Thomases include inventor Thomas Edison and children's character Thomas the Tank Engine.

Thomson

(alt. Thomsen)

English, meaning "son of Thomas." "Thomsen" means "twin" in Aramaic.

Thor

Norse, meaning "thunder." Thor was a hammer-wielding deity in Norse mythology.

Tiago

From Santiago, meaning "Saint James." Also used as a shortened form of Santiago.

Tiberius

English, meaning "from the river Tiber."

Tibor

Latin, from the river Tiber, or Hungarian for "a short meeting."

Tieman

(alt. Tiemann)

Gaelic, meaning "lord."

Tilden

(alt. Till)

English, meaning "fertile valley."

Timothy

(alt. Tim, Timmie, Timmy, Timon)

Greek, meaning "God's honor." Famous Timothys include actors Timothy Dalton, Timothy Spall, and Christopher Timothy.

Tito

(alt. Titus, Tizian)

Latin, meaning "defender." Associated with singer Tito Jackson, from the Jackson Five.

Tobias

(alt. Toby)

Hebrew, meaning "God is good."

Tod

(alt. Todd)

English, meaning "fox." Famous Tods include Todd Flanders in *The Simpsons* and Todd Alquist in *Breaking Bad*.

Tonneau

French, meaning "barrel."

Torey

Norse, meaning "Thor."

Torin

Gaelic, meaning "chief."

Torquil

Gaelic, meaning "helmet." In Scandinavia the name is also derived from Thor, after the god of thunder and lightning.

Toshi

Japanese, meaning "reflection."

Travis

French, meaning "crossover." Famous Travises include actor Travis Fimmel and drummer Travis Barker.

Trevor
(alt. Tvevin)

Welsh origin, meaning "great settlement."

Trey
(alt. Tyree)

French, meaning "three." Sometimes used as a nickname for a third-born child.

Tristan
(alt. Tristram)

Celtic from the Celtic hero. Also one of the Knights of the Round Table.

Troy

Gaelic, meaning "descended from the soldier." Troy was a legendary city in ancient Greece.

Tudor

Variant of Theodore, meaning "God's gift." Also the name of the British dynasty which included Henry VIII and Elizabeth I.

Tyler

English, meaning "tile maker."

Tyrell

French, meaning "puller." Associated with House Tyrell from *Game of Thrones*.

Tyrone

Gaelic, meaning "Owen's county."

Tyson

English, meaning "son of Tyrone." Mike Tyson is widely regarded as one of the best heavyweight boxers of all time, as well as the most ferocious and controversial.

U Boys' names

Uberto
(alt. Umberto)
Italian, variant of Hubert, meaning "bright or shining intellect."

Udo
German, meaning "power of the wolf."

Ulf
German, meaning "wolf." Also the name of a Danish Viking chief.

Ulrich
German, meaning "noble ruler."

Ultan
Irish, meaning "from Ulster."

Ulysses
Greek, meaning "wrathful." Made famous by the mythological voyager from ancient Greece.

Upton
English, meaning "high town."

Urho
Finnish, meaning "brave."

Uri
(alt. Uriah, Urias)
Hebrew, meaning "my light." Famous Uris include magician Uri Geller.

Uriel
Hebrew, meaning "angel of light." One of the archangels in the Bible.

Usher
English, from the word "usher." Associated with the R&B star Usher.

Uzi
Hebrew, meaning "my strength." A type of submachine gun.

Uzzi
(alt. Uzziah)
Hebrew, meaning "the Lord is my strength." Also the name of several characters in the Bible.

Boys' names

Vadim

Russian, meaning "scandal maker." Vadim the Bold was a legendary warrior in Eastern Europe during the ninth century.

Valdemar

German, meaning "renowned leader."

Valente

Latin, meaning "valiant."

Valentine

(alt. Valentin, Valentino; abbrev. Val)

English, from the word "valentine." St. Valentine's Day is named after Valentinus, who was said to have healed the broken heart of his jailer's daughter. One of the more popular dancers on *Dancing With The Stars* is Valentin Chmerkovskiy.

Valerio

Italian, meaning "to be strong."

Van

Dutch, meaning "son of." Famous Vans include the band Van Halen, singer Van Morrison, and the brand of shoe.

Vance

English, meaning "marshland." Vance Astrovik is the real name of the comic book hero Justice.

Vangelis

Greek, meaning "good news." Vangelis is a modern Greek composer.

Varro

Latin, meaning "strong."

Varun

Hindi, meaning "water god." Shortened form of Varuna, who is the Hindu god of all water.

Vasilis
(alt. Vasilly)

Greek, meaning "kingly."

Vaughan

Welsh, meaning "little."

Vernell

French, meaning "green and flourishing."

Verner

German, meaning "army defender." The German form of Werner, although Verner is a more common spelling in Europe.

Vernon
(alt. Vernie)

French, meaning "alder grove." Vernon Dursley is a character in the "Harry Potter" series.

Versilius

Latin, meaning "flier."

Vester

Latin, meaning "wooded." Associated with the guitar maker.

Victor
(alt. Vic, Viktor)

Latin, meaning "champion." Author Victor Hugo wrote *Les Miserables*. Viktor Krum is a "Harry Potter" character.

Vidal
(alt. Vidar)

Spanish, meaning "life-giving." Vidal Sassoon is famed as a hairstylist.

Vijay

Hindi, meaning "conquering."

Vikram

Hindi, meaning "sun."

Ville

French, meaning "town."

Vincent
(abbrev. Vin, Vince, Vinnie)

English, meaning "victorious." Famous Vincents include actor Vince Vaughn, artist Vincent van Gogh, and soccer player turned actor Vinnie Jones.

Virgil

Latin, meaning "staff bearer." From the ancient Roman poet of the same name.

Vito

Spanish, meaning "life." Vito Corleone is a character from *The Godfather*.

Vittorio

Italian, meaning "victory."

Vitus

Latin, meaning "life." Associated with St. Vitus, or the condition Saint Vitus Dance.

Vivian

(alt. Vyvian; abbrev. Viv)

Latin, meaning "lively." Used as a name for boys and girls.

Vladimir

Slavic, meaning "prince." Famous Vladimirs include Russian President Vladimir Putin, and legendary warrior Vladimir the Impaler—also known as Dracula.

Volker

German, meaning "defender of the people."

Von

Norse, meaning "hope." In Germany, "von" also means "of" or "from," and is used to denote origin, such as Ulrich von Liechtenstein.

"Bad boy" names

Ace	Conan
Arnie	Guy
Axel	Rhett
Bruce	Spike
Buzz	Tyson

Boys' names

Wade

English, meaning "to move forward" or "to go." Wade Robson is a contemporary dance choreographer.

Waldemar

German, meaning "famous ruler."

Walden

English, meaning "valley of the Britons." Famed as the title of the book by Henry Thoreau.

Waldo

Old German, meaning "rule." "Where's Waldo" is a popular children's book character.

Walker

English, meaning "a fuller."

Wallace

English, meaning "foreigner" or "stranger." One of the duo *Wallace and Gromit*.

Wally

German, meaning "ruler of the army."

Walter

(alt. Walt)

German, meaning "ruler of the army." Famous Walters include *Breaking Bad*'s Walter White, and the movie *The Secret Life of Walter Mitty*.

Ward

English, meaning "guardian."

Wardell

Old English, meaning "watchman's hill."

Warner

German, meaning "army guard." Made famous as the name of the movie studio Warner Brothers.

Warren

German, meaning "guard" or "the game park." Warren Buffett is a business tycoon and philanthropist.

Warwick

Old English, meaning "buildings near the weir." Associated with actor Warwick Davis.

Washington

English, meaning "clever" or "clever man's settlement." George Washington was the first President of the USA.

Wassily

Greek, meaning "royal" or "kingly." Wassily Kandinsky was an abstract artist.

Watson

English, meaning "son" or "son of Walter." Dr. Watson is a character from the "Sherlock Holmes" stories.

Waverley
(alt. Waverly)

English, meaning "quaking aspen."

Waylon

English, meaning "land by the road." Associated with country singer Waylon Jennings.

Wayne

English, meaning "a cartwright." Famous Waynes include comedian Wayne Brady and rapper Lil Wayne.

Webster

English, meaning "weaver."

Weldon

English, meaning "from the hill of well" or "hill with a well."

Wendell
(alt. Wendel)

German, meaning "a wend." Wendell Berry is a novelist.

Werner

German, meaning "army guard." Werner Heisenberg was a Nobel prize winner and inspiration for the alter ego of Walter White in *Breaking Bad*.

Weston

English, meaning "from the west town."

Wheeler

English, meaning "wheel maker."

Whitley

English, meaning "white wood."

Whitman

Old English, meaning "white man." Made famous by author and poet Walt Whitman.

Whitney

Old English, meaning "white island."

Wilber

(alt. Wilbur)

Old German, meaning "bright will." Wilbur Wright helped invent the first powered airplanes.

Wiley

Old English, meaning "beguiling" or "enchanting."

Wilford

Old English, meaning "the ford by the willows." Associated with actor Wilford Brimley.

Wilfred

(alt. Wilfredo, Wilfrid; abbrev. Wilf)

English, meaning "to will peace."

Wilhelm

(alt. Willem)

German, meaning "strong willed warrior." The "Wilhelm Scream" is a movie sound effect used in hundreds of movies.

Wilkes

(alt. Wilkie)

Old English, meaning "strong willed protector" or "strong and resolute protector." John Wilkes Booth was the assassin of President Lincoln.

William

(abbrev. Bill, Billy, Will, Willie, Willy)

English (Teutonic), meaning "strong protector" or "strong willed warrior." Famous Williams include William Shakespeare, Prince William of Great Britain, and rapper Will.i.am.

Willis

English, meaning "server of William." Actor Bruce Willis is known for his roles in *Die Hard* and *The Fifth Element*.

Willoughby

Old Norse and Old English, meaning "from the farm by the trees."

Wilmer

English (Teutonic), meaning "famously resolute." Actor Wilmer Valderrama is known for his role in *That 70s Show*.

Wilmot

English, meaning "resolute mind."

Wilson

English, meaning "son of William." Famous Wilsons include legendary R&B singer Wilson Pickett.

Wilton

Old Norse and English, meaning "from the farm by the brook/ streams."

Windell

(alt. Wendell)

German, meaning "wanderer" or "seeker." Actor Windell Middlebrooks is known for his role on *Scrubs*.

Windsor

Old English, meaning "river bank" or "landing place." The British Royal family is known as the House of Windsor.

Winfield

English, meaning "from the field of Wina."

Winslow

Old English, meaning "victory on the hill." Associated with the sitcom *Family Matters*.

Winter

Old English, meaning "to be born in the winter."

Winthrop

Old English, meaning "village of friends."

Winton

Old English, meaning "a friend's farm."

Wirrin

Aboriginal, meaning "a tea tree."

Wistan

Old English, meaning "battle stone" or "mark of the battle."

Wittan

Old English, meaning "farm in the woods" or "farm by the woods."

Wolf

(alt. Wolfe)

English, meaning "strong as a wolf." A wild animal in the dog family.

Wolfgang

Teutonic, meaning "the path of wolves." The composer Mozart's full name was Wolfgang Amadeus Mozart.

Wolfrom

Teutonic, meaning "raven wolf."

Wolter

Dutch, a form of Walter meaning "ruler of the army."

Woodburn

Old English, meaning "a stream in the woods."

Woodrow

English, meaning "from the row of houses by the wood." Woodrow Wilson was the 28th President of the United States.

Woodward

English, meaning "guardian of the forest."

Woody

American, meaning "path in the woods." Famous Woodys include filmmaker Woody Allen and the character of Woody from the "Toy Story" trilogy.

Worcester

Old English, meaning "from a Roman site." A tangy sauce of the same name.

Worth

American, meaning "worth much" or "wealthy place" or "wealth and riches."

Wren

Old English, meaning "tiny bird."

Wright

Old English, meaning "to be a craftsman" or "from a carpenter." Wilbur and Orville Wright were the inventors of powered aircraft.

Wyatt

Teutonic, meaning "from wood" or "from the wide water." Famous Wyatts include director Rupert Wyatt, wild west sheriff Wyatt Earp, and comedian Wyatt Cenac.

Wynn
(alt. Wyn)

Welsh, meaning "very blessed" or "the fair blessed one," and Old English, meaning "friend."

 **X** Boys' names

Xadrian

American, a combination of X and Adrian, meaning "from Hadria."

Xanthus

Greek, meaning "golden haired."

Xavier

Latin, meaning "to the new house."

Xenon

Greek, meaning "the guest." One of the noble gases.

Xerxes

Persian, meaning "ruler of the people" or "respected king." Name of a king who attempted to invade the Greek mainland, but failed.

Xylander

Greek, meaning "man of the forest."

Y Boys' names

Yaal

Hebrew, meaning "ascending" or "one to ascend."

Yadid

Hebrew, meaning "the beloved one."

Yadon

Hebrew, meaning "against judgment." Associated with the *Pokémon* character.

Yahir

Spanish, meaning "handsome one."

Yair

Hebrew, meaning "the enlightening one" or "illuminating." The spelling Jair appears in the Bible.

Yakiya

Hebrew, meaning "pure" or "bright."

Yanis

(alt. Yannis)

Greek, a form of John meaning "gift of God."

Yarden

Hebrew, meaning "to flow downward."

Ye

Chinese, meaning "bright one" or "light."

Yehuda

Hebrew, meaning "to praise and exalt." Often translated as Judah, who was a son of Jacob in the Bible.

Yered

Hebrew, a form of Jared, meaning "descending."

Yerik

Russian, meaning "God-appointed one."

Yervant

Armenian, meaning "king of people."

Yitzak
(alt. Yitzaak)

Hebrew, meaning "laughter" or "one who laughs."

Ynyr

Welsh, meaning "to honor."

Yobachi

African, meaning "one who prays to God" or "prayed to God."

Yogi

Japanese, meaning "one who practices yoga" or "from yoga." Made famous by the cartoon character Yogi Bear.

Yona

Native American, meaning "bear," and Hebrew, meaning "dove." A name used to refer to ancient people who spoke Greek.

York

Celtic, meaning "yew tree" or "from the farm of the yew tree." Also an historic city in the UK.

Yosef

Hebrew, meaning "added by God" or "God shall add." Hebrew form of Joseph.

Yuri

Aboriginal, meaning "to hear"; Japanese, meaning "one to listen"; Russian, a form of George meaning "farmer."

Yves

French, meaning "miniature archer" or "small archer." Fashion brand YSL was founded by Yves Saint Laurent.

Z Boys' names

Zachariah
(alt. Zac, Zach, Zachary)
Hebrew, meaning "remembered by the Lord" or "God has remembered." Famous Zachs include actors Zach Braff and Zach Galifianakis.

Zad
Persian, meaning "my son."

Zadok
Hebrew, meaning "righteous one." "Zadok the Priest" is a well known coronation anthem and has been sung at every crowning of a king or queen in the UK since 1727.

Zador
Hungarian, meaning "violent demeanor." Zador was the priest who anointed Solomon in the Bible.

Zafar
Arabic, meaning "triumphant."

Zaid
African, meaning "increase the growth" or "growth."

Zaide
Yiddish, meaning "the elder ones." Also the name of an unfinished opera by Mozart.

Zain
(alt. Zane)
Arabic, meaning "the handsome son." Actor Billy Zane is known for his roles in Titanic and The Phantom.

Zaire
African, meaning "river from Zaire." Zaire is the old name for Democratic Republic of the Congo.

Zarek

Persian, meaning "God protect our king." Associated with the Marvel comic book character.

Zuma

Arabic, meaning "peace."

A name for all seasons

Spring	Summer	Fall	Winter
Alvern	Augustus	Aki	Aquilo
Attwell	Balder	Akiko	Caldwell
Avir	Cain	Demitrius	Colden
Bradwell	Dax	Dionysus	Crispin
Jarek	Leo	Forrest	Darke
Kell	Sky	George	Eirwen
Marcus	Somers	Goren	Gennaio
Rain	Sunny	Hunter	Jack
Tamiko	Theros	Red	Mistral
Weldon		Storm	Rain

part three

Girls' Names

 **Girls' names**

A'mari

Variation of the Swahili or Muslim name Amira, meaning "princess."

Aanya

Sanskrit, meaning "the inexhaustible." Also variation of the Russian name Anya.

Aaryanna

Derivative of the Latin and Greek name Ariadne, meaning "the very holy one."

Abigail

(alt. Abagail, Abbigail, Abigale, Abigayle; abbrev. Abbey, Abbie, Abby, Abi)

Hebrew, meaning "my father's joy." A character in the Bible and the name of several Hawaiian princesses. The biblical Greek version of the name is Abigaia.

Abilene

(alt. Abelena, Abilee)

Latin and Spanish, meaning "hazelnut."

Abra

Female variation of Abraham. Also Sanskrit, meaning "clouds."

Abril

Spanish for the month of April; Latin, meaning "open."

Acacia

Greek, meaning "point" or "thorn." Also a species of flowering trees and shrubs.

Acadia

Greek, meaning "paradise." Originally, a French colony in Canada.

Ada

(alt. Adair, Adia)

Hebrew, meaning "adornment." Ada Lovelace is widely credited for being the world's first computer programmer, in the nineteenth century.

Adalee

German, meaning "noble." Also a contraction of Ada and Lee.

Adalia

Hebrew, meaning "God is my refuge." A genus of ladybug.

Addison

(alt. Addisyn, Addyson; abbrev. Addie, Addy, Adi)

English, meaning "son of Adam." Can be used for girls or boys.

Adelaide

(alt. Adalyn, Adalynn, Adelaida, Adeline, Adelina, Adelyn; abbrev. Addie, Addy, Adi)

Old German, meaning "noble kind." Popular after the rule of William IV and Queen Adelaide of England in the nineteenth century. Adeline Whitney was a children's author in that period.

Adele

(alt. Adela, Adelia, Adell, Adella, Adelle)

German, meaning "noble" or "nobility." Made famous by the singer Adele.

Aden

(alt. Addien)

Hebrew, meaning "decoration."

Aderyn

Welsh, meaning "bird." Also the name of several places in Wales.

Adesina

Nigerian, meaning "she paves the way." Usually given to a first-born daughter.

Adina

(alt. Adena)

Hebrew, meaning "high hopes" or "precious." Found in the Bible.

Adira

Hebrew, meaning "noble" or "powerful." Also the north Italian city.

Adley

English, meaning "son of Adam." Can be used for girls or boys.

Adrian

Italian, from the northern city of Adria. The name of an ancient Roman river. Can be used for girls, though more common for boys.

Adrienne

(alt. Adriane, Adriana, Adrianna, Adrianne)

Greek, meaning "from the city of Hadria," or Latin meaning "dark." A feminine form of Adrian.

Aegle

Greek, meaning "brightness" or "splendor." The name of several characters in ancient Greek mythology.

Aerin

Variant of Erin, meaning "peace-making." Taken from J. R. R. Tolkien's novels.

Aerith

Modern American, from the video game *Final Fantasy VII*.

Aero
(alt. Aeron)

Greak, meaning "flight."

Aerolynn

Combination of the Greek Aero, meaning "water," and the English Lynn, meaning "waterfall."

Africa

Celtic, meaning "pleasant," as well as the name of the continent.

Afsaneh

Iranian, meaning "a fairy tale."

Afsha

Persian, meaning "one who sprinkles light." Afsha Azad is known for her role in the "Harry Potter" film series.

Afton

Originally a name of a river in Scotland.

Agatha
(abbrev. Aggie)

From Saint Agatha, the patron saint of bells, meaning "good." Made famous by mystery novelist Agatha Christie.

Aglaia

Greek, meaning "brilliance." One of the three ancient Greek graces.

Agnes

Greek, meaning "virginal" or "pure." Saint Agnes of Rome is the patron saint of girls.

Agrippina

Latin, meaning "born feet first." The name of several influential ancient Roman women.

Aida

Arabic, meaning "reward" or "present." The title of an opera by Giuseppe Verdi.

Aidanne
(alt. Aidan, Aidenn)

Gaelic, meaning "fire."

Ailbhe

Irish, meaning "noble" or "bright."

Aileen
(alt. Aelinn, Aleen, Aline, Alline)

Gaelic variant of Helen, meaning "light."

Ailith
(alt. Ailish)
Old English, meaning "seasoned warrior."

Ailsa
Scottish, meaning "pledge from God." Also the name of a Scottish island.

Aina
Scandinavian, meaning "forever."

Aine
(alt. Aino)
Celtic, meaning "happiness." The Celtic goddess of summer.

Ainsley
(alt. Ansley)
Scottish/Gaelic, meaning "one's own meadow." Ainsley Hayes is a character in *West Wing*. Can be used for girls or boys.

Aisha
(alt. Aeysha)
Arabic, meaning "woman"; Swahili, meaning "life." Aisha was one of the prophet Muhammad's wives.

Aishwarya
Arabic, meaning "woman." Aishwarya Rai Bachchan is a famous Bollywood actor.

Aislinn
(alt. Aislin, Aisling, Aislyn, Alene, Allene)
Irish Gaelic, meaning "dream." A tribute to aisling, which was an old poetic genre in Ireland.

Aiyanna
(alt. Aiyana)
Native American, meaning "forever flowering."

Aja
Hindi, meaning "goat."

Akela
(alt. Akilah)
Hawaiian, meaning "noble." Hindi, meaning "alone." Akela is the wolf from *The Jungle Book*.

Akilina
Greek or Russian, meaning "eagle."

Akiva
Hebrew, meaning "protect and shelter."

Alaina
(alt. Alana, Alane, Alani, Alanna, Alayna, Aleena, Allannah, Allyn)
Feminine of Alan, originating from the Greek for "rock" or "comely." Also a spelling alternative for Eleanor.

Alana
(alt. Alanna, Allannah)

Gaelic, meaing "beauty"; Hawaiian, meaning "beautiful offering"; Old German, meaning "precious."

Alanis
(alt. Alarice)

Greek, meaning "rock" or "comely." Associated with singer Alanis Morissette.

Alba

Latin for "white." Also the Gaelic name for Scotland.

Alberta
(alt. Albertha, Albertine)

Feminine of Albert, from the Old German for "noble, bright, famous." Also a province in Canada.

Albina

Latin, meaning "white" or "fair." Name of an Etruscan goddess of the dawn.

Alda

German, meaning "old" or "prosperous." Saint Alda was an Italian mystic in the eleventh century.

Aldis

English, meaning "battle seasoned."

Aleta
(alt. Aletha)

Greek, meaning "footloose." Queen Aleta Ellis is a character from *The Legend of Prince Valiant*.

Alethea
(alt. Aletheia)

Greek, meaning "truth."

Alexandra
(alt. Alejandra, Alejandrina, Alejhandra, Aleksandra, Alessandra, Alexandrea, Alexandria, Aliandra; abbrev. Alex, Alexa, Alexi, Alexia, Alexina, Ali, Allie, Ally, Lexi, Lexie, Sandra, Sandy, Sasha, Sascha, Shura, Sondra, Xandra, Zandra)

Feminine of Alexander, from the Greek interpretation of "man's defender." Also one of the ancient Greek goddess Hera's names. Perhaps the name with the most short forms, from many languages, which are often used as names in their own right.

Alexis
(alt. Alexus, Alexys)

Greek, meaning "helper." Alexis was an ancient Greek poet of comedy.

Aleydis

Variant of Alice, meaning "nobility." Alternative name for Saint Alice of Scharbeek, the patron saint of the blind and paralyzed.

Alfreda

Old English, meaning "elf power." The modern spelling of AElfthryth of Crowland.

Alibeth

Variant of Elizabeth, meaning "pledged to God." Popular name during the Middle Ages.

Alice

(alt. Alika, Aliki, Alize, Alyce, Alys, Alyse)

English, meaning "noble" or "nobility." Made famous by the novel *Alice in Wonderland*.

Alicia

(alt. Ahlicia, Alecia, Alesha, Alesia, Alessia, Alizia, Alisha, Alycia, Alysha, Alysia)

Latin, originally derived from Alice, meaning "nobility." Famous Alicias include singer Alicia Keys, actor Alicia Silverstone, and the birth name of singer Pink.

Alida

(alt. Aleida)

Latin, meaning "small-winged one."

Alima

Arabic, meaning "cultured."

Alina

(alt. Alena, Aleana)

Slavic form of Helen, meaning "light."

Alison

(alt. Allison, Allisyn, Allyson, Alyson; abbrev. Ali, Allie, Ally)

Variant of Alice, meaning "nobility." Originally the name was Alis in the Middle Ages, with the suffix "on," which means "little."

Alivia

Variant of Olivia, meaning "olive tree."

Aliya

(alt. Aaliyah, Aleah, Alia, Aliah, Aliyah)

Arabic, meaning "exalted" or "sublime." Aliya bint Ali was the last queen consort of Iraq.

Alla

Variant of Ella or Alexandra. Also a possible reference to Allah.

Allegra

Italian, meaning "joyous."

Allura

French, from the word for entice, meaning "the power of attraction."

Alma

Latin for "giving nurture"; Italian for "soul"; and Arabic for "learned." Also commonly written as Alma Mater, meaning "nourishing mother" or "fostering mother."

Almeda

(alt. Almeta)

Latin, meaning "ambitious."

Almera

(alt. Almira)

Feminine of Elmer, from the Arabic for "aristocratic"; Old English meaning "noble."

Alohi

Variant of the Hawaiian greeting Aloha, meaning "love and affection."

Alona
(alt. Alora)

Hebrew, meaning "oak tree."

Alpha

The first letter of the Greek alphabet, usually given to a firstborn daughter.

Alta

Latin, meaning "elevated."

Altagracia

Spanish, meaning "grace." Alta Gracia is also a city in Argentina.

Althaea
(alt. Altea, Altha, Althea)

Greek, meaning "healing power." Althaea was a prominent character in ancient Greek mythology.

Alva

Spanish, meaning "blonde" or "fair-skinned." In Norway and Sweden it is considered the female form of Alf, which means "elf."

Alvena
(alt. Alvina)

Old English, meaning "elf friend." In Old German it is the female form of Adelwin, meaning "noble friend."

Alvia
(alt. Alyvia)

Variant of Olivia, meaning "olive tree," or Elvira, from the ancient Spanish city.

Alyssa
(alt. Alisa, Alissa, Allyssa, Alysa)

Greek, meaning "rational." Associated with the alyssum flower.

Amadea

Feminine of Amadeus, meaning "God's love."

Amalia

German, meaning "work"; Hebrew, meaning "labor of love."

Amana

Hebrew, meaning "loyal and true." Also a genus of tulips.

Amanda
(alt. Amandine; abbrev. Mandy)

Latin, meaning "much loved." Famous Amandas include actors Amanda Bynes and Amanda Seyfried.

Amara
(alt. Amani)

Greek, meaning "lovely forever." Actor Amara Miller is known for her role in *The Descendants*.

Amarantha

Contraction of Amanda and Samantha, meaning "much loved listener."

Amari
(alt. Amaris, Amasa, Amata, Amaya)
Hebrew, meaning "pledged by God."

Amaryllis
(alt. Ameris)
Greek, meaning "fresh." Also a flower by the same name.

Amber
French, from the semiprecious stone of the same name. Famous Ambers include actor Amber Heard and model Amber Rose.

Amberly
Contraction of Amber and Leigh, meaning "stone" and "meadow."

Amberlynn
Contraction of Amber and Lynn, meaning "stone" and "waterfall."

Amelia
(alt. Aemilia, Amelie)
Greek, meaning "industrious." Famous Amelias include flying legend Amelia Earhart and two Princess Amelias of Great Britain. Amelie is the French variant and the title of a movie.

America
From the country and continents of the same name. Associated with Ugly Betty actor America Ferrera.

Amethyst
Greek, from the precious, mulberry colored stone of the same name.

Amina
Arabic, meaning "honest and trustworthy."

Aminta
Greek, meaning "defender."

Amira
(alt. Amiya, Amiyah)
Arabic, meaning "a high-born girl"; Hebrew, meaning "rich princess."

Amity
Latin, meaning "friendship and harmony." Also a name of a faction in the "Divergent" series.

Amory
Variant of the Spanish name Amor, meaning "love."

Amy
(alt. Aimee, Amee, Ami, Amie, Ammie, Amya)
Latin, meaning "beloved." Famous Amys include actor Amy Adams and singer Amy Winehouse. Aimee is the French form used by actor Aimee Garcia, singer Aimee Mann, and Aimee Osbourne of the Osbourne family.

Ana-Lisa
Contraction of Anna and Lisa, meaning "grace" or "consecrated to God."

Anafa
Hebrew, meaning "heron."

Ananda

Hindi, meaning "bliss." One of Buddha's disciples.

Anastasia

(alt. Athanasia)

Greek, meaning "resurrection." Grand Duchess Anastasia of Russia was killed in 1918, following the Russian revolution.

Anat

Jewish, meaning "water spring." Anat is an important Semitic goddess.

Anatolia

Greek, meaning "east sunrise." From the eastern Greek town of the same name.

Andrea

(alt. Andreia, Andria, Andrine, Andrina)

Feminine of Andrew, from the Greek term for "a man's woman." Famous Andreas include writers Andrea Levy and Andrea Dworkin.

Andromeda

Greek, meaning "leader of men." From the heroine of an ancient Greek legend.

Anemone

Greek, meaning "breath." Also a flowering plant.

Angela

(alt. Angel, Angeles, Angelia, Angelle, Angie)

Greek, meaning "messenger from God" or "angel." Famous Angelas include actors Angela Lansbury and Angela Bassett.

Angelica

(alt. Angelina, Angeline, Angelique, Angelise, Angelita, Anjelica, Anjelina)

Latin, meaning "angelic." Famous Angelicas include actor Anjelica Huston and *Rugrats* character Angelica Pickles.

Anise

(alt. Anisa, Anissa)

French, from the licorice-flavored plant of the same name.

Aniston

English, meaning "town of Agnes."

Anita

(alt. Anitra)

Derived from Ann, Hannah or Anahita (the Iranian water goddess), depending on the language. Famous Anitas include singer Anita Baker and *West Side Story* character Anita.

Anna

(alt. Ana)

Derived from Hannah, meaning "grace." A prophetess in the Bible.

Annabel
(alt. Anabel, Anabelle, Annabell, Annabella, Annabelle, Amabel)

Contraction of Anna and Belle, meaning "grace" and "beauty."

Annalise
(alt. Annalee, Annalisa, Anneli, Annelie, Annelise)

Contraction of Anna and Lise, meaning "grace" and "pledged to God."

Anne
(alt. Ann)

Originally a French form of Anna, meaning "grace," but used in England for many hundreds of years. Famous Annes include actor Anne Hathaway and two of the wives of Henry VIII.

Annemarie
(alt. Annamae, Annamarie, Annelle, Annmarie)

Contraction of Anna and Mary, meaning "grace" and "star of the sea." The name of actress Anne-Marie Duff.

Annette
(alt. Annetta)

Hebrew, derived from Hannah, meaning "grace." Associated with actors Annette Funicello and Annette Bening.

Annis
Greek, meaning "finished or completed." The Black Annis is a blue-faced witch in English mythology.

Annora
Latin, meaning "honor."

Anoushka
(alt. Anousha)

Russian variation of Ann, meaning "grace."

Anthea
(alt. Anthi)

Greek, meaning "flower-like." Also another name for the ancient Greek goddess Hera.

Antigone
In ancient Greek mythology, Antigone was the daughter of Oedipus.

Antoinette
(alt. Antonetta, Antonette, Antonietta; abbrev. Toni)

Female form of Anthony, meaning "invaluable grace." French queen consort Marie Antoinette was executed during the French Revolution.

Antonia
(alt. Antonella, Antonina)

Latin, meaning "invaluable." A very popular name in ancient Rome.

Anwen

Welsh, meaning "very fair."

Anya

(alt. Aanya, Aniya, Aniyah, Aniylah, Anja)

Russian, meaning "grace."

Aoife

Gaelic, meaning "beautiful joy." Associated with goddess Esuvia.

Apollonia

Feminine of Apollo, the Greek god of the sun. Saint Apollonia is the patron saint of dentistry.

Apple

From the name of the fruit. Famous Apples include technology company Apple Inc., and Gwyneth Paltrow's daughter.

April

(alt. Avril)

Latin, meaning "opening up." Also the fourth month, which has associations with the goddess Venus.

Aquilina

(alt. Aqua, Aquila)

Spanish, meaning "like an eagle." Associated with Saint Aquilina.

Ara

Arabic, meaning "brings rain." Also a star constellation. Can be used for girls or boys.

Arabella

(alt. Arabelle; abbrev. Bel, Bella)

Latin, meaning "answered prayer." The name of an opera by Richard Strauss.

Araceli

(alt. Aracely)

Spanish, meaning "altar of Heaven."

Araminta

Contraction of Arabella and Aminta, meaning "answered prayer" and "defender."

Arcadia

Greek, meaning "paradise." The daughter of ancient Roman Emperor Arcadius.

Ardelle

(alt. Ardell, Ardella)

Latin, meaning "burning with enthusiasm." Ardelle Kloss is a figure skater.

Arden

(alt. Ardis, Ardith)

Latin, meaning "burning with enthusiasm." Made famous by the cosmetics company Eliabeth Arden.

Arella

(alt. Areli, Arely)

Hebrew, meaning "angel."

Aretha

Greek, meaning "woman of virtue." Aretha Franklin is a soul singer.

Aria
(alt. Ariah, Arya)

Italian, meaning "melody." Arya Stark is a character in *Game of Thrones*.

Ariadne

Both Greek and Latin, meaning "the very holy one." In ancient Greek mythology, Ariadne was the daughter of King Minos.

Ariana
(alt. Ariane, Arianna, Arienne)

Welsh, meaning "silver."

Ariel
(alt. Ariela, Ariella, Arielle)

Hebrew, meaning "lioness of God." Ariel is the main character in Disney's *The Little Mermaid*.

Arlene
(alt. Arleen, Arline; abbrev. Arlie, Arly)

Gaelic, meaning "pledge." Associated with actor Arlene Dahl.

Armida

Latin, meaning "little armed one." Taken from the character of Armida in *Gerusalemme liberata* by Italian poet Torquato Tasso.

Artemisia
(alt. Artemis, Arti, Artie)

Greek/Spanish, meaning "perfect." Artemisia was a legendary female ancient Persian naval commander.

Arwen

Welsh, meaning "fair" or "fine." Arwen is a key Elven figure in *The Lord of the Rings*.

Ashanti

Geographical area in Africa. Also the name of the popular R&B singer Ashanti.

Ashby

English, meaning "ash tree farm."

Ashley
(alt. Ashlee, Ashleigh, Ashli, Ashlie, Ashly)

English, meaning "ash tree meadow." Famous Ashleys include actor Ashley Judd, and singers Ashley Tisdale and Ashlee Simpson. Can be used for girls or boys.

Ashlynn
(alt. Ashlyn)

Irish Gaelic, meaning "dream."

Ashton
(alt. Ashtyn)

Old English, meaning "ash tree town." Can be used for girls or boys.

Asia

Name of the continent. Also a name for an Oceanid in ancient Greek mythology.

Asma
(alt. Asmara)

Arabic, meaning "highstanding."

Aspen
(alt. Aspynn)

Name of the tree. Also the Colorado city famous for its ski resort.

Assumpta
(alt. Asumpta, Assunta)

Italian, meaning "raised up."

Asta
(alt. Asteria, Astor, Astoria)

Greek or Latin, meaning "starlike."

Astrid

Old Norse, meaning "beautiful like a God." Astrid Lundgren is the author of *Pippi Longstocking*.

Atara

Hebrew, meaning "diadem" or "crown." Also a genus of butterfly.

Athena
(alt. Athenais)

Greek, meaning "wise." Athena was the ancient Greek goddess of wisdom, mathematics, and arts and crafts.

Aubrey
(alt. Aubree, Aubriana, Aubrie)

French, meaning "elf ruler."

Audrey
(alt. Audra, Audrie, Audrina, Audry)

English, meaning "noble strength." Saint Etheldreda was known as Saint Audrey, and was a seventh-century English princess. Made famous by reality star Audrina Patridge.

Augusta
(alt. August, Augustine)

Latin, meaning "worthy of respect."

Aura
(alt. Aurea)

Greek or Latin, meaning either "soft breeze" or "gold." An aura is the perceived field of energy surrounding people and objects in various spiritual beliefs.

Aurelia
(alt. Aurelie)

Latin, meaning gold. The mother of Julius Caesar.

Aurora
(alt. Aurore)

Latin, meaning "dawn." In ancient Roman mythology, Aurora was the goddess of sunrise.

Austine
(alt. Austen, Austin)

Latin, meaning "worthy of respect."

Autumn

Latin, from the name of the harvest season.

Ava
(alt. Avia, Avie)

Latin, meaning "like a bird." Associated with actor Ava Gardner.

Avalon
(alt. Avalyn, Aveline)
Celtic, meaning "island of apples." Avalon is the mythological island in the King Arthur legend.

Axelle
Greek, meaning "father of peace."

Aya
(alt. Ayah)
Hebrew, meaning "bird."

Ayanna
(alt. Ayana)
Nigerian, meaning "beautiful flower."

Ayesha
(alt. Aisha, Aysha)
Persian, meaning "small one."

Azalea
Latin, meaning "dry earth." Also the name of a flowering shrub.

Azalia
Hebrew, meaning "aided by God."

Aziza
Hebrew, meaning "mighty"; Arabic meaning "precious." Female variation of Aziz.

Azure
(alt. Azaria)
French, meaning "sky-blue." Refers to the bright blue color of the sky on a clear day.

Names of First Ladies

Barbara (Bush)

Edith (Roosevelt)

Elizabeth (Ford)

Grace (Coolidge)

Hillary (Clinton)

Jacqueline (Kennedy)

Martha (Washington)

Mary (Lincoln)

Michelle (Obama)

Nancy (Reagan)

B Girls' names

Babette
(alt. Babe)

French version of Barbara; Greek meaning "foreign." Babette Cole is the author of children's books *Mommy Laid an Egg* and *Princess Smartypants*.

Bailey
(alt. Baeli, Bailee)

English, meaning "law enforcer."

Bambi
(alt. Bambina)

Shortened version of the Italian "bambina," meaning "child." Made famous by the Disney movie *Bambi*.

Barbara
(alt. Barbra; abbrev. Barb, Barbie)

Greek, meaning "foreign." Famous Barbaras include journalist Barbara Walters, and singer and actor Barbra Streisand.

Basma

Arabic, meaning "smile."

Bathsheba

Hebrew, meaning "daughter of the oath." Bathsheba was a key biblical figure, and mother of King Solomon.

Bay
(alt. Baya)

From the edible plant the bay leaf, or the geographical name for a large inlet of water.

Beata

Latin, meaning "blessed."

Beatrice
(alt. Beatrix, Beatriz, Bee, Bellatrix; abbrev. Bea)

Latin, meaning "bringer of gladness." Beatrice is a character in Dante's *Divine Comedy* and Shakespeare's *Much Ado About Nothing*.

Belinda
(alt. Belen, Belina)

Contraction of Belle and Linda, meaning "beautiful." Well-known Belindas include singer Belinda Carlisle.

Bella
(alt. Béla)

Latin, meaning "beautiful." Bella (Isabella) Swan is the main female character in the "Twilight" series.

Belle
(alt. Bell)

French, meaning "beautiful." Popularized by the Disney princess in *Beauty and the Beast*.

Belva

Latin, meaning "beautiful view." The inspiration for one of the characters in the musical *Chicago* was real-life murderer Belva Gaertner.

Bénédicta
(alt. Benedetta; abbrev. Bennie)

Latin, the feminine of Benedict, meaning "blessed." Associated with Benedicta Henrietta of the Palatinate.

Benita
(alt. Bernita; abbrev. Bennie)

Spanish, meaning "blessed."

Berit
(alt. Beret)

Scandinavian, meaning "splendid" or "gorgeous."

Bernadette
(alt. Bernadine; abbrev. Bernie)

French, meaning "courageous." Saint Bernadette was known for her visions of the Virgin Mary.

Bernice
(alt. Berenice, Berniece, Burnice)

Greek, meaning "she who brings victory." The name of Herod's daughter in the Bible.

Bertha
(alt. Berta, Berthe, Bertie)

German, meaning "bright." There are four saints called Bertha, all from the Middle Ages.

Beryl

Greek, meaning "pale, green gemstone." The name of a precious mineral.

Bess
(alt. Bessie)

Shortened form of Elizabeth, meaning "consecrated to God." Queen Elizabeth I's nickname was Good Queen Bess.

Beth

Hebrew, meaning "house." Also shortened form of Elizabeth, meaning "consecrated to God."

Bethany
(alt. Bethan)

Hebrew, referring to a geographical location in the Bible.

Bethel

Hebrew, meaning "house of God." A city in the Bible.

Bettina

(alt. Battina, Betiana, Betina, Bettine; abbrev. Betty, Ina, Tina)

Latin, derived from Benedetta or German derived from Elizabeth. Bettina Bush was the voice for *Rainbow Brite*.

Betty

(alt. Betsy, Bette, Bettie, Bettye)

Originally a shortened version of Elizabeth, meaning "consecrated to God," now often used as a name in its own right. Famous Bettys include cartoon character Betty Boop, actor Betty Grable, and glamor model Bettie Page.

Beulah

Hebrew, meaning "married." The name of the place that exists between Earth and Heaven.

Beverly

(alt. Beverlee, Beverley)

English, meaning "beaver stream." Made famous by Beverly Hills, CA, and actor Beverley Mitchell.

Beyoncé

American, made popular by the singer.

Bianca

(alt. Blanca)

Italian, meaning "white." Bianca is a character from Shakespeare's *Othello*.

Bijou

French, meaning "precious ring."

Billie

(alt. Bill, Billy, Billye)

Originally used for girls as a shortened version of Wilhelmina, meaning "determined." Now used almost universally as a standalone name, made popular as the stage name chosen by jazz singer Billie Holiday and tennis legend Billie Jean King.

Bina

Hebrew, meaning "knowledge."

Birgit

(alt. Birgitta)

German, meaning "power and strength." Used as a variation of Bridget.

Blaer

Icelandic, meaning "light breeze."

Blair

Scottish Gaelic, meaning "flat, plain area." Well-known Blairs include actor Blair Underwood.

Blake
(alt. Blakely, Blakelyn)

English, meaning either "pale skinned" or "dark." Associated with actor Blake Lively. Can be used for girls or boys.

Blanche
(alt. Blanch)

French, meaning "white or pale." Famous Blanches include the characters of Blanche Devereaux in *The Golden Girls*, and Blanche DuBois in *A Streetcar Named Desire*.

Bliss

English, meaning "intense happiness."

Blithe

English, meaning "joyous."

Blodwen

Welsh, meaning "white flower." The name of a Welsh opera.

Blossom

English, meaning "flowerlike." *Blossom* was a 1990s sitcom.

Blythe
(alt. Bly)

English, meaning "happy and carefree." Blythe Danner starred in sitcom *Will and Grace* and is the mother of actor Gwyneth Paltrow.

Bobbi
(alt. Bobbie, Bobby)

Shortened version of Roberta, meaning "bright fame." Associated with cosmetics brand Bobbi Brown.

Bonita

Spanish, meaning "pretty." "La Isla Bonita" is a song by Madonna.

Bonnie
(alt. Bonny)

Scottish, meaning "fair of face." One half of the outlaw duo Bonnie and Clyde.

Brandy
(alt. Brandee, Brandi, Brandie)

Dutch, meaning "burnt wine." Name of the liquor.

Brea
(alt. Bree, Bria)

Shortened form of Brianna, meaning "strong." Also the name of an ancient Irish god.

Brenda

Old Norse, meaning "sword."

Brianna
(alt. Breana, Breann, Breanna, Breanne, Brenna, Brenyn, Briana, Brianne, Bryanna)

Irish Gaelic, meaning "strong."

Bridget
(alt. Bridgett, Bridgette, Brigette, Brigid, Brigitta, Brigitte)

Irish Gaelic, meaning "strength and power." Famous Bridgets include actors Bridget Fonda and Brigitte Bardot, and the novel and movie *Bridget Jones's Diary*.

Brier
(alt. Briar)

French, meaning "heather." Sleeping Beauty's pseudonym is Briar Rose in the Disney movie.

Brit
(alt. Britt, Britta)

Celtic, meaning "spotted" or "freckled." Name of actor Britt Ekland.

Britannia

Latin, meaning "Britain." Britannia is the female personification of Great Britain.

Brittany
(alt. Britany, Britney, Britni, Brittani, Brittanie, Brittney, Brittni, Brittny)

Latin, meaning "from Britain." Famous Brittanys include the French province, singer Britney Spears, and actor Brittany Murphy.

Bronwen
(alt. Bronwyn)

Welsh, meaning "fair breast." The spelling of Bronwen is more common for baby girls, and Bronwyn for baby boys.

Brooke
(alt. Brook)

English, meaning "small stream." Brooke Shields is an actor and model. Can be used for girls or boys.

Brooklyn
(alt. Brooklynn)

Name of a New York borough. Associated with model Brooklyn Decker.

Brunhilda
(alt. Brunhilde, Brynhildr)

German, meaning "armor-wearing fighting maid." Brynhildr was an important character in Old German mythology.

Bryn
(alt. Brynn)

Welsh, meaning "mount" or "hill."

Bryony
(alt. Briony)

English, from bryonia, the name of a European vine.

Buffy

American alternative of Elizabeth, meaning "consecrated to God." The protagonist of the sci-fi series *Buffy the Vampire Slayer*.

C Girls' names

Cadence
(alt. Candenza)
Latin, meaning "with rhythm." Also used beginning with K.

Cai
Vietnamese, meaning "feminine."

Caitlin
(alt. Cadyn, Caitlann, Caitlyn, Caitlyn, Kaitlin)
Greek, meaning "pure." Catelyn Stark is a central character from *Game of Thrones*. Also used beginning with K, as for Kaitlin Doubleday.

Calandra
Greek, meaning "lark." A small Mediterranean bird.

Calantha
(alt. Calanthe)
Greek, meaning "lovely flower."

Caledonia
Latin, meaning Scotland.

Calla
Greek, meaning "beautiful." Associated with the calla lily.

Callie
(alt. Caleigh, Cali, Calleigh, Cally)
Greek, meaning "beauty." Callie Khouri is a screenwriter.

Calliope
(alt. Kalliope)
Greek, meaning "beautiful voice." From the muse of epic poetry in Greek mythology.

Callista
(alt. Calista, Callisto, Kallista)
Greek, meaning "most beautiful." Best-known as the name of actor Calista Flockhart.

Camas

Native American, from the root and bulb of the same name.

Cambria

Welsh, from the alternate name for Wales.

Camden
(alt. Camdyn)

English, meaning "winding valley." Also a part of London, England.

Cameo

Italian, meaning "skin." Associated with the notion of a cameo role in film or television.

Cameron
(alt. Camryn)

Scottish Gaelic, meaning "bent nose." Used for boys and girls. The best known female Cameron (Diaz) was recently reported to be the highest-paid female actor over the age of 40.

Camilla
(alt. Camelia, Camellia, Camila, Camille, Camillia)

Latin, meaning "spiritual serving girl." Made famous by model Camilla Alves, and Camilla, Duchess of Cornwall, who is married to Prince Charles.

Candace
(alt. Candice, Candis, Kandace)

Latin, meaning "brilliant white." Famous Candaces include actor Candace Cameron Bure, basketball player Candace Parker, and Candace Bushnell, author of Sex in the City.

Candida

Latin, meaning "white."

Candra

Latin, meaning "glowing."

Candy
(alt. Candi, Kandy)

Shortened form of Candace, meaning "brilliant white." Also a name for sweets or confectionery.

Caoimhe

Celtic, meaning "gentleness." Has many different pronunciations, including "Kyva" and "Keeva," depending on where in Ireland you hear it.

Caprice

Italian, meaning "ruled by whim." Made famous by model and actor Caprice.

Cara

Latin, meaning "darling." Cara Delevingne is a model and Cara Black a bestselling mystery novelist.

Carey
(alt. Cari, Carie, Carri, Carrie, Cary)

Welsh, meaning "near the castle." Famous Careys include actor Carey Mulligan and singer Mariah Carey.

Carina
(alt. Corina)

Italian, meaning "dearest little one." Also the name of a star constellation.

Carissa
(alt. Carisa)

Greek, meaning "grace."

Carla
(alt. Charl, Karla)

Feminine of the Old Norse Carl, meaning "free man." Carla Bruni-Sarkozy is the singer-songwriter married to former French president Nicolas Sarkozy.

Carlin
(alt. Carleen, Carlene)

Gaelic, meaning "little champion."

Carlotta
(alt. Carlota)

Italian, meaning "free man." Carlotta is a character from *The Phantom of the Opera*.

Carly
(alt. Carlee, Carley, Carli, Carlie, Karly, Karlie)

Feminine of the German Charles, meaning "man." Famous Carlys include singers Carly Simon and Carly Rae Jepson, and model Karlie Kloss.

Carmel
(alt. Carmela, Carmelita, Carmella)

Hebrew, meaning "garden." American Carmelita Jeter is the Olympic medal winning 100 meters sprinter.

Carmen
(alt. Carma, Carmina)

Latin, meaning "song." The opera *Carmen* was composed by Georges Bizet.

Carol
(alt. Carole, Carrol, Carroll, Caryl, Karol)

Originally the short form of Caroline, meaning "man." Famous Carols include actor Carol Burnett.

Caroline
(alt. Carolann, Carolina, Carolyn, Carolynn)

German, meaning "man." A feminine form of Charles. Caroline Kennedy is the daughter of John F. Kennedy.

Carrington

English, meaning "Charles's town."

Carys
(alt. Cerys)

Welsh, meaning "love."

Casey
(alt. Casy, Casie, Kasey)

Irish Gaelic, meaning "watchful." Used for girls and boys.

Cassandra

(alt. Casandra, Cassandre, Kassandra; abbrev. Cassie)

Greek, meaning "one who prophesies doom" or "entangler of men." Cassandra was a seer in ancient Greek mythology.

Cassia

(alt. Casia, Casie, Cassie)

Greek, meaning "cinnamon."

Cassidy

Irish, meaning "clever."

Catherine

(alt. Catalina, Catarina, Caterina, Catharine, Cathleen, Cathrine, Cathryn; abbrev. Cate, Cathy, Cathie, Caity, Caty)

Greek, meaning "pure." Famous Catherines include Catherine, Duchess of Cambridge, actor Catherine Zeta Jones, and Russia's Catherine the Great. Cathleen is the Irish variant of Catherine, and Catalina the Spanish version. All variations and abbreviations can also be spelled starting with a K rather than a C.

Cayley

(alt. Cayla, Caylee, Caylen)

Gaelic, meaning "slim" and "fair."

Cecilia

(alt. Cecelia, Cecile, Cecilie, Cecily, Cicely, Cicily)

Latin, meaning "blind one."

Celena

Greek, meaning "goddess of the moon." Also a spelling variation for Selena.

Celeste

(alt. Celestina, Celestine)

Latin, meaning "heavenly." Associated with actor Celeste Holm.

Celine

(alt. Celia, Celina)

French version of Celeste, meaning "heavenly." Associated with singer Celine Dion.

Cerise

French, meaning "cherry." The color cerise is a deep, pink-red color.

Chanah

(alt. Chana)

Hebrew, meaning "grace." Also a spelling variation for Hannah.

Chance

Middle English, meaning "good fortune."

Chandler

(alt. Chandell)

English, meaning "candle maker." Can be used for girls or, more commonly, boys.

Chandra
(alt. Chanda, Chandry)

Sanskrit, meaning "like the moon."
Chandra is a god of the moon in
Hinduism.

Chanel
(alt. Chanelle)

French, meaning "pipe." Name of
the French fashion house founded by
designer Coco Chanel.

Chantal
(alt. Chantel, Chantelle, Chantilly)

French, meaning "stony spot."

Chardonnay

French, from the wine variety of the
same name.

Charis
(alt. Charice, Charissa, Charisse)

Greek, meaning "grace." One of the
graces in ancient Greek mythology.

Charity

Latin, meaning "brotherly love."

Charlene
(alt. Charleen, Charline)

German, meaning "man." Associated
with actor Charlene Tilton.

Charlotte
(alt. Charnette, Charolette; abbrev.
Charlie, Charley, Charlize, Charly,
Lottie)

French, meaning "little and
feminine." Famous Charlottes
include author Charlotte Bronte,
singer Charlotte Church, and the
novel Charlotte's Web by E. B. White.
Charlie is also the abbreviation for
the boys' name Charles.

Charmaine

Latin, meaning "clan." Derived
from Charmain, a favorite servant of
Cleopatra.

Chastity

Latin, meaning "purity."

Chava
(alt. Chaya)

Hebrew, meaning "beloved."

Chelsea
(alt. Chelsee, Chelsey, Chelsi, Chelsie)

English, meaning "port or landing
place." Famous Chelseas include
comedian Chelsea Handler and
advocate Chelsea Clinton.

Cher

French, meaning "beloved." Made
famous by the singer Cher.

Cherie
(alt. Cheri, Cherise)

French, meaning "dear."

Cherish
(alt. Cherith)

English, meaning "to treasure." The
title of a song by Madonna.

Chermona

Hebrew, meaning "sacred mountain."

Cherry

(alt. Cherri)

French, meaning "cherry fruit."

Cheryl

(alt. Cheryle)

English, meaning "little and womanly." Made famous by dancer Cheryl Burke from *Dancing With The Stars*.

Chesney

English, meaning "place to camp." Can be used for girls or, more commonly, boys.

Cheyenne

(alt. Cheyanne)

Native American, from the tribe of the same name in Wyoming.

Chiara

(alt. Ceara, Chiarina, Ciara)

Italian, meaning "light." Associated with the singer Ciara.

China

From the country of the same name.

Chiquita

Spanish, meaning "little one."

Chloe

(alt. Cloe)

Greek, meaning "pale green shoot." Famous Chloes include actors Chloe Grace Moretz and Chloe Sevigny, and author Toni Morrison—whose birth name was Chloe Wofford.

Chloris

(alt. Cloris)

Greek, meaning "pale." Made famous by actor and comedian Cloris Leachman.

Christabel

(alt. Christobel)

Latin and French, meaning "fair Christian." The title of a poem by Samuel Taylor Coleridge.

Christina

(alt. Christine, Christen, Christene, Christian, Christiana, Christiane, Christin, Cristina; abbrev. Chris, Chrissy, Christa, Christie, Christy, Crissy, Cristy)

Greek, meaning "anointed Christian." Famous Christinas include singer Christina Aguilera and actors Christina Ricci and Christine Taylor.

Chuma

Aramaic, meaning "warmth."

Cierra

(alt. Ciera)

Irish, meaning "black."

Cinderella

French, meaning "little ashgirl."
Subject of the children's fairy tale.

Cinnamon

Greek, from the exotic spice of the
same name.

Citlali
(alt. Citlalli)

Nahuatl, meaning "star." An ancient
Aztec name.

Citrine

Latin, from the gemstone of the same
name.

Claire
(alt. Clara, Clare, Claira)

Latin, meaning "bright." Associated
with actor Claire Danes.

Clarabelle
(alt. Claribel)

Contraction of Clare and Isobel,
meaning "bright" and "consecrated
to God." Clarabelle is a Disney cow
cartoon character.

Clarissa
(alt. Clarice, Clarisse)

Variation of Claire, meaning "bright."
The title character from the sitcom
Clarissa Explains It All.

Clarity

Latin, meaning "lucid."

Claudia
*(alt. Claudetta, Claudette, Claudie,
Claudine)*

Latin, meaning "lame." The first
female president of Haiti was
Claudette Werleigh.

Clematis

Greek, meaning "vine." A type of
flowering plant.

Clementine
(alt. Clemency, Clementina, Clemmie)

Latin, meaning "mild and merciful."
Also the small orange fruit.

Cleopatra

Greek, meaning "her father's
renown." Famed as an ancient
Egyptian queen.

Clio
(alt. Cleo, Cliona)

Greek, from the ancient Greek muse
of the same name.

Clodagh

Irish, meaning "river."

Clotilda
(alt. Clothilda, Clothilde, Clotilde)

German, meaning "renowned
battle." Saint Clotilde was known for
her works of charity.

Clover

English, from the flower of the same
name.

Coby

Diminutive of Jacob, meaning "supplanter." More commonly used as a boys' name.

Coco

Spanish, meaning "help." Name of the French fashion designer Coco Chanel.

Cody

English, meaning "pillow."

Colleen
(alt. Coleen)

Irish Gaelic, meaning "girl." Colleen Camp is an actor.

Collette
(alt. Colette)

Greek/French, meaning "people of victory." Sidonie-Gabrielle Colette was the author of Gigi.

Constance
(alt. Constanza, Constantina, Konstance; abbrev. Connie)

Latin, meaning "steadfast." Oscar Wilde's wife was Constance Lloyd. Famous Connies include actors Connie Britton and Connie Nielsen, and journalist Connie Chung.

Consuelo
(alt. Consuela)

Spanish, meaning "comfort." Originally from the Virgin Mary, who was Our Lady of Consolation in Spanish.

Cora
(alt. Kora)

Greek, meaning "maiden."

Coral
(alt. Coralie, Coraline, Corelia, Corene)

Latin, from the marine life of the same name.

Corazon

Spanish, meaning "heart" or "darling."

Cordelia
(alt. Cordia, Cordie)

Latin, meaning "heart." Famous fictional Cordelias include characters in Shakespeare's King Lear and TV's Buffy the Vampire Slayer.

Corey
(alt. Cori, Corrie, Cory)

Irish Gaelic, meaning "the hollow."

Corin
(alt. Corine)

Latin, meaning "spear."

Corinne
(alt. Corinna, Corrine)

French version of Cora, meaning "maiden." Associated with singer Corinne Bailey Rae.

Corliss

English, meaning "cheery."

Cornelia

Latin, meaning "like a horn." The name of several influential ancient Roman women.

Cosette

French, meaning "people of victory." Name of a key character in Victor Hugo's *Les Misérables*.

Cosima
(alt. Cosmina)

Greek, meaning "order." One of the clones in *Orphan Black*.

Courtney
(alt. Cortney)

English, meaning "court-dweller." Famous Courtneys include actor Courtney Cox and singer Courtney Love.

Creola

French, meaning "American-born, English descent." Associated with the Creole language and people.

Crescent

French, meaning "increasing."

Cressida

From the Trojan heroine in Greek mythology of the same name.

Crystal
(alt. Christal, Chrystal, Cristal, Krystal)

Greek, meaning "ice." A kind of manufactured precious stone.

Csilla

Hungarian, meaning "defenses."

Cyd

Shortened form of Sidney, meaning "wide island." Cyd Charisse was a dancer and actor.

Cynara

Greek, meaning "thistly plant."

Cynthia
(abbrev. Cinda, Cindi, Cindy, Cyndi)

Greek, meaning "goddess from the mountain." Famous Cynthias include actor Cynthia Nixon and designer Cynthia Rowley. Famous Cindys include 1980s supermodel Cindy Crawford and singer Cindi Lauper.

Cyra

Persian, meaning "sun." Also a genus of ladybugs.

Cyrilla

Latin, meaning "lordly." Also a type of flowering plant.

D

Girls' names

Dacey

Irish Gaelic, meaning "from the south."

Dada

Nigerian, meaning "curly haired." Associated with the art movement Dadaism.

Daenerys

Literary, from the fictional character in *Game of Thrones*.

Dagmar

German, meaning "day's glory." Dagmar was the stage name of Virginia Egnor.

Dagny

Nordic, meaning "new day."

Dahlia

Scandinavian, from the flowering plant of the same name.

Dai

Welsh, meaning "darling." Used for girls or, more commonly, boys.

Daisy
(alt. Daisey, Dasia)

English, meaning "eye of the day." A flowering plant.

Dakota

Native American, meaning "allies." Associated with actor Dakota Fanning, and the states of North and South Dakota.

Dalia
(alt. Daliah, Dalila)

Hebrew, meaning "delicate branch." A Lithuanian goddess.

Dallas

Scottish Gaelic, from the village of the same name. Also the city in Texas.

Damaris

Greek, meaning "calf." A character in the Bible.

Damita

Spanish, meaning "little noblewoman."

Dana

(alt. Dania, Danna, Dayna)

English, meaning "from Denmark"; Persian, meaning "a perfect and valuable pearl."

Danae

Greek, from the mythological heroine of the same name.

Danica

(alt. Danika)

Latin, meaning "from Denmark." Famous Danicas include racing driver Danica Patrick, and actor and author Danica McKellar.

Danielle

(alt. Danelle, Daniela, Daniella, Danila, Danita, Danyell; abbrev. Dani, Danni)

The feminine form of the Hebrew Daniel, meaning "God is my judge." The name of actor Danielle Fischel.

Daphne

(alt. Dafne, Daphna)

Greek, meaning "laurel tree." Daphne was a water nymph in Greek mythology.

Dara

Hebrew/Persian, meaning "wisdom." A character in the Bible.

Darby

(alt. Darbi, Darbie)

Irish, meaning "park with deer."

Darcy

(alt. Darcey, Darci, Darcie)

Irish Gaelic, meaning "dark." Famous Darcys include ballerina Darcey Bussell, and Pride and Prejudice character Mr. Darcy.

Daria

Greek, meaning "rich." Associated with cartoon series Daria.

Darla

English, meaning "darling." Made famous by the child star Darla Hood.

Darlene

(alt. Darleen, Darline)

American, meaning "darling." Darlene Gillespie is a member of the Mickey Mouse Club.

Daryl

(alt. Darryl)

Old English, and possibly also Old French, meaning "loved." Daryl is usually the female spelling and Darryl the male. Daryl Hannah is an actor.

Davina

Hebrew, meaning "loved one."
Davina Claire is a character on *The
Vampire Diaries*.

Dawn

(alt. Dawna)
English, meaning "to become day."

Daya

Hebrew, meaning "bird of prey." A
form of teaching in the Sikh religion.

Deanna

*(alt. Dayana, Deana, Deanna,
Deanne)*
English, meaning "girl from the
valley." The name of singer and actor
Deanna Durbin.

Deborah

*(alt. Debbra, Debra, Debrah; abbrev.
Debbi, Debbie, Debby, Debi)*
Hebrew, meaning "bee." A
prophetess in the Bible.

December

Latin, meaning "tenth month."

Dee

(alt. Dea)
Welsh, meaning "swarthy." Also
a shortened form of many names
beginning with "De-."

Deidre

(alt. Deidra, Deirdre)
Irish, meaning "raging woman."

Deja

(alt. Dejah)
French, meaning "already." The
French term for "already seen" is
"déjà vu."

Delaney

(alt. Delany)
Irish Gaelic, meaning "offspring of
the challenger."

Delia

Greek, meaning "from Delos."
Associated with the ancient Greek
island of Delos.

Delilah

(alt. Delina)
Hebrew, meaning "seductive."
Famous Delilahs include the lover of
Samson in the Bible, and the songs
"Delilah" by Tom Jones and "Hey
There Delilah" by Plain White T's.

Della

(alt. Dell)
Shortened form of Adele, meaning
"nobility." Donald Duck's twin sister
is called Della Duck.

Delores

(alt. Deloris)
Spanish, meaning "sorrows."

Delphine

*(alt. Delpha, Delphia, Delphina,
Delphinia)*
Greek, meaning "dolphin."

Delta

Greek, meaning "fourth child." Also the fourth letter of the Greek alphabet.

Demetria

(alt. Demetrice, Dimitria)

Greek, from the mythological heroine of the same name.

Demi

French, meaning "half." Name of the actor Demi Moore.

Dena

(alt. Deena)

English, meaning "from the valley."

Denise

(alt. Denice, Denisa, Denisse)

French, meaning "to be devoted to Bacchus." Name of the actor Denise Richards.

Desdemona

Greek, meaning "wretchedness." Desdemona is Othello's love interest in Shakespeare's *Othello*.

Desiree

(alt. Desirae, Des'ree)

French, meaning "much desired." Associated with singer Des'ree.

Desma

Greek, meaning "blinding oath."

Destiny

(alt. Destany, Destinee, Destiney, Destini)

French, meaning "fate." Associated with the former girl group Destiny's Child.

Deva

Hindi, meaning "God-like." Deva is also a name for several Buddhist, Hindu, and New Age spiritual entities or people.

Devin

(alt. Devinne)

Irish Gaelic, meaning "poet." Used as a girls' or, more commonly, boys' name.

Devon

English, from the county of the same name. Also female variant of Devin, meaning "poet."

Diamond

English, meaning "brilliant." One of the hardest and most valuable substances on Earth.

Diana

(alt. Dian, Diane, Dianna, Dianne)

Roman, meaning "divine." Made famous by Diana, the former Princess of Wales.

Diandra

Greek, meaning "two males."

Dilys

Welsh, meaning "reliable."

Dimona

Hebrew, meaning "south." A town in the Bible.

Dinah
(alt. Dina)

Hebrew, meaning "justified." A character in the Bible.

Dionne

Greek, from the mythological heroine of the same name. Famous Dionnes include singers Dionne Warwick and Dionne Bromfield, and the infamous Dionne quintuplets.

Divine

Italian, meaning "heavenly." Associated with divinity or Dante's Divine Comedy.

Dixie

French, meaning "tenth." Also an old term for the South.

Dodie

Hebrew, meaning "well-loved." Dodie Smith was the author of 101 Dalmations.

Dolores
(alt. Doloris)

Spanish, meaning "sorrows."

Dominique
(alt. Domenica, Dominica, Domonique)

Latin, meaning "Lord." The name of a song by Soeur Sourire.

Donata

Latin, meaning "given."

Donna
(alt. Dona, Donnie)

Italian, meaning "lady." Famous Donnas include singer Donna Summer and actor Donna Reed.

Dora

Greek, meaning "gift." The title character in Dora the Explorer.

Doran

Irish Gaelic, meaning "fist" or "stranger."

Dorcas

Greek, meaning "gazelle." Character in the Bible.

Doreen
(alt. Dorene, Dorine)

Irish Gaelic, meaning "brooding"; Greek, meaning "gift."

Doris
(alt. Dorris)

Greek, from the place of the same name. Made famous by singer and actor Doris Day.

Dorothy

(alt. Dorathy, Doretha, Dorotha, Dorothea, Dorthy; abbrev. Dolly, Dottie, Dotty)

Greek, meaning "gift of God." Most commonly associated with Dorothy from *The Wizard of Oz*.

Dorrit

(alt. Dorit)

Greek, meaning "gift of God." *Little Dorrit* is a novel by Charles Dickens.

Dory

(alt. Dori)

French, meaning "gilded." Associated with Dory from *Finding Nemo* and its sequel *Finding Dory*.

Dove

(alt. Dovie)

English, from the bird of the same name. Used as a symbol of peace.

Drew

Greek, meaning "masculine." Can be used for girls or boys (as a nickname for Andrew). Made famous by actor Drew Barrymore.

Drusilla

(alt. Drucilla)

Latin, meaning "of the Drusus clan."

Dulcie

(alt. Dulce, Dulcia)

Latin, meaning "sweet."

Dusty

(alt. Dusti)

Old German, meaning "brave warrior." Famous as the name of singer Dusty Springfield.

E Girls' names

Earla

English, meaning "leader."

Eartha

English, meaning "earth." Associated with singer Eartha Kitt.

Easter

Egyptian, from the festival and Pacific island of the same name.

Ebba

English, meaning "fortress of riches." A Top 10 name for baby girls in Sweden.

Ebony
(alt. Eboni)

Latin, meaning "deep, black wood." Made famous by the song "Ebony and Ivory" by Paul McCartney and Stevie Wonder.

Echo

Greek, meaning "reflected sound." Echo was the name of a nymph in Greek mythology.

Eda
(alt. Edda)

English, meaning "wealthy and happy." An ancient goddess of time and wealth.

Edelmira

Spanish, meaning "admired for nobility."

Eden
(alt. Edie, Eddie)

Hebrew, meaning "pleasure."

Edina

Scottish, meaning "from Edinburgh."

Edith
(alt. Edyth)

English, meaning "prosperity through battle." Edith Wharton was a Pulitzer Prize-winning author.

Edna

Hebrew, meaning "enjoyment."

Edrea

English, meaning "wealthy and powerful." Edrea Vorsal is an opera singer.

Edwina

English, meaning "wealthy friend." Associated with socialite Edwina Mountbatten.

Effie

Greek, meaning "pleasant speech." Effie Trinket is a character in "The Hunger Games" series.

Eglantine

French, from the flowering shrub of the same name.

Eileen
(alt. Eibhlín)

Irish, meaning "shining and brilliant." Associated with the song "Come on Eileen" by Dexys Midnight Runners.

Ekaterina
(alt. Ekaterini)

Slavic, meaning "pure."

Elaine
(alt. Elaina, Elayne)

French, meaning "bright, shining light." Elaine Stritch is an actor and singer.

Elba

Italian, from the island of the same name.

Elberta

English, meaning "high-born."

Eldora

Spanish, meaning "covered with gold."

Eleanor
(alt. Alienor, Aliana, Elana, Elanor, Eleanora, Eleanore, Elena, Eleni, Elenor, Elenora, Elina, Elinor, Elinore; abbrev. Elie, Ellie)

Greek, meaning "light." Queen Eleanor of Aquitane was married to England's Henry II and was one of the most influential, wealthy, and powerful women of the Middle Ages.

Electra
(alt. Elektra)

Greek, meaning "shining." Famous as a character in ancient Greek myth.

Elfrida
(alt. Elfrieda)

English, meaning "elf power." Elfrida Andree is a composer.

Eliane
(alt. Eliana)

Hebrew, meaning "Jehovah is God."

Elissa
(alt. Elise)

French, meaning "pledged to God." The other name of Dido, the ancient Roman Queen of Carthage.

Eliza
(alt. Elisha, Elise)

Hebrew, meaning "pledged to God." Made famous by the character Eliza Doolittle from the play *Pygmalion* and film adaptation *My Fair Lady*.

Elizabeth
(alt. Elisabet, Elisabeth, Elizabella, Elsbeth, Elspet; abbrev. Bess, Bessie, Bet, Beth, Betty, Libby, Liz, Lizzie)

Hebrew, meaning "pledged to God." The name of the current Queen of England, Elizabeth II. The previous Queen Elizabeth I was also known as "Good Queen Bess."

Elke

German, meaning "nobility."

Ella

German, meaning "completely."

Elle
(alt. Ellie)

French, meaning "she." Elle Macpherson was one of the original 1980s supermodels, known as "The Body."

Ellen
(alt. Elin, Eline, Ellyn)

Greek, meaning "shining." Associated with comedian and TV host Ellen DeGeneres.

Ellice
(alt. Elyse)

Greek, meaning "the Lord is God."

Elma
(alt. Elna)

Latin, meaning "soul." Elma Napier is a pioneering Caribbean politician.

Elmira
(alt. Elmyra)

Arabic, meaning "aristocratic lady." Elmyra Duff is a cartoon character.

Elodie

French, meaning "marsh flower."

Eloise
(alt. Elois, Eloisa, Elouise)

French, meaning "renowned in battle."

Elsa
(alt. Else, Elsie)

Hebrew, meaning "pledged to God." Elsa is a character from Disney's *Frozen*.

Elula

Hebrew, meaning "August."

Elva

Irish, meaning "noble."

Elvina

English, meaning "noble friend."

Elvira

(alt. Elvera)

Spanish, from the place of the same name. Associated with the 1980s film Elvira, Mistress of the Dark.

Ember

(alt. Embry)

English, meaning "spark."

Emeline

German, meaning "industrious."

Emerald

English, meaning "green gemstone." A precious stone.

Emery

(alt. Emory)

German, meaning "ruler of work." A dark rock used in the manufacture of nail files.

Emilia

Latin, meaning "rival, eager." Associated with Game of Thrones actor Emilia Clarke.

Emily

(alt. Emelie, Emilee, Emilie, Emlyn)

Latin, meaning "rival, eager." Famous Emilys include actor Emily Blunt and author Emily Dickinson.

Emma

(alt. Emme, Emmi, Emmie, Emmy)

German, meaning "embraces everything." Made famous by Jane Austen's novel Emma.

Emmanuelle

Hebrew, meaning "God is among us."

Emmeline

(alt. Emmelina; abbrev. Emi, Emme, Emmie, Emmy)

German, meaning "embraces everything." Emmeline Pankhurst was a British activist and suffragette, named by Time magazine as "One of the 100 Most Important People of the Twentieth Century."

Ena

Shortened form of Georgina, meaning "farmer."

Enid

(alt. Eneida)

Welsh, meaning "life spirit." Enid Blyton was an English children's novelist.

Enola

Native American, meaning "solitary." Associated with the song "Enola Gay."

Enya

Irish Gaelic, meaning "fire." Irish singer Enya's birth name was Eithne.

Erica
(alt. Ericka, Erika)

Scandinavian, meaning "ruler forever." Erica Durance is an actor.

Erin
(alt. Eryn)

Irish Gaelic, meaning "from the isle to the west." An old name for Ireland. Erin Brockovich is a legal clerk and activist, portrayed by Julia Roberts in the film of the same name.

Eris

Greek, from the mythological heroine of the same name. Eris is responsible for chaos, strife, and discord.

Erlinda

Hebrew, meaning "spirited."

Erma

German, meaning "universal."

Ermine

French, meaning "weasel." The fur of a stoat or weasel is known as ermine.

Erna

English, meaning "sincere." A character in Norse mythology.

Ernestine
(alt. Ernestina)

English, meaning "sincere." Ernestine Gilbreth Carey is the author of *Cheaper By the Dozen*.

Esme

French, meaning "esteemed." Esme Cullen is a character in *Twilight*.

Esmeralda

Spanish, meaning "emerald." Esmeralda is a lead character in *The Hunchback of Notre Dame*.

Esperanza

Spanish, meaning "hope."

Estelle
(alt. Estela, Estell, Estella)

French, meaning "star." Associated with R&B singer Estelle.

Esther
(alt. Esta, Ester, Etha, Ethna, Ethne)

Persian, meaning "star." A character in the biblical Book of Esther.

Eternity

Latin, meaning "forever."

Ethel
(alt. Ethyl)

English, meaning "noble." Ethel Merman was an actor and singer, best known for rousing musical theater.

Etta
(alt. Etter, Ettie)

Shortened form of Henrietta, meaning "ruler of the house." Famous Ettas include singer Etta James (real name Janesetta), and DC Comic character Etta Candy.

Eudora

Greek, meaning "generous gift." Princess Tiana's mother Eudora is a character in Disney's *Princess and the Frog*.

Eugenia

(alt. Eugenie)

Greek, meaning "well born." Princess Eugenie is a granddaughter of Queen Elizabeth II.

Eulalia

(alt. Eula, Eulah, Eulalie)

Greek, meaning "sweetspeaking." Associated with Saint Eulalia.

Eunice

(alt. Unice)

Greek, meaning "victorious." Eunice Kennedy Shriver was John F. Kennedy's sister and the founder of the Special Olympics.

Euphemia

Greek, meaning " favorable speech."

Eva

Hebrew, meaning "life." Eva Peron was the real-life inspiration for the musical *Evita*.

Evadne

Greek, meaning "pleasing one."

Evangeline

(alt. Evangelina)

Greek, meaning "good news." The very first musical comedy was called *Evangeline*, in 1874.

Evanthe

Greek, meaning "good flower."

Eve

(alt. Evie)

Hebrew, meaning "life." The Bible story names Eve as the first woman to walk on the Earth.

Evelina

(alt. Evelia)

German, meaning "hazelnut." The title of a novel by eighteenth-century author Fanny Burney.

Evelyn

(alt. Evalyn, Evelin, Eveline, Evelyne)

German, meaning "hazelnut." Famous Evelyns include singer Evelyn "Champagne" King, deaf virtuoso percussionist Evelyn Glennie and novelist Evelyn Waugh (who was in fact a man).

Everly

(alt. Everleigh, Everley)

English, meaning "grazing meadow."

Evette

French, meaning "yew wood."

Evonne

(alt. Evon)

French, meaning "yew wood." Made famous by Australian tennis pro Evonne Goolagong.

Girls' names

Fabia
(alt. *Fabiana, Fabienne, Fabiola, Fabriana*)

Latin, meaning "from the Fabian clan."

Fabrizia
Italian, meaning "works with hands."

Faith
English, meaning "loyalty." Famous Faiths include singers Faith Hill and Faith Evans.

Faiza
Arabic, meaning "victorious."

Fallon
Irish Gaelic, meaning "descended from a ruler."

Fanny
(alt. *Fannie*)

Latin, meaning "from France." The heroine of Jane Austen's *Mansfield Park* is Fanny Price.

Farica
German, meaning "peaceful ruler."

Farrah
English, meaning "lovely and pleasant." Associated with actor Farrah Fawcett and reality TV star Farrah Abraham.

Fatima
Arabic, meaning "baby's nurse."

Faustine
Latin, meaning "fortunate."

Fawn
French, meaning "young deer." Also the light brown color.

Fay
(alt. *Fae, Faye*)

French, meaning "fairy." Famous Fays include author Fay Weldon and original *King Kong* actor Fay Wray.

Felicia
(alt. Felecia, Felice, Felicita, Felisha)

Latin, meaning "lucky and happy." Famous Felicias include actors Felicia Day and Felicia Farr, and *American Idol*'s Felicia Barton.

Felicity

Latin, meaning "fortunate."

Fenella

Irish Gaelic, meaning "white shoulder." Made famous by actor Fenella Fielding.

Fenia

Scandinavian, from the mythological giantess of the same name.

Fern
(alt. Fearn, Fearne, Ferne, Ferrin)

English, from the plant of the same name.

Fernanda

German, meaning "peace and courage."

Ffion
(alt. Fion)

Irish Gaelic, meaning "fair and pale" or "foxglove." Very popular name for baby girls in Wales.

Fia

Italian, meaning "flame." Also a nickname for Fiona.

Fifi

Hebrew, meaning "Jehovah increases."

Filomena

Greek, meaning "loved one."

Finlay
(alt. Finley)

Irish Gaelic, meaning "fair-headed courageous one." Used for girls or, more commonly, boys.

Finola
(alt. Fionnula)

Irish Gaelic, meaning "fair shoulder." Associated with actor Finola Hughes.

Fiona
(alt. Fiora)

Irish Gaelic and Scottish, meaning "fair and pale." Princess Fiona is a character in *Shrek*.

Flanna
(alt. Flannery)

Irish Gaelic, meaning "russet hair" or "red hair."

Flavia

Latin, meaning "yellow hair."

Fleur
(alt. Flor)

French, meaning "flower." Fleur Delacour is a character in the "Harry Potter" series.

Flora

Latin, meaning "flower." A fairy godmother in Disney's *Sleeping Beauty* (she was the red one).

Florence

(alt. Florencia, Florene, Florine; abbrev. Flo, Florrie, Flossie, Floy)

Latin, meaning "in bloom." Associated with the Italian city of the same name.

Florida

Latin, meaning "flowery." Also the southern state.

Frances

(alt. Francine, Francis; abbrev. Fanny, Fran, Frankie, Frannie, Franny)

Latin, meaning "from France." Famous Franceses include actor Frances McDormand and playwright Frances Hodgson Burnett.

Francesca

(alt. Franchesca, Francisca)

Latin, meaning "from France." Francesca Simon is a children's author.

Freda

(alt. Freida, Frida, Frieda)

German, meaning "peaceful." Associated with artist Frida Kahlo.

Frederica

German, meaning "peaceful ruler." Popular name for modern European princesses.

Fuchsia

German, from the flower of the same name.

G Girls' names

Gabrielle
(alt. Gabriel, Gabriela, Gabriella; abbrev. Gabbi, Gabby)
Hebrew, meaning "heroine of God." A character in *Xena: Warrior Princess*.

Gaia
(alt. Gaea)
Greek, meaning "the earth." Gaia was the ancient Greek Mother Goddess.

Gail
(alt. Gale, Gayla, Gayle)
Hebrew, meaning "my father rejoices." Gail O'Grady is an actor and producer.

Gala
French, meaning "festive merrymaking."

Galiena
German, meaning "high one."

Galina
Russian, meaning "shining brightly."

Garnet
(alt. Garnett)
English, meaning "red gemstone." Can be used as a twin name alongside Ruby.

Gay
(alt. Gaye)
French, meaning "glad and lighthearted."

Gaynor
Welsh, meaning "white and smooth." Associated with singer Gloria Gaynor.

Gemini
Greek, meaning "twin." The third astrological sign in the Zodiac.

Gemma
(alt. Jemma)

Italian, meaning "precious stone." Well-known Gemmas include actor Gemma Arterton.

Gene

Greek, meaning "well born." Usually a boys' name, as with actor and dancer Gene Kelly, but can be used for girls.

Genesis

Greek, meaning "beginning." Associated with the first book of the Old Testament, and the band Genesis.

Geneva
(alt. Genevra)

French, meaning "juniper tree." A city in Switzerland.

Genevieve
(alt. Genie)

German, meaning "white wave." Saint Genevieve is said to have saved Paris.

Georgia
(alt. Georgie)

Greek, meaning "farmer." Also the southern US state and a European country.

Georgina
(alt. Georgene, Georgette, Georgiana, Georgianna, Georgine, Giorgina; abbrev. Giget, Gigi)

Greek, meaning "farmer." Georgina Chapman is an actor and fashion designer. *Gigi* is the title of the novel and musical.

Geraldine
(abbrev. Geri)

German, meaning "spear ruler." Geraldine Chaplin is an actor and Geri Halliwell is "Ginger Spice" of the Spice Girls.

Gerda

Nordic, meaning "shelter." A character from Hans Christian Andersen's *Snow Queen*.

Germaine

French, meaning "from Germany." Germaine Greer is an author and activist.

Gertrude
(alt. Gertie)

German, meaning "strength of a spear." Made famous by author Gertrude Stein.

Gia
(alt. Ghia)

Italian, meaning "God is gracious."

Gianina
(alt. Giana)

Hebrew, meaning "God's graciousness."

Gilda

English, meaning "gilded." A character from Verdi's opera *Rigoletto*.

Gilia

Hebrew, meaning "joy of the Lord." Also a genus of flowering plants.

Gillian

Latin, meaning "youthful." Famous Gillians include actor Gillian Anderson and author Gillian Cross.

Ginger

Latin, from the root of the same name.

Giovanna

Italian, meaning "God is gracious."

Giselle
(alt. Gisela, Gisele, Giselle, Gisselle)

German, meaning "pledge." Famous Giselles include the romantic ballet and supermodel Gisele Bündchen.

Gita
(alt. Geeta)

Sanskrit, meaning "song." The Bhagavad Gita is an important part of Hindu scripture, and is often simply known as the Gita.

Giulia
(alt. Giuliana)

Italian, meaning "youthful." Associated with TV host Giuliana Rancic.

Gladys
(alt. Gladyce)

Welsh, meaning "lame." Gladys Knight is a singer.

Glenda

Welsh, meaning "fair and good."

Glenna
(alt. Glennie)

Irish Gaelic, meaning "glen."

Gloria
(alt. Glory)

Latin, meaning "glory." Famous Glorias include singers Gloria Estefan and Gloria Gaynor.

Glynda
(alt. Glinda)

Welsh, meaning "fair." Name of the good witch in *The Wizard of Oz*.

Glynis

Welsh, meaning "small glen." Glynis Nunn is a heptathlon athlete.

Golda
(alt. Goldia, Goldie)

English, meaning "gold." Golda Meir is the former Israeli Prime Minister.

Grace
(alt. Graça, Gracie, Gracin, Grayce)

Latin, meaning "grace." The actor Grace Kelly became Princess Grace of Monaco.

Grainne
(alt. Grania)

Irish Gaelic, meaning "love." Also an ancient goddess of corn.

Gratia
(alt. Grasia)

Latin, meaning "blessing." Gratia was the ancient Greek goddess of charm, beauty, and fertility.

Greer
(alt. Grier)

Latin, meaning "alert and watchful."

Gregoria

Latin, meaning "alert."

Greta
(alt. Gretel)

Greek, meaning "pearl." One of the characters in the fairy tale *Hansel and Gretel*.

Gretchen

German, meaning "pearl." Gretchen Mol is an actor.

Griselda
(alt. Griselle)

German, meaning "gray fighting maid."

Gudrun

Scandinavian, meaning "battle."

Guinevere

Welsh, meaning "white and smooth." The legendary Queen consort of King Arthur.

Gwenda

Welsh, meaning "fair and good."

Gwendolyn
(alt. Gwen, Gwendolen, Gwenel)

Welsh, meaning "fair bow." Gwendolyn Brooks is a poet.

Gwyneth
(alt. Gwynneth, Gwynyth)

Welsh, meaning "happiness." Made famous by actor Gwyneth Paltrow.

Gwynn
(alt. Gwyn)

Welsh, meaning "fair blessed."

Gypsy

English, meaning "of the Roman tribe." Associated with the movie *Gypsy*.

H Girls' names

Hadassah

Hebrew, meaning "myrtle tree." The Hebrew name for Esther in the Bible.

Hadley

English, meaning "heather meadow." Hadley Richardson was the wife of Ernest Hemingway.

Hadria

Latin, meaning "from Hadria." The name of two ancient cities in Italy.

Hala

Arabic, meaning "halo." A female weather demon in Serbian mythology.

Haley
(alt. Hailee, Hailey, Hailie, Haleigh, Hali, Halie, Haylee, Hayleigh, Hayley, Haylie)

English, meaning "hay meadow." Famous Haleys include singer Haley Reinhart and singer Hayley Mills.

Halima
(alt. Halimah, Halina)

Arabic, meaning "gentle." The prophet Mohammad's foster mother was called Halimah.

Hallie
(alt. Halle, Halley)

German, meaning "ruler of the home or estate." Associated with actor Halle Berry.

Hannah
(alt. Haana, Hana, Hanna)

Hebrew, meaning "grace." Famous Hannahs include actor Hannah Gordon and musical comedy Hannah Montana.

Harley
(alt. Harlene)

English, meaning "the long field." Used for girls and boys. Made famous by the Harley-Davidson motorbike company.

Harlow

English, meaning "army hill."

Harmony

Latin, meaning "harmony."

Harper

English, meaning "minstrel." Has risen in popularity after its use by Victoria and David Beckham for their daughter Harper Seven.

Harriet
(alt. Harriett, Harriette, Hattie)

German, meaning "ruler of the home or estate." Famous Harriets include activist Harriet Tubman and author Harriet Beecher Stowe.

Haven

English, meaning "a place of sanctuary."

Hayden

Old English, meaning "hedged valley."

Hazel
(alt. Hazle)

English, from the tree of the same name. Also an eye color.

Heather

English, from the flower of the same name. Famous Heathers include actors Heather Graham and Heather Locklear, and model Heather Mills.

Heaven

English, meaning "everlasting bliss."

Hedda

German, meaning "warfare." *Hedda Gabler* is a play by Henrik Ibsen.

Hedwig

German, meaning "warfare and strife." Also Harry Potter's constant owl companion.

Heidi
(alt. Heidy)

German, meaning "nobility." The title of a children's book *Heidi* by Johanna Spyri.

Helen
(alt. Halen, Helena, Helene, Hellen)

Greek, meaning "light." In Greek mythology Helen of Troy was considered to be the most beautiful woman in the world.

Helga

German, meaning "holy and sacred."

Heloise

French, meaning "renowned in war." Heloise d'Argenteuil was a nun and writer.

Henrietta
(alt. Henriette)

German, meaning "ruler of the house." Henrietta Maria of France was queen consort to England's King Charles I.

Hephzibah

Hebrew, meaning "my delight is in her." A character in the Bible.

Hera

Greek, meaning "queen." Hera is the ancient Greek Queen of the Gods and the goddess of marriage, women, and births.

Hermia
(alt. Hermina, Hermine, Herminia)

Greek, meaning "messenger." A character from Shakespeare's play *A Midsummer Night's Dream*.

Hermione

Greek, meaning "earthly." Harry Potter's closest (and smartest) female friend.

Hero

Greek, meaning "brave one of the people."

Hertha

English, meaning "earth." Another name for Nerthus, the goddess of fertility in ancient German mythology.

Hesper
(alt. Hesperia)

Greek, meaning "evening star." The first evening star in ancient Greece.

Hester
(alt. Hestia)

Greek, meaning "star." Hester Prynne is a character from *The Scarlet Letter*.

Hilary
(alt. Hillary)

Greek, meaning "cheerful and happy." Famous Hilarys include actor Hilary Swank and politician Hillary Rodham Clinton.

Hilda
(alt. Hildur)

German, meaning "battle woman." The first female pilot to own a license was Hilda Hewlett.

Hildegarde
(alt. Hildegard)

German, meaning "battle stronghold."

Hildred

German, meaning "battle counselor."

Hilma

German, meaning "helmet."

Hollis

English, meaning "near the holly bushes."

Holly
(alt. Holli, Hollie)

English, from the tree of the same name. Famous Hollys include writer Holly Black and actor Holly Hunter.

Honey

English, meaning "sweet nectar."

Honor
(alt. Honora, Honoria, Honour)

Latin, meaning "woman of worth and respect." Actor Honor Blackman played Bond girl Pussy Galore in *Goldfinger*.

Hope

English, meaning "desire and expectation." One of the three virtues: faith, hope, and charity.

Hortense
(alt. Hortencia, Hortensia)

Latin, meaning "of the garden." The name of Napoleon Bonaparte's mother.

Hulda

German, meaning "loved one." A prophetess in the Bible.

Hyacinth

Greek, from the flower of the same name. A hero in ancient Greek mythology.

Long names	Short names
Alexandria	Bea
Bernadette	Bo
Christabelle	Fay
Constantine	Jan
Evangeline	Jo
Gabrielle	Kay
Henrietta	Kim
Jacqueline	May
Marguerite	Mia
Wilhelmina	Val

I Girls' names

Ianthe
(alt. Iantha)
Greek, meaning "purple flower."

Ida
(alt. Idell, Idella)
English, meaning "prosperous." Ida B. Wells was a prominent African-American civil rights activist and journalist.

Idona
Nordic, meaning "renewal."

Ignacia
Latin, meaning "ardent."

Ila
French, meaning "island." In Hindu mythology, Ila is a character able to change sexes at will.

Ilana
Hebrew, meaning "tree." Famous Ilanas include pianist Ilana Vered and a character on TV series *Lost*.

Ilaria
Italian, meaning "cheerful."

Ilene
American, meaning "light." Ilene Woods was the voice of Disney's *Cinderella*.

Iliana
(alt. Ileana)
Greek, meaning "Trojan."

Ilona
Hungarian, meaning "light." The name of the Queen of the Fairies in Magyar mythology.

Ilsa
German, meaning "pledged to God." The character played by Ingrid Bergman in *Casablanca*.

Ima

German, meaning "embraces everything."

Iman

Arabic, meaning "faith." Associated with the model, actor and entrepreneur known simply as Iman.

Imelda

German, meaning "all-consuming fight." Imelda Staunton is an Oscar nominated British actor who appeared in the "Harry Potter" films.

Imogen
(alt. Imogene)

Latin, meaning "last-born."

Ina

Latin, meaning "to make feminine." Famous Inas include author and presenter Ina Garten, childbirth pioneer Ina May Gaskin, and the Ina language of Brazil.

Inaya

Arabic, meaning "taking care."

India
(alt. Indie)

Hindi, from the country of the same name. India Arie is a singer.

Indiana

Latin, meaning "from India." Also the Midwestern state.

Indigo

Greek, meaning "deep blue dye." One of the seven colors of the rainbow.

Indira
(alt. Inira)

Sanskrit, meaning "beauty." Indira Gandhi was the first and only female Prime Minister of India.

Inez
(alt. Ines)

Spanish, meaning "pure."

Inga
(alt. Inge, Ingeborg, Inger)

Scandinavian, meaning "guarded by Ing."

Ingrid

Scandinavian, meaning "beautiful." Made famous by actor Ingrid Bergman.

Io
(alt. Eye)

Greek, from the mythological priestess and heroine of the same name.

Ioanna

Greek, meaning "grace."

Iola
(alt. Iole)

Greek, meaning "cloud of dawn." *Iola Leory* by Frances Harper is one of the first published novels by a black female author.

Iolanthe

Greek, meaning "violet flower." The title of a comic opera by Gilbert and Sullivan.

Iona

Greek, from the island of the same name.

Ione

Greek, meaning "violet." Also a genus of orchid.

Iphigenia

Greek, meaning "sacrifice." The ancient Greek victim of slaughter, who became known as the mother of all strong children.

Ira
(alt. Iva)

Hebrew, meaning "watchful."

Irene
(alt. Irelyn, Irena, Irina, Irini)

Greek, meaning "peace." Singer Irene Cara won an Academy Award for Best Original Song.

Iris

Greek, meaning "rainbow." Also a flower and the Greek goddess who travels with the speed of wind from one end of the rainbow to the other, and from sea to sky, and connects the gods with humanity.

Irma

German, meaning "universal."

Isabel
(alt. Isabela, Isabell, Isabella, Isabelle, Isobel, Izabella, Izabelle; abbrev. Izzie, Izzy)

Spanish, meaning "pledged to God." The name of various historical members of European royal families, including Queen Isabella I of Spain.

Isadora

Latin, meaning "gift of Isis."

Ishana

Hindi, meaning "desire." One of the names for Shiva in the Hindu faith.

Isis

Egyptian, from the goddess of the same name. She was worshipped as the ideal mother and wife, and the goddess of nature and magic.

Isla
(alt. Isa, Isela, Isley)

Scottish Gaelic, meaning "river." Isla Fischer is an actor.

Isolde

Welsh, meaning "fair lady." A character in Richard Wagner's opera *Tristan und Isolde*.

Istas

Native American, meaning "snow."

Ivana

(alt. Iva, Ivanka)

Slavic, meaning "Jehovah is gracious." Associated with model Ivana Trump.

Ivory

Latin, meaning "white as elephant tusks."

Ivy

English, from the plant of the same name. Beyoncé and Jay-Z's daughter is Blue Ivy.

Ixia

South African, from the flower of the same name.

Girls' names

Jacinda
(alt. Jacinta)
Spanish, meaning "hyacinth." Jacinda Barrett is an actor.

Jacqueline
(alt. Jacalyn, Jacklyn, Jaclyn, Jacquelin, Jacquelyn, Jacquline, Jaquelin, Jaqueline; abbrev. Jackie, Jacky, Jacqui)
French, meaning "he who supplants." Famous Jacquelines include actor Jacqueline Bisset, cellist Jacqueline du Pré, First Lady Jacqueline (Jackie) Kennedy Onassis, and singer Jackie Evancho.

Jade
(alt. Jada, Jaida, Jayda, Jayde)
Spanish, meaning "green stone." Associated with TV host Jade McCarthy.

Jaden
(alt. Jadyn, Jaiden, Jayden)
Contraction of Jade and Hayden, meaning "green hedged valley." Used for girls as well as for boys.

Jael
Hebrew, meaning "mountain goat." A character in the Bible.

Jaime
(alt. Jaima, Jaimie, Jami, Jamie)
Spanish, meaning "he who supplants." J'aime is also French for "I love."

Jamila
Arabic, meaning "lovely." Jamila Gavin is a children's author.

Jan
(alt. Jana, Janae, Janay, Jann, Janna, Joana)

Hebrew, meaning "the Lord is gracious"; Arabic, meaning "dear"; and Persian, meaning "life."

Jane
(alt. Jayne)

Feminine form of John, meaning "the Lord is gracious." Famous Janes include actors Jane Lynch, Jane Seymour, and Jayne Mansfield.

Janelle
(alt. Janel, Janell, Jenelle)

American, derived from Jane, meaning "the Lord is gracious." Janelle Monae is a singer and Janell Burse is a professional basketball player.

Janet
(alt. Janette)

Scottish, meaning "the Lord is gracious." Famous Janets include singer Janet Jackson and Olympic champion swimmer Janet Evans.

Janice
(alt. Janis)

American, meaning "the Lord is gracious." Janice Dickinson is a former supermodel.

Janie
(alt. Janey, Janney, Jannie)

Derived from Jane or short form of Janet, meaning "the Lord is gracious." Famous Janies include Motown songwriter Janie Bradford, country singer Janie Frickie and Janie Hendrix, the sister of musician Jimi.

Janine
(alt. Janeen)

English, meaning "the Lord is gracious." Associated with actor Janine Turner.

Janoah
(alt. Janiya, Janiyah)

Hebrew, meaning "quiet and calm."

January

Latin, meaning "the first month." January Jones is an actor.

Jasmine
(alt. Jasmin, Jazim, Jazmine)

Persian, meaning "jasmine flower." Also the princess in Disney's *Aladdin*.

Jay

Latin, meaning "jaybird."

Jayna

Sanskrit, meaning "bringer of victory."

Jean
(alt. Jeane, Jeanie, Jeanne, Jeannie)

Scottish, meaning "the Lord is gracious." Jean Harlow was a glamorous acting star of the 1930s. Also associated with the sitcom *I Dream of Jeannie*.

Jeana
(alt. Jeanna)

Latin, meaning "queen."

Jeanette
(alt. Jeannette, Janette)

French, meaning "the Lord is gracious." Jeanette MacDonald is an actor.

Jeanine
(alt. Jeannine)

Latin, meaning "the Lord is gracious."

Jemima

Hebrew, meaning "dove." Famous Jemimas include writer Jemima Khan, actor Jemima Kirke, and the children's character Jemima Puddle-Duck.

Jena

Arabic, meaning "little bird."

Jennifer
(alt. Jenifer; abbrev. Jenna, Jennie, Jenny)

Cornish alternative to Guinevere, meaning "white and smooth." Famous Jennifers include actors

Jennifer Lawrence, Jennifer Aniston, Jenna Elfman, Jenna Dewan, singer Jennifer Hudson and the character of Jenna Maroney in *30 Rock*.

Jerrie
(alt. Jeri, Jerri, Jerrie, Jerry)

German, meaning "spear ruler." Jerry Hall is a model and actor, known also for her marriage to Mick Jagger.

Jerusha

Hebrew, meaning "married." Jerusha Hess is a film maker.

Jeryl

English, meaning "spear ruler." Associated with actor Jeryl Prescott.

Jessamy
(alt. Jessame, Jessamine, Jessamyn)

Persian, meaning "jasmine flower." Also a children's book by Barbara Sleigh.

Jessica
(alt. Jesica, Jessika; abbrev. Jess, Jessa, Jessie)

Hebrew, meaning "He sees." Famous Jessicas include actors Jessica Alba and Jessica Lange, singer Jessie J and the character Jess from *Girls*.

Jesusa

Spanish, meaning "mother of the Lord."

Jette
(alt. Jetta, Jettie)
Danish, meaning "black as coal."

Jewel
(alt. Jewell)
French, meaning "delight." Associated with singer songwriter Jewel.

Jezebel
(alt. Jezabel, Jezabelle)
Hebrew, meaning "pure and virginal." The misbehaving wife of King Ahab in the Bible.

Jill
Latin, meaning "youthful."

Jillian
Latin, meaning "youthful." Jillian Michaels is a personal trainer and TV personality.

Jimena
Spanish, meaning "heard."

Joan
Hebrew, meaning "the Lord is gracious." Famous Joans include Saint Joan of Arc, actor Joan Collins, and comedian Joan Rivers.

Joanna
(alt. Joana, Joanie, Joann, Joanne, Johanna, Joni; abbrev. Jo)
Hebrew, meaning "the Lord is gracious." Famous Joannas include author J. K. Rowling (real name Joanne), and actors Joanna Lumley and Joanna Page.

Jocasta
Italian, meaning "lighthearted." A character in ancient Greek mythology.

Jocelyn
(alt. Jauslyn, Jocelyne, Joscelin, Joslyn; abbrev. Joss)
German, meaning "cheerful." Famous Jocelyns include renowned American socialite Jocelyn Wildenstein, singer Jocelyn Brown, and English soul singer songwriter Joss Stone.

Jody
(alt. Jodee, Jodi, Jodie)
Shortened form of Judith, meaning "Jewish." Made famous by actor Jodie Foster.

Joelle
(alt. Joela)
Hebrew, meaning "Jehovah is the Lord."

Joie
French, meaning "joy."

Jolene

Contraction of Joanna and Darlene, meaning "gracious darling." The title of a song by Dolly Parton.

Jolie
(alt. Joely)

French, meaning "pretty." Made famous by actor and director Angelina Jolie.

Jonisa
(alt. Jonisha)

Hebrew and French, meaning "God is gracious."

Jordan
(alt. Jordana, Jordin, Jordyn)

Hebrew, meaning "descend." Made famous by singer Jordan Sparks.

Jorgina

Dutch, meaning "farmer."

Josephine
(alt. Josefina, Josephina; abbrev. Jo, Josie, Joss)

Hebrew, meaning "Jehovah increases." Famous Josephines include actor Josephine Baker, author Josephine Bell, and comedian Josie Lawrence.

Jovita
(alt. Jovie)

Latin, meaning "made glad." Associated with Saint Jovita.

Joy

Latin, meaning "joy." Joy Behar is a comedian.

Joyce

Latin, meaning "joyous." Famous Joyces include author Joyce Carol Oates and actors Joyce Blair and Joyce DeWitt.

Juanita
(alt. Juana)

Spanish, meaning "the Lord is gracious." Associated with the ice maiden Mummy Juanita.

Jubilee

Hebrew, meaning "ram's horn" or "special anniversary." The celebration of an anniversary.

Judith
(alt. Judit; abbrev. Jude, Judi, Judy)

Hebrew, meaning "Jewish." Famous Judiths include the character in the Bible and actors Judy Garland and Judi Dench.

Jules

French, meaning "Jove's child." Also an abbreviation of Julian used for boys.

Julia
(alt. Juli, Julie)

Latin, meaning "youthful." Famous Julias include actor Julia Roberts, TV chef Julia Childs, and actor and singer Julie Andrews.

Julianne
(alt. Juliana, Juliann, Julianna)

Latin, meaning "youthful." Julianne Moore and Julianna Margulies are both actors.

Juliet
(alt. Joliet, Juliette)

Latin, meaning "youthful." A character in Shakespeare's play *Romeo and Juliet*.

June
(alt. Juna)

Latin, after the month of the same name. The name of several American actors famous in the period 1930–60, and country singer June Carter Cash.

Juniper

Dutch, from the shrub of the same name used in the production of gin.

Juno
(alt. Juneau)

Latin, meaning "queen of heaven." Juno was an ancient Roman goddess of marriage and Rome.

Justice

English, meaning "to deliver what is just." The female spirit of Justice is depicted with balance scales, a blindfold, and a sword.

Justine
(alt. Justina)

Latin, meaning "fair and righteous." Famous Justines include the Christian saint, and actor Justine Bateman.

K Girls' names

Kala
(alt. Kaela, Kaiala, Kaila)
Sanskrit, meaning "black one." The great ape that saved Tarzan as a baby.

Kali
(alt. Kailey, Kaleigh, Kaley, Kalie, Kalli, Kally, Kaylee, Kayleigh)
Sanskrit, meaning "black one." Also the Hindu goddess of time and change.

Kalila
Arabic, meaning "beloved."

Kalina
Slavic, meaning "flower."

Kama
Sanskrit, meaning "love." Associated with the Hindu goal of intellectual fulfillment.

Kami
Japanese, meaning "lord."

Kamilla
(alt. Kamilah)
Slavic, meaning "serving girl."

Kana
Hawaiian, from the demi-god of the same name who could take the form of a rope that could stretch from Molokai to Hawaii.

Kara
Latin, meaning "dear one." The bracelet worn by members of the Sikh faith.

Karen
(alt. Caren, Carin, Caron, Caryn, Karan, Karin, Karina, Karon, Karren; abbrev. Kari)
Greek, meaning "pure." Famous Karens include singer Karen Carpenter, actor Karen Gillan and TV host and scientist Kari Byron.

Karimah
Arabic, meaning "giving."

Karissa
(alt. Carissa, Korissa)
Greek, meaning "very dear."

Karishma
(alt. Karisma)
Sanskrit, meaning "miracle." Karisma Kapoor is an actor.

Karma
Hindi, meaning "destiny." Karma is the principle of good and bad deeds being returned to you.

Kate
(alt. Kat, Katie, Kathi, Kathie, Kathy, Kati, Katy)
Derived from or used as a shortened form of Catherine or Katherine, meaning "pure." Actors Kate Winslet and Kate Hudson were given the name Kate. The Duchess of Cambridge, formerly Kate Middleton, was given the name Catherine.

Katherine
(alt. Katharine, Kathrine, Kathryn, Katrina, Katya, Katyea; abbrev. Kate, Kathy, Katie, Katy, Kay, Kitty)
Greek, meaning "pure." Also spelled with a C rather than a K, both forms are frequently used. Katya is the Russian form of Katherine.

Kathleen
(alt. Kathlyn)
Greek, meaning "pure." Kathleen Robertson is an actor.

Katniss
From one of the common names of the aquatic plant genus Sagittaria. Made famous by the character Katniss Everdeen from "The Hunger Games" trilogy.

Kaya
Sanskrit, meaning "nature," or Turkish, meaning "rock." Also a sweet coconut jam.

Kayla
(alt. Kaylah)
Greek, meaning "pure." Also Gaelic, meaning "slim" and "fair."

Kaylee
(alt. Kayley, Kayleigh, Kayli, Kaylin)
Derived from Kayla, meaning "pure." Kayley is a character from The Magic Sword: Quest for Camelot.

Keeley
(alt. Keely)
Irish, meaning "battle maid." Keeley Hawes is an actor.

Keila
Hebrew, meaning "citadel."

Keira
Irish Gaelic, meaning "dark." Name of actor Keira Knightley.

Keisha
(alt. Keesha)
Arabic, meaning "woman." Name of actor Keisha Pulliam.

Kelila

Hebrew, meaning "crown of laurel."

Kelis

American, meaning "beautiful." Kelis is an R&B singer.

Kelly

(alt. Keli, Kelley, Kelli, Kellie)

Irish Gaelic, meaning "battle maid." Famous Kellys include singer Kelly Clarkson and TV personality Kelly Osbourne.

Kelsey

(alt. Kelcie, Kelsea, Kelsi, Kelsie)

English, meaning "island."

Kendall

(alt. Kendal)

English, meaning "the valley of the Kent."

Kendra

English, meaning "knowing." Kendra Wilkinson is a reality TV star.

Kenna

Irish Gaelic, meaning "handsome."

Kennedy

(alt. Kenadee, Kennedi)

Irish Gaelic, meaning "helmet head." Made famous by the Kennedy family.

Kenya

African, from the country of the same name.

Kenzie

Shortened form of Mackenzie, meaning "son of the wise ruler."

Kerensa

Cornish, meaning "love." Also used as a spelling variation of Karen.

Kerrigan

Irish, meaning "black haired."

Kerry

(alt. Keri, Kerri, Kerrie)

Irish, from the county of the same name. Name of actor Kerry Washington.

Khadijah

(alt. Khadejah)

Arabic, meaning "premature baby." Khadija bint Khuwaylid was the first wife of Muhammad and known as the "Mother of Islam."

Kiana

(alt. Kia, Kiana)

American, meaning "fibre." Associated with TV personality Kiana.

Kiara

Italian, meaning "light." Saint Kiara saved an Irish town from a fire through prayer.

Kiki

Spanish, meaning "home ruler." "Let's Have a Kiki" is a song by the Scissor Sisters. Kiki Dee was the stage name of a pop singer from the 1970s.

Kimberly

(alt. Kimberleigh, Kimberley; abbrev. Kim)

Old English, meaning "royal forest." Also a town in South Africa. Famous Kimberlys include reality star Kim Kardashian, singer Lil' Kim, and actor Kim Basinger.

Kingsley

(alt. Kinsley)

English, meaning "king's meadow." Used for boys as well as girls.

Kinsey

English, meaning "king's victory."

Kira

Greek, meaning "lady." The antagonist in the popular Japanese anime *Death Note*.

Kiri

Maori, meaning "tree bark." Dame Kiri Te Kanawa is an opera singer.

Kirsten

(alt. Kirstin; abbrev. Kirstie, Kirsty)

Scandinavian, meaning "Christian." Kirsten Dunst and Kirstie Alley are actors and Kirsten Gillibrand a politican.

Kizzy

Hebrew, meaning the plant cassia.

Klara

Hungarian, meaning "bright."

Komal

Hindi, meaning "soft and tender."

Kristen

(alt. Kristan, Kristin, Kristine; abbrev. Kri, Krista, Kristi, Kristie, Kristy)

Greek, meaning "Christian." Famous Kristens include actor Kristen Stewart and reality TV star Kris Jenner.

Kwanza

(alt. Kwanzaa)

African, meaning "beginning." Also the name of the weeklong African-American festival in December and January.

Kyla

(alt. Kya, Kylah, Kyle)

Scottish, meaning "narrow spit of land." The name of actor Kyla Pratt.

Kylie

(alt. Kiley, Kylee)

Irish Gaelic, meaning "graceful." The name of singer Kylie Minogue.

Kyra

Greek, meaning "lady."

Kyrie

Greek, meaning "the Lord." Also a prayer sung at the beginning of Christian masses.

L Girls' names

Lacey
(alt. Laci, Lacie, Lacy)
French, from the town of the same name. Famous Laceys include actor Lacey Turner and dancer Lacey Schwimmer.

Ladonna
Italian, meaning "lady." A spelling alternative to Madonna.

Lady
English, meaning "bread kneader." A character from Disney's *Lady and the Tramp*.

Laila
(alt. Layla, Leila, Lejla, Lela, Lelah, Lelia)
Arabic, meaning "night." Famous Lailas include boxer Laila Ali, and the song "Layla" by Eric Clapton.

Lainey
(alt. Laine, Laney)
French, meaning "bright light."

Lakeisha
(alt. Lakeshia)
American, meaning "woman." A contraction of La and Keisha.

Lakshmi
(alt. Laxmi)
Sanskrit, meaning "good omen." The Hindu goddess of wealth.

Lana
Greek, meaning "light." Famous Lanas include singer Lana Del Rey, and actor Lana Turner.

Lani
(alt. Lanie)
Hawaiian, meaning "heaven and sky."

Lara
Latin, meaning "famous." Famous Laras include actor Lara Flynn Boyle, Tomb Raider star Lara Croft, and an ancient Roman nymph.

Laraine

French, meaning "from Lorraine."

Larissa

(alt. Larisa)

Greek, meaning "light-hearted." Larissa was a nymph in ancient Greek mythology.

Lark

(alt. Larkin)

English, meaning "playful songbird."

Larsen

(alt. Larsan)

Scandinavian, meaning "son of Lars."

Latifa

Arabic, meaning "gentle and pleasant."

Latika

(alt. Lotika)

Hindi, meaning "a plant." Also a character in Slumdog Millionaire.

Latisha

Latin, meaning "happiness."

Latona

(alt. Latonia)

Latin, from the mythological ancient Roman heroine of the same name who had twin boys with Zeus.

Latoya

Spanish, meaning "victorious one." Name of singer LaToya Jackson.

Latrice

(alt. Latricia)

Latin, meaning "noble."

Laura

(alt. Lora)

Latin, meaning "laurel." Famous Lauras include actor Laura Dern, author Laura Ingalls Wilder, and designer Laura Ashley.

Laurel

Latin, meaning "laurel tree." Also a term used for young women in the Mormon Church.

Lauren

(alt. Lauran, Loren)

Latin, meaning "laurel." Famous Laurens include actors Lauren Bacall and Lauran Grace.

Laveda

(alt. Lavada)

Latin, meaning "cleansed."

Lavender

Latin, from the plant of the same name. A character from the "Harry Potter" series.

Laverne

(alt. Lavern, Laverna)

Latin, from the goddess of the same name. Famous Lavernes include Laverne Andrews, of the Andrews Sisters, and sitcom Laverne & Shirley.

Lavinia

(alt. Lavina)

Latin, meaning "woman of Rome." In Roman mythology Lavinia is a heroine whose hair caught fire, creating a prophecy.

Lavonne

(alt. Lavon)

French, meaning "yew wood."

Leah

(alt. Lea, Leia)

Hebrew, meaning "weary." Name of Glee star Lea Michele.

Leandra

Greek, meaning "lion man." A character in Don Quixote.

Leanne

(alt. Leann, Leanna, Leeann)

Contraction of Lee and Ann, meaning "meadow grace." Famous Leannes include singers LeAnn Rimes and Lee Ann Womack.

Leda

Greek, meaning "gladness." The ancient Greek heroine Leda was seduced by Zeus in the form of a swan.

Lee

(alt. Leigh)

English, meaning "pasture or meadow."

Leilani

Hawaiian, meaning "flower from heaven." Name of actor Leilani Jones.

Leith

Scottish Gaelic, meaning "broad river."

Lena

(alt. Leena, Lina)

Latin, meaning "light." Famous Lenas include actor and filmmaker Lena Dunham and actor Lena Headey.

Lenna

(alt. Lennie)

German, meaning "lion's strength." The Lenna photograph is a standard test image used in image processing.

Léonie

(alt. Leona, Leone)

Latin, meaning "lioness." Leonie Adams is a poet.

Leonora

(alt. Lenora, Lenore, Leonor, Leonore, Leora)

Greek, meaning "light." Leonora Braham is an opera singer.

Leslie

(alt. Leslee, Lesley)

Scottish Gaelic, meaning "the gray castle." Famous Leslies include actor and dancer Leslie Caron, and singer Leslie Feist. Lesley is more commonly the female spelling and Leslie the male.

Leta

Latin, meaning "glad and joyful." Leta Hollingworth is a child psychologist.

Letha

Greek, meaning "forgetfulness." Also a type of butterfly.

Letitia

(alt. Leticia, Lettice, Lettie)

Latin, meaning "joy and gladness." Saint Leticia was a Spanish virgin martyr.

Lexia

(alt. Lexi, Lexie)

Greek, meaning "defender of mankind." Also a genus of butterfly.

Lia

Italian, meaning "bringer of the gospel." Lia Williams is an actor.

Liana

French, meaning "to twine around."

Libby

(alt. Libbie)

Originally a shortened form of Elizabeth, meaning "pledged to God." Name of singer Libby Holman.

Liberty

English, meaning "freedom." Made famous by the Statue of Liberty in New York, NY.

Lida

Slavic, meaning "loved by the people."

Liese

(alt. Liesel, Liesl)

German, meaning "pledged to God." Liesl is a character in the *Sound of Music*.

Lila

(alt. Lilah)

Arabic, meaning "night." In the Hindu faith, Lila refers to playtime or pastimes.

Lilac

Latin, from the flower of the same name. Also the pale purple color.

Lilia

(alt. Lilias)

Scottish, meaning "lily."

Lilith

Arabic, meaning "ghost." In Jewish mythology Lilith was thought to be a female demon.

Lillian

(alt. Lilian, Liliana, Lilla, Lillianna)

Latin, meaning "lily." Famous Lillians include actor Lillian Gish, playwright Lillian Hellman, and nursing pioneer Lillian Wald.

Lily
(alt. Lili, Lillie, Lilly)

Latin, from the flower of the same name. Famous Lilys include singer Lily Allen, actor Lily Collins, and model Lily Cole.

Linda
(alt. Lynda)

Spanish, meaning "pretty." Famous Lindas include actor Linda Blair and singer Linda Ronstadt.

Linden
(alt. Lindie, Lindy)

European, from the tree of the same name.

Lindsay
(alt. Lindsey, Linsey, Lynsey)

English, meaning "island of linden trees." Famous Lindsays include actor Lindsay Lohan and skier Lindsay Vonn. Can be used for both girls and boys.

Linette
(alt. Lynette)

Welsh, meaning "idol."

Linnea
(alt. Linnae, Linny)

Scandinavian, meaning "lime or linden tree." An extremely popular name for baby girls in Sweden.

Liora
(alt. Lior)

Hebrew, meaning "I have a light." Also a spelling alternative to Leora.

Lisa
(alt. Leesa, Lise, Liza)

Hebrew, meaning "pledged to God." Famous Lisas include singer Lisa Bonet, actor Lisa Kudrow, and The Simpsons character Lisa Simpson.

Lish

Shortened form of Elisha, meaning "my God is salvation."

Lissa

Greek, meaning "bee." Also a shortened form of Melissa.

Lissandra
(alt. Lisandra)

Greek, meaning "man's defender."

Liv

Nordic, meaning "defense." Also a short form of Olivia. Actor Liv Tyler is an original Liv, although she did change her last name!

Livia

Latin, meaning "olive." Livia Drusilla was the wife of Roman Emperor Augustus.

Logan

Irish Gaelic, meaning "small hollow." Used more commonly for boys.

Lois

German, meaning "renowned in battle." Made famous by *Superman* heroine Lois Lane.

Lolita

(alt. Lola; abbrev. Lollie)

Spanish, meaning "sorrows." The title of a novel by Vladimir Nabokov.

Lona

Latin, meaning "lion." Lona is a moon deity in Hawaiian mythology.

Lorelei

(alt. Loralai, Loralie)

German, meaning "dangerous rock." Associated with the Lorelei myth in Germany.

Lorenza

Latin, meaning "from Laurentium."

Loretta

(alt. Loreto)

Latin, meaning "laurel." Loretta Devine is an actor.

Lori

(alt. Laurie, Lorie, Lorri)

Latin, meaning "laurel." Name of actor Lori Petty.

Lorna

Scottish, from the place of the same name. The title character in R. D. Blackmore's novel *Lorna Doone*.

Lorraine

(alt. Loraine)

French, meaning "from Lorraine." Famous Lorraines include actor Lorraine Bracco, paranormal investigator Lorraine Warren, and playwright Lorraine Hansberry.

Lottie

(alt. Lotta, Lotte)

French, meaning "little and womanly." Also a shortened form of Charlotte.

Lotus

Greek, meaning "lotus flower."

Louise

(alt. Lou, Louie, Louisa, Luisa)

German, meaning "renowned in battle." Famous Louises include actors Louise Fletcher and Louise Lasser.

Lourdes

French, from the town of the same name. Chosen by Madonna for her daughter.

Love

English, meaning "deep affection and attraction."

Lowri

Welsh, meaning "crowned with laurels."

Luanne
(alt. Luann, Luanna)

German, meaning "renowned in battle"; Hawaiian, meaning "enjoyment." Famous Luannes include author Luanne Rice and *Real Housewife* LuAnn de Lesseps.

Lucia
(alt. Luciana)

Italian, meaning "light."

Lucille
(alt. Lucile, Lucilla)

French, meaning "light." Name of actor Lucille Ball.

Lucinda

English, meaning "light." Famous Lucindas include actor Lucinda Jenney and singer Lucinda Williams.

Lucretia
(alt. Lucrece)

Spanish, meaning "light." Important figure in ancient Roman history.

Lucy
(alt. Lucie)

Latin, meaning "light." Associated with sitcom *I Love Lucy*.

Ludmilla

Slavic, meaning "beloved of the people."

Luella
(alt. Lue)

English, meaning "renowned in battle." Luella Bartley is a designer.

Lulu
(alt. Lula)

German, meaning "renowned in battle." Name of the singer.

Luna

Latin, meaning "moon." Luna was the personification of the moon in ancient Roman mythology.

Lupita

Spanish, from the town of the same name. Lupita Nyong'o is an actor.

Luz

Spanish, meaning "light."

Lydia
(alt. Lidia)

Greek, meaning "from Lydia." Lydia Bennet is one of the five sisters in Jane Austen's *Pride and Prejudice*.

Lynn
(alt. Lyn, Lynna, Lynne)

Spanish, meaning "pretty"; English, meaning "waterfall." Name of the actor Lynn Redgrave.

Lyra

Latin, meaning "lyre." The main female character in Philip Pullman's trilogy *His Dark Materials*.

M Girls' names

Mab
(alt. Mabe)
Irish Gaelic, meaning "joy."
Queen Mab is a character from
Shakespeare's *Romeo and Juliet*.

Mabel
(alt. Mabelle, Mable)
Latin, meaning "loveable." Dates
from the fifth century.

Macaria
Spanish, meaning "blessed."

Mackenzie
(alt. Mackenzy, McKenzie)
Irish Gaelic, meaning "son of the
wise ruler." Used for girls and boys.

Macy
(alt. Macey, Maci, Macie)
French, meaning "Matthew's estate."
Famous Macys include department
store Macy's and reality TV star Maci
Bookout.

Mada
English, meaning "from Magdala."
In Hindu mythology, Mada is an
enormous monster who is able to
swallow the universe.

Madden
(alt. Maddyn)
Irish, meaning "little dog." Associated
with the video game series.

Madeline
(alt. Madaline, Madalyn, Madeleine,
Madelyn, Madilyn; abbrev. Maddi,
Maddie, Madie)
Greek, meaning "from Magdala."
Associated with Ludwig Bemelmans's
"Madeline" novels.

Madge
Greek, meaning "pearl." Also
the short form of Marjorie
and the nickname of singer
Madonna.

Madhuri

Hindi, meaning "sweet girl."

Madison

(alt. Maddison, Madisen, Madisyn)

English, meaning "son of the mighty warrior." Made famous by *Splash* character Madison, and President James Madison.

Madonna

Latin, meaning "my lady." Made famous by pop legend Madonna and the Virgin Madonna.

Maeve

Irish Gaelic, meaning "intoxicating." Queen Maeve appears in Irish mythology and Maeve Binchy was an Irish author.

Mafalda

Spanish, meaning "battlemighty." Mafalda Hopkirk is a character in the "Harry Potter" series.

Magali

Greek, meaning "pearl."

Magdalene

(alt. Magdalen, Magdalena)

Greek, meaning "from Magdala." Associated with Mary Magdalene from the Bible.

Maggie

Shortened form of Margaret, meaning "pearl." Famous Maggies include actors Maggie Gyllenhaal and Maggie Grace, and *The Simpsons* character Maggie Simpson.

Magnolia

Latin, from the flowering plant of the same name. Also the name of a movie.

Mahala

(alt. Mahalia)

Hebrew, meaning "tender affection."

Maia

(alt. Maja)

Greek, meaning "mother." An important character in ancient Greek mythology.

Maida

English, meaning "maiden."

Maisie

(alt. Maisey, Maisy, Maizie, Masie, Mazie)

Greek, meaning "pearl." Name of actor Maisie Williams.

Malin

(alt. Maline)

Hebrew, meaning "of Magda." Famous Malins include actor Malin Akerman, singer Malin Berggren, and infamous alleged Swedish witch Malin Matsdotter.

Maliyah
(alt. Malia)

Hawaiian, meaning "beloved." Also the name of one of President Barack Obama's daughters.

Malka

Hebrew, meaning "queen."

Mallory
(alt. Malorie)

French, meaning "unhappy." The name of children's author Malorie Blackman.

Malvina

Gaelic, meaning "smooth brow."

Mamie
(alt. Mammie)

Shortened form of Margaret, meaning "pearl." Famous Mamies include former First Lady Mamie Eisenhower, actor Mamie Gummer, and infamous midwife Mamie Cadden.

Mandy
(alt. Mandie)

Shortened form of Amanda, meaning "much loved." Famous Mandys include actor Mandy Moore, performer Mandy Miller, and the song "Mandy" by Barry Manilow.

Manisha

Sanskrit, meaning "desire." Manisha is the goddess of wisdom in the Hindu faith.

Mansi

Hopi, meaning "plucked flower."

Manuela

Spanish, meaning "the Lord is among us."

Mara

Hebrew, meaning "bitter." Famous Maras include actors Mara Wilson and Rooney Mara, and author Mara Bergman.

Marcy
(alt. Marci, Marcie, Marcia, Marcela, Marceline, Marcella, Marcelle)

Latin, meaning "war-like." Famous Marcias include actor Marcia Cross and voice actor Marcia Wallace.

Margaret
(alt. Margarete, Margaretta, Margarette, Margret, Margarita, Margeurite; abbrev. Maggie, Margot, Meg)

Greek, meaning "pearl." Famous Margarets include author Margaret Atwood, actor Margaret Rutherford, and former Prime Minister of Great Britain Margaret Thatcher. Margot is the abbreviation of the French form, Marguerite, used by dancer Margot Fonteyn.

Maria
(alt. Mariah)

Latin, meaning "bitter." Famous Marias include tennis pro Maria Sharapova, performer Maria Von Trapp, and singer Mariah Carey.

Marian

(alt. Marianne, Mariam, Mariana, Marion)

French, meaning "bitter grace." Maid Marian is a character from the Robin Hood legend.

Maribel

Hebrew, meaning "beautiful."

Marie

French, meaning "bitter." Famous Maries include French Queen consort Marie Antoinette, physicist Marie Curie, and singer Marie Osmond.

Mariel

(alt. Mariela, Mariella, Marika)

Dutch, meaning "bitter."

Marietta

(alt. Marieta)

French, meaning "bitter." Marietta Stow was a suffragist.

Marigold

English, from the flowering plant of the same name. Associated with the movie *The Best Exotic Marigold Hotel*.

Marilyn

(alt. Marilee, Marilene, Marilynn)

English, meaning "bitter." Made famous by actor and singer Marilyn Monroe.

Marin

American, from the county of the same name.

Marina

(alt. Marine)

Latin, meaning "from the sea."

Mariposa

Spanish, meaning "butterfly."

Marisa

(alt. Maris, Marissa)

Latin, meaning "of the sea." Famous Marisas include actors Marisa Tomei, Marissa Ribisi, and Marissa Jaret Winokur.

Marisol

Spanish, meaning "bitter sun." Associated with Maria de la Soledad, which is a Spanish title for the Virgin Mary.

Marjolaine

French, meaning "marjoram."

Marjorie

(alt. Margery, Marjory; abbrev. Madge, Marge, Margie, Margit, Margy)

French, meaning "pearl." Famous Marjories include actors Marjorie Reynolds and Marjorie Main, socialite Marjorie Bridges, and autobiographer Margery Kempe.

Marlene
(alt. Marla, Marlen, Marlena)

Hebrew, meaning "bitter." Name of the actor Marlene Dietrich.

Marley
(alt. Marlee)

American, meaning "bitter." Made famous by singer Bob Marley.

Marlo
(alt. Marlowe)

American, meaning "bitter."

Marnie
(alt. Marney)

Scottish, meaning "from the sea." Famous Marnies include the character of Marnie from *Girls*, the movie *Marnie* by Alfred Hitchcock, and the birth name of ballerina Darcey Bussell.

Marseille

French, from the city of the same name.

Marsha

English, meaning "war-like." Famous Marshas include singer Marsha Hunt, playwright Marsha Norman, and *Brady Bunch* character Marsha.

Martha
(alt. Marta)

Aramaic, meaning "lady." A character in the Bible.

Martina
(alt. Martine)

Latin, meaning "war-like." Famous Martinas include singer Martina McBride, and tennis pros Martina Hingis and Martina Navratilova.

Marvel

French, meaning "something to wonder at." Also a comic book brand.

Mary

Hebrew, meaning "bitter." Famous Marys include the Virgin Mary and Mary Magdalene from the Bible, and author Mary Shelley.

Masada

Hebrew, meaning "foundation."

Matilda
(alt. Mathilda, Mathilde; abbrev. Tilly)

German, meaning "battlemighty." *Matilda* is a novel by Roald Dahl, and a movie from the book.

Mattea

Hebrew, meaning "gift of God."

Maude
(alt. Maud)

German, meaning "battlemighty." Maude Flanders is a character from *The Simpsons*.

Maura

Irish, meaning "bitter."

Maureen
(alt. Maurine)
Irish, meaning "bitter."

Mavis
French, meaning "thrush." Mavis is a character in *Hotel Transylvania*.

Maxine
(abbrev. Maxie)
Latin, meaning "greatest." Maxine Andrews was one of the singing group the Andrews Sisters.

May
(alt. Mae, Maya, Maye, Mayra)
Hebrew, meaning "gift of God." Also the fifth month.

Mckenna
(alt. Mackenna)
Irish Gaelic, meaning "son of the handsome one." Used more commonly for boys.

Medea
(alt. Madea, Meda)
Greek, meaning "ruling." Associated with the Tyler Perry character Madea.

Meg
Shortened form of Margaret, meaning "pearl." Famous Megs include actor Meg Ryan, and the characters of Meg from Disney's *Hercules* and Meg Griffin from *Family Guy*.

Megan
(alt. Meagan, Meghan)
Welsh, meaning "pearl." Famous Megans include actors Megan Fox and Megan Mullally.

Mehitabel
Hebrew, meaning "benefited by God."

Mehri
Persian, meaning "kind."

Melanie
(alt. Melania, Melany, Melonie; abbrev. Mel)
Greek, meaning "dark-skinned." Famous Melanies include actor Melanie Griffith and singers Melanie Brown and Melanie Chisholm of the Spice Girls.

Melba
Australian, meaning "from Melbourne." Made famous by Melba toast and the dessert Peach Melba.

Melia
(alt. Meliah)
German, meaning "industrious."

Melina
Greek, meaning "honey." Name of actor Melina Kanakaredes.

Melinda
Latin, meaning "honey." Philanthropist Melinda Gates is the wife of Microsoft founder Bill Gates.

Melisande
(alt. Melisende)

French, meaning "bee." Melisandre is a character from *Game of Thrones*.

Melissa
(alt. Melisa, Mellissa)

Greek, meaning "bee." Famous Melissas include singer Melissa Etheridge and actor Melissa Joan Hart.

Melody
(alt. Melodie)

Greek, meaning "song."

Melvina

Celtic, meaning "chieftain."

Menora
(alt. Menorah)

Hebrew, meaning "candlestick." A Menorah is a candalabrum with seven branches, used in Jewish worship; a symbol of Judaism.

Mercedes

Spanish, meaning "mercies." Made famous by the car company Mercedes Benz.

Mercy

English, meaning "mercy."

Meredith
(alt. Meridith)

Welsh, meaning "great ruler." Meredith Brooks is a singer.

Merle

French, meaning "blackbird." Also the term for the patterning on the coat of a dog.

Merry

English, meaning "lighthearted."

Meryl
(alt. Merrill)

Irish Gaelic, meaning "seabright." The name of actor Meryl Streep and ice dancer Meryl Davis.

Meta

German, meaning "pearl."

Mia

Italian, meaning "mine." Famous Mias include actors Mia Farrow and Mia Wasikowskaa, and singer M.I.A.

Michaela
(alt. Makaela, Makaila, Makayla, McKayla, Micaela, Mikaela, Mikaila, Mikala, Mikayla)

Hebrew, meaning "who is like the Lord." The name of gymnast McKayla Maroney.

Michelle
(alt. Machelle, Mechelle, Michaele, Michal, Michele; abbrev. Micki, Mickie, Micky)

French, meaning "who is like the Lord." Famous Michelles include First Lady Michelle Obama, and actor Michelle Rodriguez.

Migdalia

Greek, meaning "from Magdala."

Mignon

French, meaning "cute." Also a cut of steak.

Mika
(alt. Micah)

Hebrew, meaning "who resembles God." Associated with singer Mika.

Milada

Czech, meaning "my love."

Milagros

Spanish, meaning "miracles." Also a type of Mexican folk charm.

Milan

Italian, from the city of the same name.

Mildred

English, meaning "gentle strength." The title character from the movie and TV series *Mildred Pierce*.

Milena

Czech, meaning "love and warmth."

Miley

American, meaning "smiley." Name of singer and actor Miley Cyrus.

Millicent
(alt. Milicent; abbrev. Millie, Milly)

German, meaning "high-born power." Famous Millicents include suffragist Millicent Fawcett, British spy Milicent Bagot, and the musical *Thoroughly Modern Millie*.

Mimi

Italian, meaning "bitter." Mimi is a character from Giacome Puccini's opera *La boheme*.

Mina
(alt. Mena)

German, meaning "love"; Persian, meaning "colored glass."

Mindy
(alt. Mindi)

Latin, meaning "honey." Famous Mindys include comedian Mindy Kaling, singer Mindy McCready, and actor Mindy Sterling.

Minerva

Roman, from the goddess of the same name. Minerva was the goddess of wisdom, arts, and defense.

Ming

Chinese, meaning "bright." Associated with the Ming Dynasty in China.

Minnie
(alt. Minna)

German, meaning "helmet." Made famous by Disney's Minnie Mouse.

Mira
(alt. Meera)

Latin, meaning "admirable."

Mirabel
(alt. Mirabella, Mirabelle)

Latin, meaning "wonderful." Also a type of plum.

Miranda
(alt. Meranda)

Latin, meaning "admirable." Famous Mirandas include actors Miranda Richardson and Miranda Hart, and model Miranda Kerr.

Mirella
(alt. Mireille, Mirela)

Latin, meaning "admirable." Mirella Freni is an opera singer.

Miriam

Hebrew, meaning "bitter." A prophetess in the Bible.

Mirta

Spanish, meaning "crown of thorns."

Missy
(alt. Missie)

Shortened form of Melissa, meaning "bee." The name of singer and producer Missy Elliot.

Misty
(alt. Misti)

English, meaning "mist." Associated with Misty from Pokémon.

Mitzi

German, meaning "bitter." Name of actor Mitzi Gaynor.

Miu

Japanese, meaning "beautiful feather."

Moira
(alt. Maira)

Irish, meaning "bitter." Associated with actor Moira Kelly.

Molly
(alt. Mollie)

American, meaning "bitter." Famous Mollys include actors Molly Ringwald and Molly Sims.

Mona

Irish Gaelic, meaning "aristocratic." The vampire from *Mona the Vampire*.

Monica
(alt. Monika, Monique)

Latin, meaning "adviser." Famous Monicas include intern Monica Lewinsky, tennis pro Monica Seles, and *Friends* character Monica Geller.

Monroe

Gaelic, meaning "mouth of the river Rotha." Made famous by singer and actor Marilyn Monroe.

Montserrat
(alt. Monserrate)

Spanish, from the town of the same name. Montserrat Caballe is an opera singer.

Morag

Scottish, meaning "star of the sea."
Also the name of the Loch Moror
monster in Scotland.

Morgan
(alt. Morgann)

Welsh, meaning "great and bright."
Used for girls and boys.

Moriah

Hebrew, meaning "the Lord is my
teacher."

Morwenna

Welsh, meaning "maiden." Saint
Morwenna is the patron saint of
Cornwall, England.

Moselle
(alt. Mozell, Mozella, Mozelle)

Hebrew, meaning "savior."

Mulan

Chinese, meaning "wood orchid."
The name of the Disney movie *Mulan*.

Muriel

Irish Gaelic, meaning "seabright."
Name of the novelist Muriel Spark.

Mya
(alt. Maya, Myah)

Greek, meaning "mother." Famous
Myas include author Maya Angelou,
comedian Maya Rudolph, and
the Mayan people of Central
America.

Myfanwy

Welsh, meaning "my little lovely
one."

Myra

Latin, meaning "scented oil." Name
of the pioneering lawyer Myra
Bradwell.

Myrna
(alt. Mirna)

Irish Gaelic, meaning "tender and
beloved." Associated with actor
Myrna Fahey.

Myrtle

Irish, from the shrub of the same
name. Myrtle Wilson is a character
from *The Great Gatsby*.

N

Girls' names

Nadia
(alt. Nadya)
Russian, meaning "hope."
Nadia Comaneci was the first gymnast to be awarded a perfect score of 10 in an Olympic event.

Nadine
French, meaning "hope."
Name of the socialite Nadine Caridi.

Nahara
Aramaic, meaning "light."

Naima
Arabic, meaning "water nymph."

Nalani
Hawaiian, meaning "serenity of the skies."

Nancy
(alt. Nanci, Nancie; abbrev. Nan, Nanna, Nannie)
Hebrew, meaning "grace." Famous Nancys include former First Lady Nancy Reagan and figure skater Nancy Kerrigan.

Nanette
(alt. Nannette)
French, meaning "grace." Associated with musical No, No, Nanette.

Naomi
(alt. Naoma, Noemi)
Hebrew, meaning "pleasant." Famous Naomis include actor Naomi Watts, author Naomi Wolf, and an important character in the Bible.

Narcissa
Greek, meaning "daffodil." Narcissa Malfoy is a character in the "Harry Potter" series.

Nastasia

Greek, meaning "resurrection." Can also refer to a baby born on Christmas Day.

Natalie

(alt. Natalia, Natalya, Nathalie)

Latin, meaning "birth day." Natalie Wood was an actor.

Natasha

(alt. Natasa; abbrev. Nat, Tasha)

Russian, meaning "birth day." A character from Leo Tolstoy's War and Peace.

Neda

English, meaning "wealthy." An ancient Greek nymph.

Nedra

English, meaning "underground."

Neema

Swahili, meaning "born of prosperity."

Neka

Native American, meaning "goose."

Nell

(alt. Nelda, Nella, Nellie, Nelly)

Originally a shortened form of Eleanor, meaning "light." The title of a movie. Singer Nelly Furtado was given the name at birth, but Nell Gwynn, mistress of King Charles II, was an Eleanor.

Nemi

Italian, from the lake of the same name.

Neoma

Greek, meaning "new moon."

Nereida

Spanish, meaning "sea nymph."

Nerissa

Greek, meaning "sea nymph." A character in Shakespeare's The Merchant of Venice.

Nettie

(alt. Neta)

Shortened form of Henrietta, meaning "ruler of the house."

Neva

Spanish, meaning "snowy."

Nevaeh

American, meaning "heaven" (and spelled that way backwards).

Niamh

(alt. Neve)

Irish, meaning "brightness." An Irish goddess.

Nicola

(abbrev. Nicki, Nicky, Nikki)

Greek, meaning "victory of the people." Famous Nicolas include actor Nicola Peltz and singer Nicola Roberts.

Nicole
(alt. Nichol, Nichole, Nicolette, Nicolle, Nikole)

Greek, meaning "victory of the people." Famous Nicoles include actor Nicole Kidman, socialite Nicole Richie, and singer Nicole Scherzinger.

Nidia
Spanish, meaning "graceful."

Nigella
Irish Gaelic, meaning "champion." Name of chef Nigella Lawson.

Nikita
Greek, meaning "unconquered." Also a song by Elton John.

Nila
Egyptian, meaning "Nile." Associated with Nila wafers.

Nilda
German, meaning "battle woman."

Nina
Spanish, meaning "girl." Nina Simone is a singer.

Nissa
Hebrew, meaning "sign."

Nita
Spanish, meaning "gracious."

Nixie
German, meaning "water sprite."

Noelle
(alt. Noel)

French, meaning "Christmas." Noelle is usually the female form and Noel the male form.

Nola
(alt. Nuala)

Irish Gaelic, meaning "white shoulder." Often refers to someone with white or very blonde hair.

Nona
Latin, meaning "ninth."

Nora
(alt. Norah)

Shortened form of Eleanor, meaning "light." The name of screenwriter Nora Ephron, singer Norah Jones, and author Nora Roberts.

Noreen
(alt. Norine)

Irish, meaning "light." Noreen Murray was a scientist who helped develop the vaccine against hepatitis B.

Norma
Latin, meaning "pattern." Marilyn Monroe's birth name was Norma Jean Mortenson.

Normandie
(alt. Normandy)
French, from the province of the same name.

Novia
(alt. Nova)
Latin, meaning "new."

Nydia
Latin, meaning "nest."

Nysa
(alt. Nyssa)
Greek, meaning "ambition." A district in ancient Greek mythology.

Old name, new fashion

Bella	Hazel
Carolyn	Matilda
Clara	Nora
Dorothy	Penelope
Emmeline	Rosalie

Girls' names

Oceana
(alt. Ocean, Océane, Ocie)
Greek, meaning "ocean."

Octavia
Latin, meaning "eighth."
Famous Octavias include actor
Octavia Spencer, and Octavia in
Shakespeare's *Antony and
Cleopatra*.

Oda
(alt. Odie)
Shortened form of Odessa, meaning
"long voyage"; German, meaning
"wealth" or "inheritance."

Odele
(alt. Odell)
English, meaning "woad hill." Woad
is a dye for the color indigo.

Odelia
Hebrew, meaning "I will praise the
Lord." Associated with Saint Odelia.

Odessa
Greek, meaning "long voyage."

Odette
(alt. Odetta)
French, meaning "wealthy." Name
of the "good" swan in *Swan
Lake*.

Odile
(alt. Odilia)
French, meaning "prospers in battle."
Name of the "bad" swan in *Swan
Lake*.

Odina
Feminine form of Odin, meaning
"creative inspiration," from the
Nordic god of the same name.

Odyssey
Greek, meaning "long journey."
Title of the epic poem by
Homer.

Oksana

Russian, meaning "praise to God."

Ola
(alt. Olie)

Greek, meaning "man's defender."

Olena
(alt. Olene)

Russian, meaning "light."

Olga

Russian, meaning "holy." Name of the model and actor Olga Kurylenko, and gymnast Olga Korbut.

Olivia
(alt. Olivev, Oliviana, Olivié, Ollie; abbrev. Liv, Livia)

Latin, meaning "olive." Famous Olivias include actors Olivia Munn and Olivia Wilde, and *Scandal* character Olivia Pope.

Olwen

Welsh, meaning "white footprint."

Olympia
(alt. Olimpia)

Greek, meaning "from Mount Olympus." Name of actor Olympia Dukakis.

Oma
(alt. Omie)

Arabic, meaning "leader." In some communities, Oma refers to a grandmother.

Omyra

Latin, meaning "scented oil."

Oneida
(abbrev. Ona, Onnie)

Native American, meaning "long awaited." The name of a tribe.

Onyx

Latin, meaning "veined gem." Also a semiprecious stone.

Oona
(alt. Oonagh)

Irish, meaning "unity."

Opal

Sanskrit, meaning "gem." Also a precious stone.

Ophelia
(alt. Ophélie)

Greek, meaning "help." A character in Shakespeare's *Hamlet*.

Oprah

Hebrew, meaning "young deer." Name of the legendary TV host Oprah Winfrey.

Ora

Latin, meaning "prayer." Also a platinum metal.

Orabela

Latin, meaning "prayer."

Oralie
(alt. Oralia)

French, meaning "golden."

Orane

French, meaning "rising."

Orchid

Greek, from the flower of the same name.

Oriana
(alt. Oriane)

Latin, meaning "dawning." One of the many nicknames of Queen Elizabeth I.

Orla
(alt. Orlaith, Orly)

Irish Gaelic, meaning "golden lady."

Orlean

French, meaning "plum." The city of New Orleans in Louisiana.

Orsa
(alt. Osia, Ossie)

Latin, meaning "bear."

Otthid

Greek, meaning "prospers in battle."

Ottilie
(alt. Ottie)

French, meaning "prospers in battle." Name of the opera singer Ottilie Metzger.

Ouida

French, meaning "renowned in battle."

Ozette

Native American, from the village of the same name.

P

Girls' names

Padma

Sanskrit, meaning "lotus." Padma Lakshmi is an Indian born American cookery book writer, actor and TV host.

Paige
(alt. Page)

French, meaning "serving boy." Paige Turco is an actor.

Paisley

Scottish, from the town of the same name. The name of a fabric pattern.

Palma
(alt. Palmira)

Latin, meaning "palm tree."

Paloma

Spanish, meaning "dove." Famous Palomas include singer Paloma Faith and designer Paloma Picasso.

Pamela
(alt. Pamala, Pamella; abbrev. Pam, Pammie)

Greek, meaning "all honey." Famous Pamelas include actors Pamela Anderson and Pamela Adlon, and author Pamela (P. L.) Travers.

Pandora

Greek, meaning "all gifted." Associated with the myth of Pandora's box in ancient Greek mythology.

Pangiota

Greek, meaning "all is holy."

Pansy

French, from the flower of the same name.

Paradisa
(alt. Paradis)

Greek, meaning "garden orchard."

Paris
(alt. Parisa)

Greek, from the mythological hero of the same name. Famous Parises include the city in France and socialite Paris Hilton.

Parker

English, meaning "park keeper." Parker Posey is an actor.

Parthenia

Greek, meaning "virginal."

Parthenope

Greek, from the mythological Siren of the same name. Parthenope Nightingale was sister of nurse Florence Nightingale.

Parvati

Sanskrit, meaning "daughter of the mountain." The Hindu goddess of love and devotion. Also a character in the "Harry Potter" series.

Pascale

Latin, meaning "Easterchild." Also a boys' name, usually spelt Pascal.

Patience

French, meaning "the state of being patient."

Patricia
(abbrev. Pat, Patsy, Patti, Pattie, Patty, Trisha)

Latin, meaning "noble." Famous Patricias include actors Patricia Arquette and Patricia O'Neal.

Paula

Latin, meaning "small." Famous Paulas include singer Paula Abdul, actor Paula Patton, and chef Paula Deen.

Pauline
(alt. Paulette, Paulina)

Latin, meaning "small." Associated with actor Pauline Collins.

Paxton

Latin, meaning "peaceful town."

Paz

Spanish, meaning "peace."

Pazia

Hebrew, meaning "golden."

Peace

English, meaning "peace."

Pearl
(alt. Pearle, Pearlie, Perla)

Latin, meaning "pale gemstone."

Peggy
(alt. Peggie)

Greek, meaning "pearl." The name of actor Peggy Lipton and figure skater Peggy Fleming; also the movie *Peggy Sue Got Married*.

Pelia

Hebrew, meaning "marvel of God."

Penelope

(abbrev. Penni, Pennie, Penny)

Greek, meaning "bobbin worker." Penelope was also the loyal wife of Odysseus in Greek mythology.

Peony

Greek, from the flower of the same name.

Perdita

Latin, meaning "lost." A character in William Shakespeare's play *The Winter's Tale*.

Peri

(alt. Perri)

Hebrew, meaning "outcome." Associated with Peri spirits in Persian mythology.

Perry

French, meaning "pear tree."

Persephone

Greek, meaning "bringer of destruction." The Queen of the Underworld in ancient Greek mythology.

Petra

(alt. Petrina)

Greek, meaning "rock."

Petula

Latin, meaning "to seek." Name of the singer Petula Clark.

Petunia

Greek, from the flower of the same name.

Peyton

(alt. Payton)

Old English, meaning "fighting man's estate." Associated with TV series *Peyton Place*.

Phaedra

Greek, meaning "bright."

Philippa

(abbrev. Pippa)

Greek, meaning "horse lover." Philippa Gregory is an author.

Philomena

(alt. Philoma)

Greek, meaning "loved one." Title of the book and movie *Philomena*.

Phoebe

Greek, meaning "shining and brilliant." Name of actor Phoebe Cates, and *Friends* character Phoebe Buffay.

Phoenix

Greek, meaning "red as blood." The city in Arizona and the mythical bird.

Phyllis
(alt. Phillia, Phyllida, Phylis)
Greek, meaning "leafy bough."
Name of comedian Phyllis Diller.

Pia
Latin, meaning "pious."

Pilar
Spanish, meaning "pillar."

Piper
English, meaning "pipe player." Piper Laurie is an actor.

Plum
Latin, from the fruit of the same name.

Polly
Hebrew, meaning "bitter." Associated with the classic Polly Pocket toy.

Pomona
Latin, meaning "apple." Name of the goddess of fruitful abundance in ancient Roman mythology.

Poppy
Latin, from the flower of the same name. Name of model Poppy Delevingne, sister of Cara Delevingne.

Portia
(alt. Porsha)
Latin, meaning "from the Portia clan." Portia de Rossi is an actor.

Posy
(alt. Posie)
English, meaning "small flower."

Precious
Latin, meaning "of great worth." Title of the movie *Precious*.

Priela
Hebrew, meaning "fruit of God."

Primrose
English, meaning "first rose."

Princess
English, meaning "daughter of the monarch."

Priscilla
(alt. Priscila)
Latin, meaning "ancient." Name of the actor Priscilla Presley.

Priya
Hindi, meaning "loved one."

Prudence
(abbrev. Pru, Prudie)
Latin, meaning "caution." Prudence is the mother of all virtues.

Prunella
Latin, meaning "small plum." Name of the actor Prunella Scales.

Psyche
Greek, meaning "breath." The name of a TV show *Psyche*.

Girls' names

Qiturah
Arabic, meaning "incense."

Queen
(alt. Queenie)
English, meaning "queen." The name of rapper and actor Queen Latifah.

Quiana
American, meaning "silky." Name of the model Quiana Grant.

Quincy
(alt. Quincey)
French, meaning "estate of the fifth son."

Quinn
(alt. Quinnie)
Irish Gaelic, meaning "counsel." Quinn is a character from *Glee*.

R Girls' names

Rachel

(alt. Rachael, Rachelle, Raquel; abbrev. Rach)

Hebrew, meaning "ewe." Famous Rachels include the character in the Bible, actors Rachel Weisz and Rachel Bilson, and the *Glee* character Rachel Berry.

Radhika

Sanskrit, meaning "prosperous."

Rae

(alt. Ray)

Feminine form of Ray, meaning "ray," or shortened form of Rachel, meaning "ewe." Rae Armantrout is a poet.

Rahima

Arabic, meaning "compassionate." Name of smallpox survivor Rahima Banu.

Raina

(alt. Rain, Raine, Rainey, Rayne)

Latin, meaning "queen."

Raissa

(alt. Raisa)

Yiddish, meaning "rose." Name of former Russian First Lady Raisa Gorbacheva.

Raleigh

(alt. Rayleigh)

English, meaning "meadow of roe deer."

Rama

(alt. Ramey, Ramya)

Hebrew, meaning "exalted." Associated with the Vishnu's avatars in the Hindu faith.

Ramona

(alt. Romona)

Spanish, meaning "wise guardian." Associated with the "Ramona" books, and the movie *Ramona and Beezus*.

Ramsey

(alt. Ramsay)

English, meaning "raven island."

Rana

(alt. Rania, Rayna)

Arabic, meaning "beautiful thing."

Randy

(alt. Randi)

Shortened form of Miranda, meaning "admirable." More commonly used for boys, as a short form of Randall.

Rani

Sanskrit, meaning "queen."

Raphaela

(alt. Rafaela, Raffaella)

Spanish, meaning "healing God."

Rashida

Turkish, meaning "righteous." Name of actor Rashida Jones.

Raven

(alt. Ravyn)

English, from the bird of the same name. Raven-Symoné is an actor.

Razia

Arabic, meaning "contented."

Reagan

(alt. Reagen, Regan)

Irish Gaelic, meaning "descendant of Riagán." Associated with former President and First Lady Ronald and Nancy Reagan.

Reba

Shortened form of Rebecca, meaning "joined." Name of singer and actor Reba McEntire.

Rebecca

(alt. Rebekah; abbrev. Reb, Reba, Becca, Bex)

Hebrew, meaning "joined." Famous Rebeccas include the character from the Bible, designer Rebecca Minkoff, and one-hit-wonder Rebecca Black.

Reese

(alt. Reece)

Welsh, meaning "fiery and zealous." Name of actor Reese Witherspoon.

Regina

(abbrev. Geena, Gena, Gina)

Latin, meaning "queen." Famous Reginas include actors Regina Hall and Regina King, and singer Regina Spektor. Geena Davis is an actor.

Reina

(alt. Reyna, Rheyna)

Spanish, meaning "queen."

Rena

(alt. Reena, Rina)

Hebrew, meaning "serene."

Renata

Latin, meaning "reborn." Renata Tebaldi is an opera singer.

Rene

Greek, meaning "peace." Rene Russo is an actor.

Renée
(alt. Renae)

French, meaning "reborn." Name of actor Renée Zellweger.

Renita
(alt. Renira)

Latin, meaning "resistant."

Reshma
(alt. Resha)

Sanskrit, meaning "silk."

Reta
(alt. Retha, Retta)

Portuguese, meaning "straight." Also a shortened form of Margaret.

Rhea

Greek, meaning "earth." Also a type of ostrich-like bird. Name of actor Rhea Perlman.

Rheta

Greek, meaning "eloquent speaker." Flora Rheta Schreiber is an author.

Rhiannon
(alt. Rhian)

Welsh, meaning "witch." A prominent figure in Welsh mythology.

Rhoda

Greek, meaning "rose." Title of the sitcom *Rhoda*.

Rhona

Nordic, meaning "rough island." Rhona Mitra is a model and actor.

Rhonda
(alt. Ronda)

Welsh, meaning "noisy." "Help Me Rhonda" is a song by the Beach Boys.

Ría
(alt. Rie, Riya)

Shortened form of Victoria, meaning "victor."

Ricki
(alt. Rieko, Rika, Rikki)

Shortened form of Frederica, meaning "peaceful ruler." Name of the TV host Ricki Lake.

Rihanna
(alt. Reanna, Rhianna)

Welsh, meaning "witch." Name of singer Rihanna.

Riley

Irish Gaelic, meaning "courageous."

Rilla

German, meaning "small brook."

Rima

Arabic, meaning "antelope." Name of the comic book character *Rima the Jungle Girl*.

Riona

Irish Gaelic, meaning "like a queen."

Ripley

English, meaning "shouting man's meadow."

Risa

Latin, meaning "laughter."

Rita

Shortened form of Margaret, meaning "pearl." Famous Ritas include actors Rita Hayworth and Rita Moreno, and singer Rita Coolidge.

River

(alt. Riviera)

English, from the body of water of the same name. Famous Rivers include actor River Phoenix, singer Rivers Cuoma, and comedian Joan Rivers.

Roberta

(abbrev. Bobbi, Bobby, Robbie, Robi, Roby)

English, meaning "bright fame." Name of singer Roberta Flack.

Robin

(alt. Robbin, Robyn)

English, meaning "bright fame." Famous Robins include actor Robin Wright Penn, and singers Robyn and Robin Thicke. Used for both girls and boys.

Rochelle

(alt. Richelle, Rochel)

French, meaning "little rock." Name of actor Rochelle Aytes.

Rogue

French, meaning "beggar." Also an "X-Men" character.

Rohina

(alt. Rohini)

Sanskrit, meaning "sandalwood."

Roisin

Irish Gaelic, meaning "little rose."

Rolanda

German, meaning "famous land." Rolanda Watts is a voice actor.

Roma

Italian, meaning "Rome." Also the name of an ancient Roman deity, and a group of nomadic people.

Romaine

(alt. Romina)

French, meaning "from Rome."

Romola

(alt. Romilda, Romily)

Latin, meaning "Roman woman." Name of the actor Romola Garai.

Romy

Shortened form of Rosemary, meaning "dew of the sea." Famous Romys include actor Romy Rosemont and the movie Romy and Michele's High School Reunion.

Rona
(alt. Ronia, Ronja, Ronna)
Nordic, meaning "rough island."

Ronnie
(alt. Roni, Ronnie)
English, meaning "strong counsel."

Rosa
Italian, meaning "rose." Made famous by Civil Rights activist Rosa Parks.

Rosabel
(alt. Rosabella)
Contraction of Rose and Belle, meaning "beautiful rose."

Rosalie
(alt. Rosale, Rosalia, Rosalina)
French, meaning "rose garden." Actor Andie MacDowell's birth name is actually Rosalie.

Rosalind
(alt. Rosalinda)
Spanish, meaning "pretty rose." A character in Shakespeare's play *As You Like It*.

Rosalyn
(alt. Rosaleen, Rosaline, Roselyn)
Contraction of Rose and Lynn, meaning "pretty rose."

Rosamond
(alt. Rosamund)
German, meaning "renowned protector." Famous Rosamunds include actor Rosamund Pike and author Rosamunde Pilcher.

Rose
(alt. Rosie, Rosia)
Latin, from the flower of the same name. Famous Roses include actors Rose Byrne and Rose McGowan, and the character of Rose DeWitt Bukater from *Titanic*.

Roseanne
(alt. Rosana, Rosanna, Rosanne, Roseann, Roseanna)
Contraction of Rose and Anne, meaning "graceful rose." Name of comedian and actor Roseanne Barr.

Rosemary
(alt. Rosemarie; abbrev. Rosie, Rosy)
Latin, meaning "dew of the sea." Famous Rosemarys include actor Rosemary Clooney and the film *Rosemary's Baby*.

Rosita
Spanish, meaning "rose." Also a character on *Sesame Street*.

Rowena
(alt. Rowan)
Welsh, meaning "slender and fair." Rowena was a powerful and beautiful seductress in ancient Welsh mythology.

Roxanne
(alt. Roxana, Roxane, Roxanna; abbrev. Roxie)

Persian, meaning "dawn." Also a song by Police. Famous Roxies include the character of Roxie Hart from the musical *Chicago*, inventor Roxey Ann Caplin, and the band Roxy Music.

Rubina
(alt. Rubena)

Hebrew, meaning "behold, a son."

Ruby
(alt. Rubi, Rubie)

English, meaning "red gemstone." Made famous by the song "Ruby Tuesday" by the Rolling Stones.

Ruth
(alt. Ruthe, Ruthie)

Hebrew, meaning "friend and companion." Famous Ruths include the character from the Bible and Supreme Court Justice Ruth Bader Ginsburg.

Ryan

Gaelic, meaning "little king." Used for girls or, more commonly, boys.

"Bad girl" names

Delilah	Roxy
Desdemona	Salome
Jezebel	Scarlett
Lilith	Tallulah
Pandora	Trixie

S Girls' names

Saba
(alt. Sabah)

Greek, meaning "from Sheba."

Sabina
(alt. Sabine)

Latin, meaning "from the Sabine tribe." The title given to political women in ancient Rome.

Sabrina

Latin, meaning "the River Severn." Famous Sabrinas include the movie *Sabrina*, the sitcom *Sabrina, the Teenage Witch*, and the character from *Charlie's Angels*.

Sadie
(alt. Sade, Sadye)

Hebrew, meaning "princess." Name of designer Sadie Frost.

Saffron

English, from the reddish-yellow spice of the same name.

Safiyya
(alt. Safiya)

Arabic, meaning "sincere friend." One of Muhammad's wives in the Qu'ran.

Sage
(alt. Saga, Saige)

Latin, meaning "wise and healthy." Also an aromatic herb.

Sahara

Arabic, meaning "desert."

Sakura

Japanese, meaning "cherry blossom."

Sally
(alt. Sallie)

Hebrew, meaning "princess." Name of the actor Sally Field.

Salome
(alt. Salma)

Hebrew, meaning "peace." The name of a seductress in the Bible.

Samantha
(abbrev. Sam, Sammie, Sammy)

Hebrew, meaning "told by God." Famous Samanthas include TV host Samantha Brown and actors Samantha Lewes and Samantha Morton.

Samara
(alt. Samaria, Samira)

Hebrew, meaning "under God's rule."

Sanaa

Arabic, meaning "brilliance." Also the capital of Yemen.

Sandra
(alt. Saundra; abbrev. Sandy)

Shortened form of Alexandra, meaning "defender of mankind." Famous Sandras include actor Sandra Bullock and the character Sandy from *Grease*.

Sangeetha
(alt. Sangeeta)

Hindi, meaning "musical."

Sanna
(alt. Saniya, Sanne, Sanni)

Hebrew, meaning "lily."

Santana
(alt. Santina)

Spanish, meaning "holy." Name of the *Glee* character Santana Lopez.

Sapphire
(alt. Saphira)

Hebrew, meaning "blue gemstone." Associated with *Push* (or *Precious*) author Sapphire.

Sarah
(alt. Sara, Sarai, Sariah)

Hebrew, meaning "princess." Famous Sarahs include actors Sarah Michelle Gellar and Sarah Hyland, and reality TV star Sarah Palin.

Sasha
(alt. Sacha, Sascha)

Russian, meaning "man's defender." Name of President Barack Obama's daughter.

Saskia
(alt. Saskie)

Dutch, meaning "the Saxon people"; Danish, meaning "valley of light."

Savannah
(alt. Savanah, Savanna, Savina)

Spanish, meaning "treeless."

Scarlett
(alt. Scarlet)

English, meaning "scarlet." Scarlett O'Hara is the protagonist of Margaret Mitchell's novel *Gone With The Wind*.

Scout

French, meaning "to listen." Also the lead character in Harper Lee's novel *To Kill a Mockingbird*.

Sedona

(alt. Sedonia, Sedna)

Spanish, from the city of the same name.

Selah

(alt. Sela)

Hebrew, meaning "cliff"; Hebrew, meaning "stop and listen."

Selby

English, meaning "manor village."

Selena

(alt. Salena, Salima, Salina, Selene, Selina)

Greek, meaning "moon goddess." Famous Selenas include singers Selena Gomez and Selena Quintanilla-Perez (known simply as Selena), and actor Selena Royle.

Selma

German, meaning "Godly helmet." Name of actor Selma Blair.

Seneca

Native American, meaning "from the Seneca tribe."

Sephora

Hebrew, meaning "bird"; Greek, meaning "beauty."

September

Latin, meaning "seventh month." The ninth month.

Seraphina

(alt. Serafina, Seraphia, Seraphine)

Hebrew, meaning "ardent." Saint Serafina was known for her strong faith despite illness and suffering.

Serena

(alt. Sarina, Sereana)

Latin, meaning "tranquil." Name of tennis pro Serena Williams.

Serenity

Latin, meaning "serene." Also a sci-fi movie.

Shakira

Arabic, meaning "thankful." Name of the singer Shakira.

Shania

(alt. Shaina, Shana, Shaniya)

Hebrew, meaning "beautiful." Name of the singer Shania Twain.

Shanice

American, meaning "from Africa." Name of the singer Shanice.

Shaniqua

(alt. Shanika)

African, meaning "warrior princess."

Shanna

English, meaning "old."

Shannon
(alt. Shannan, Shanon)

Irish Gaelic, meaning "old and ancient." Shannon Elizabeth is an actor

Shantal
(alt. Shantel, Shantell)

French, from the place of the same name.

Shanti
(alt. Shantih)

Hindi, meaning "peaceful."

Sharlene

German, meaning "man."

Sharon
(alt. Sharen, Sharona, Sharron)

Hebrew, meaning "a plain." Famous Sharons include reality TV star Sharon Osbourne and actors Sharon Stone and Sharon Tate.

Shasta

American, from the mountain and Native American tribe of the same name.

Shauna
(alt. Sharna, Shawna)

Irish, meaning "the Lord is gracious." Sharna Burgess is a dancer.

Shayla
(alt. Shaylie, Shayna, Sheyla)

Irish, meaning "blind."

Shea

Irish Gaelic, meaning "from the fairy fort." The tree and nut of the same name.

Sheena

Irish, meaning "the Lord is gracious." Name of the singer Sheena Easton.

Sheila
(alt. Shelia, Shila)

Irish, meaning "blind." Name of singer Sheila E.

Shelby
(alt. Shelba, Shelbie)

English, meaning "estate on the ledge."

Shelley
(alt. Shellie, Shelly)

English, meaning "meadow on the ledge." Famous Shelleys include actor Shelley Fabares and Shelley Duvall, and author Mary Shelley.

Shenandoah

Native American, meaning "after an Oneida chief." Also the name of a national park.

Sheridan

Irish Gaelic, meaning "wild man."

Sheryl
(alt. Sherryl; abbrev. Sheri, Sherie, Sherri, Sherrie)

German, meaning "man." Famous Sheryls include singer Sheryl Crow, businesswoman Sheryl Sandberg, and host Sheryl Underwood. Also comedian and host Sherri Shepherd.

Shiloh

Hebrew, meaning "his gift." Name of Angelina Jolie and Brad Pitt's daughter.

Shirley
(alt. Shirlee)

English, meaning "bright meadow." Famous Shirleys include singer Dame Shirley Bassey, actor Shirley MacLaine, and child star Shirley Temple.

Shivani

Sanskrit, meaning "wife of Shiva."

Shona

Irish Gaelic, meaning "God is gracious."

Shoshana
(alt. Shoshanna)

Hebrew, meaning "lily." Shoshanna Shapiro is a character from *Girls*.

Shura

Russian, meaning "man's defender"; Arabic, meaning "consultation."

Sian
(alt. Sianna)

Welsh, meaning "the Lord is gracious."

Sibyl
(alt. Sybil)

Greek, meaning "seer and oracle." Sibyl was a prophetess in ancient Greek mythology.

Sidney
(alt. Sydney)

English, meaning "from St. Denis." Name of the city in Australia.

Sidonie
(alt. Sidonia, Sidony)

Latin, meaning "from Sidonia."

Siena
(alt. Sienna)

Latin, from the town of the same name.

Sierra

Spanish, meaning "saw."

Signa
(alt. Signe)

Scandinavian, meaning "victory."

Sigrid

Nordic, meaning "fair victory." Sigrid the Haughty was an important figure in ancient Norse mythology.

Silja

Scandinavian, meaning "blind."

Simcha

Hebrew, meaning "joy."

Simone
(alt. Simona)

Hebrew, meaning "listening intently."
Famous Simones include singer Nina
Simone, and philosopher Simone de
Beauvoir.

Sinead

Irish, meaning "the Lord is gracious."
Name of singer Sinead O'Connor.

Siobhan

Irish, meaning "the Lord is gracious."
Siobhan Fallon Hogan is an actor.

Siren
(alt. Sirena)

Greek, meaning "entangler." In
ancient Greek mythology, sirens
were beautiful and dangerous
creatures who lured sailors to their
deaths.

Siria

Spanish, meaning "glowing."

Skye
(alt. Sky)

Scottish, from the island of the same
name in Scotland.

Skylar
(alt. Skyla, Skyler)

Dutch, meaning "giving shelter."
Skylar White is a character from
Breaking Bad.

Sloane
(alt. Sloan)

Irish Gaelic, meaning "man of arms."
Famous Sloanes include Sloane
Stephens, the infamous Sloane
Rangers, and the character of Sloane
Sabbith on Newsroom.

Socorro

Spanish, meaning "to aid."

Sojourner

English, meaning "temporary stay."
Name of the women's rights
and civil rights activist Sojourner
Truth.

Solana

Spanish, meaning "sunlight."

Solange

French, meaning "with dignity."
Solange Knowles is a singer.

Soledad

Spanish, meaning "solitude."

Soleil

French, meaning "sun." Cirque du
Soleil is a performance group.

Solveig

Scandinavian, meaning "woman of the house."

Sonia
(alt. Sonja, Sonya)

Greek, meaning "wisdom." Sonia Kasuk is a designer.

Sophia
(alt. Sofia, Sofie, Sophie)

Greek, meaning "wisdom." Famous Sophias include director Sofia Coppola and actors Sofia Vergara and Sophia Loren.

Sophronia

Greek, meaning "sensible."

Soraya

Persian, meaning "princess."

Sorcha

Irish Gaelic, meaning "bright and shining."

Sorrel

English, from the herb of the same name.

Spirit

Latin, meaning "breath."

Stacey
(alt. Stacie, Stacy)

Greek, meaning "resurrection." Famous Staceys include actors Stacey Keibler and Stacey Dash, and presenter Stacey Dales.

Star
(alt. Starla, Starr)

English, meaning "star." The name of reality TV star Star Jones.

Stella

Latin, meaning "star." Stella McCartney is a designer.

Stephanie
(alt. Stefanie, Stephani, Stephany, Stephenie; abbrev. Steph)

Greek, meaning "crowned." Famous Stephanies include actor Stephanie Beacham, tennis pro Stefanie Graf, and author Stephenie Meyer.

Sukey
(alt. Sukey, Sukie)

Derived from Susan, meaning "lily."

Sula

American, meaning "peace" or "little she-bear." Also the novel *Sula* by Toni Morrison.

Summer

English, from the season of the same name. Summer Glau is an actor.

Sunday

English, meaning "the first day." Nicole Kidman and Keith Urban's daughter is Sunday Rose.

Sunny
(alt. Sun)

English, meaning "of a pleasant temperament."

Suri

Persian, meaning "red rose." Tom Cruise and Katie Holmes's daughter is Suri.

Surya

Hindi, from the sun god of the same name.

Susan

(alt. Susann, Suzan; abbrev. Sue, Susie, Suzy)

Hebrew, meaning "lily." Famous Susans include actor Susan Sarandon, singer Susan Boyle, and suffragist Susan B. Anthony.

Susannah

(alt. Susana, Susanna, Susanne, Suzanna, Suzanne)

Hebrew, meaning "lily."

Svetlana

Russian, meaning "star."

Swanhild

Saxon, meaning "battle swan."

Sylvia

(alt. Silvia, Sylvie)

Latin, meaning "from the forest." Famous Sylvias include authors Sylvia Plath and Sylvia Day, and singer Sylvia Robinson.

Great female singers

Adele (Adkins)

Aretha (Franklin)

Billie (Holiday)

Dionne (Warwick)

Dolly (Parton)

Ella (Fitzgerald)

Gladys (Knight)

Jennifer (Hudson)

Judy (Garland)

Nina (Simone)

T

Girls' names

Tabitha
(alt. Tabatha, Tabetha)
Aramaic, meaning "gazelle." A character in the Bible who was raised from the dead.

Tahira
Arabic, meaning "virginal."

Tai
Chinese, meaning "big."

Taima
(alt. Taina, Tayna)
Native American, meaning "peal of thunder."

Talia
(alt. Tali)
Hebrew, meaning "heaven's dew." Talia Shire is an actor.

Taliesin
Welsh, meaning "shining brow." The name of a Welsh poet Taliesin.

Talise
(alt. Talisa, Talyse)
Native American, meaning "lovely water." Talisa Stark is a character from *Game of Thrones*.

Talitha
Aramaic, meaning "young girl."

Tallulah
(alt. Taliyah)
Native American, meaning "leaping water." Famous Tallulahs include actors Tallulah Bankhead and Tallulah Riley, and *Bugsy Malone* character Tallulah.

Tamara
(alt. Tamera)
Hebrew, meaning "palm tree." Famous Tamaras include actors Tamara Taylor and Tamera Mowry.

Tamatha
(alt. Tametha)

American, meaning "dear Tammy."

Tamika
(alt. Tameka)

American, meaning "people."

Tamsin
(abbrev. Tami, Tammie, Tammy)

Hebrew, meaning "twin." Tammy Wynette is the name used by the legendary country singer—her real first name was Virginia.

Tanis
Spanish, meaning "to make famous."

Tanya
(alt. Tania, Tanya, Tonya)

Shortened form of Tatiana, meaning "from the Tatius clan." The name of actor Tanya Roberts and figure skater Tonya Harding.

Tara
(alt. Tahra, Tarah, Tera)

Irish Gaelic, meaning "rocky hill." Famous Taras include actors Tara Reid and Tara Fitzgerald.

Tatiana
(alt. Tatyana)

Russian, meaning "from the Tatius clan." Famous Tatianas include actors Tatyana Ali and Tatiana Maslany, and author Tatiana de Rosnay.

Tatum
English, meaning "lighthearted." Famous Tatums include actors Tatum O'Neal and Channing Tatum.

Tawny
(alt. Tawanaa, Tawnee, Tawnya)

English, meaning "golden brown."

Taya
Greek, meaning "poor one." In several languages the name also means "princess" or "goddess."

Taylor
(alt. Tayler)

English, meaning "tailor." Famous Taylors include singer Taylor Swift and actors Taylor Lautner and Taylor Schilling.

Tea
Greek, meaning "goddess." Tea Leoni is an actor.

Teagan
(alt. Teague, Tegan)

Irish Gaelic, meaning "poet."

Teal
English, from the bird of the same name. Also the blue-green color.

Tecla
Greek, meaning "fame of God."

Temperance

English, meaning "virtue."
Temperance Brennan is a character
from *Bones*.

Tempest

French, meaning "storm." The
Shakespeare play of the same name.

Teresa

(alt. Terese, Tereza, Theresa, Therese)

Greek, meaning "harvest." Famous
Teresas include nun Mother Teresa,
TV medium Theresa Caputo, and
actor Teresa Graves.

Terri

(alt. Teri, Terrie, Terry)

Derived from the short form of
Teresa, meaning "harvest." Teri
Hatcher is an actor, given this short
name at birth.

Tessa

(alt. Tess, Tessie)

Derived from the short form of
Teresa, meaning "harvest." Famous
Tessas include ice dancer Tessa
Virtue and literary heroine *Tess of the
D'Urbervilles* by Thomas Hardy.

Thais

Greek, from the mythological
heroine of the same name.

Thalia

Greek, meaning "blooming." The
name of numerous ancient Greek
muses, nymphs, and graces.

Thandie

(alt. Thana, Thandi)

Arabic, meaning "thanksgiving."
Thandie Newton is an actor.

Thea

Greek, meaning "goddess." Can be
a shortened form of Theodora or
Dorothea.

Theda

German, meaning "people." Name
of the silent movie actor Theda
Bara.

Thelma

Greek, meaning "will." Famous
Thelmas include singer Thelma
Houston, and the movie *Thelma &
Louise*.

Theodora

Greek, meaning "gift of God." The
name of numerous ancient Roman
figures.

Theodosia

Greek, meaning "gift of God."

Thisbe

Greek, from the mythological
heroine of the same name.

Thomasina

(alt. Thomasin, Thomasine, Thomasyn)

Greek, meaning "twin." The birth
name of singer Tammi Terrell was
Thomasina Montgomery.

Thora

Scandinavian, meaning "Thor's struggle." Name of the actor Thora Birch.

Tia
(alt. Tiana)

Spanish, meaning "aunt." Tia Mowry is an actor.

Tiara

Latin, meaning "jeweled headband."

Tierney

Irish Gaelic, meaning "Lord."

Tierra
(alt. Tiera)

Spanish, meaning "land."

Tiffany
(alt. Tiffani, Tiffanie)

Greek, meaning "God's appearance." Name of the one-hit-wonder singer Tiffany.

Tigris
(alt. Tiggy)

Irish Gaelic, meaning "tiger."

Tilly
(alt. Tilda, Tillie)

Shortened form of Matilda, meaning "battle-mighty."

Timothea

Greek, meaning "honoring God."

Tina
(alt. Teena, Tena)

Shortened form of Christina, meaning "anointed Christian." Famous Tinas include comedian Tina Fey and singer Tina Turner.

Tirion

Welsh, meaning "kind and gentle."

Tirzah

Hebrew, meaning "pleasantness." A character in the Bible.

Titania

Greek, meaning "giant." The Queen of the Fairies from Shakespeare's *A Midsummer Night's Dream*.

Toby
(alt. Tobi)

Hebrew, meaning "God is good." Usually a boys' name but can be used for girls.

Toni
(alt. Tony)

Latin, meaning "invaluable." Female version of Tony, or short form of Antoinette. Famous Tonis include singer Toni Braxton, author Toni Morrison, and choreographer Toni Basil.

Tonia
(alt. Tonja, Tonya)

Russian, meaning "praiseworthy."

Topaz

Latin, meaning "golden gemstone."

Tori

(alt. Tora)

Shortened form of Victoria, meaning "victory." Famous Toris include actor Tori Spelling and singer Tori Amos.

Tova

(alt. Tovah, Tove)

Hebrew, meaning "good."

Tracy

(alt. Tracey, Tracie)

Greek, meaning "harvest." Famous Tracys include singer Tracy Chapman, actor Tracey Ullman, and artist Tracey Emin.

Treva

Welsh, meaning "homestead."

Trilby

English, meaning "vocal trills." Also the name of a style of men's hat.

Trina

(alt. Trena)

Greek, meaning "pure."

Trinity

Latin, meaning "triad." Associated with the Christian Holy Trinity. The lead female character from film series "The Matrix."

Trisha

(alt. Tricia)

Shortened form of Patricia, meaning "noble." Name of singer Trisha Yearwood.

Trista

Latin, meaning "sad."

Trixie

Shortened form of Beatrix, meaning "bringer of gladness." Trixie the Triceratops is a character in *Toy Story 3*.

Trudie

(alt. Tru, Trudy)

Shortened form of Gertrude, meaning "strength of a spear." Trudie Goodwin is an actor.

Tullia

Roman, meaning "bound for glory."

Twyla

(alt. Twila)

American, meaning "star." Name of the choreographer Twyla Tharp.

Tyler

English, meaning "tiler." Used for girls and also for boys.

Tyra

Scandinavian, meaning "Thor's struggle." Tyra Banks is a model.

Tzipporah

Hebrew, meaning "bird."

U

Girls' names

Ula
(alt. Ulla)
Celtic, meaning "gem of the sea."

Ulrika
(alt. Urica)
German, meaning "power of the wolf."

Uma
Sanskrit, meaning "flax." Uma Thurman is an actor.

Una
Latin, meaning "one."

Undine
Latin, meaning "little wave."

Unique
Latin, meaning "only one."

Unity
English, meaning "oneness."

Uriela
(alt. Uriella)
Hebrew, meaning "God's light."

Ursula
Latin, meaning "little female bear." The villain from Disney's *The Little Mermaid*.

Uta
German, meaning "prospers in battle."

Girls' names

Vada

German, meaning "famous ruler."

Valdis

(alt. Valdiss, Valdys, Valdyss)

Norse, meaning "goddess of the dead," from the mythological goddess of the same name.

Valencia

(alt. Valancy, Valarece)

Latin, meaning "strong and healthy." A city in Spain.

Valentina

Latin, meaning "strong and healthy."

Valentine

Latin, from the saint of the same name.

Valerie

(alt. Valarie, Valeria, Valery, Valorie; abbrev. Val, Vale, Valia, Vallie)

Latin, meaning "to be healthy and strong." Famous Valeries include actors Valerie Bertinelli and Valerie Harper, and the song "Valerie" by Mark Ronson and Amy Winehouse.

Vandana

Sanskrit, meaning "worship."

Vanessa

(alt. Vanesa)

Greek, meaning "butterfly." Famous Vanessas include actor Vanessa Hudgens and singer Vanessa Williams.

Vanity

Latin, meaning "self-obsessed."

Vashti

Persian, meaning "beauty." A Persian queen in the Bible.

Veda

Sanskrit, meaning "knowledge and wisdom."

Vega

Arabic, meaning "falling vulture."

Velda

German, meaning "ruler."

Vella

American, meaning "beautiful."

Velma

English, meaning "determined protector." A character from *Scooby Doo*.

Venice
(alt. Venetia, Venita)

Latin, meaning "city of canals." An Italian city.

Venus

Latin, from the Roman goddess of the same name. Venus was the goddess of love, beauty, sex, and fertility.

Vera
(alt. Verla, Verlie)

Slavic, meaning "faith." Famous Veras include designer Vera Wang, actor Vera Farmiga, and singer Vera Lynn.

Verda
(alt. Verdie)

Latin, meaning "spring-like."

Verena

Latin, meaning "true." Associated with Saint Verena.

Verity

Latin, meaning "truth."

Verna
(alt. Vernie)

Latin, meaning "spring green."

Verona

Latin, from the Italian city of the same name.

Veronica
(alt. Verica, Veronique)

Latin, meaning "true image." Famous Veronicas include actors Veronica Lake and Veronica Carlson, and the "Veronica Mars" series and movie.

Veruca

Latin, meaning "wart." Veruca Salt is a character from *Charlie and the Chocolate Factory*.

Vesta

Latin, from the Roman goddess of the same name.

Vicenta

Latin, meaning "prevailing."

Victoria
(abbrev. Tori, Vicki, Vicky, Vikki, Vix)
Latin, meaning "victory." Famous Victorias include designer Victoria Beckham, England's Queen Victoria, and chain store Victoria's Secret.

Vida
Spanish, meaning "life."

Vidya
Sanskrit, meaning "knowledge." Refers to learning and knowledge in the Hindu faith.

Vienna
Latin, from the city of the same name in Austria.

Vigdis
Scandinavian, meaning "war goddess."

Vina
(alt. Vena)
Spanish, meaning "vineyard."

Viola
Latin, meaning "violet." Name of the actor Viola Davis.

Violet
(alt. Violetta)
Latin, meaning "purple." The famed nurse and survivor Violet Jessop.

Virginia
(alt. Virgie, Virginie; abbrev. Ginnie, Ginny)
Latin, meaning "maiden." Famous Virginias include author Virginia Woolf, *Raising Hope* character Virginia Chance, and the eastern states of Virginia and West Virginia.

Vita
Latin, meaning "life."

Vittoria
Variation of Victoria, meaning "victory."

Viva
Latin, meaning "alive." Name of the actor Viva.

Vivian
(alt. Vivien, Vivienne, Vyvian)
Latin, meaning "lively." Famous Vivians include actor Vivian Leigh, designer Vivienne Westwood, and photographer Vivian Maier.

Vivica
(alt. Viveca)
Scandinavian, meaning "war fortress." Name of the actor Vivica A. Fox.

Vonda
Czech, meaning "from the tribe of Vandals." Vonda Shepard is a singer.

Girls' names

Waleska
Polish, meaning "beautiful."

Wallis
English, meaning "from Wales." Name of socialite Wallis Simpson.

Wanda
(alt. Waneta, Wanita)
Slavic, meaning "tribe of the vandals." Name of comedian and actor Wanda Sykes.

Wava
English, meaning "way."

Waverly
(alt. Waverley)
Old English, meaning "meadow of aspens."

Wendy
English, meaning "friend." Famous Wendys include host Wendy Williams, the character of Wendy Darling in *Peter Pan*, and the hamburger chain Wendy's.

Whisper
English, meaning "whisper."

Whitley
Old English, meaning "white meadow."

Whitney
(alt. Witney)
Old English, meaning "white island." Famous Whitneys include singer Whitney Houston, comedian Whitney Cummings, and dancer Witney Carson.

Wilda
German, meaning "willow tree."

Wilhelmina
(abbrev. Mina, Mine, Minna, Willa, Willy, Wilma)
German, meaning "determined to protect." A popular name with the German royal family.

Willa
(alt. Willene, Willia)
German, meaning "helmet." Willa Cather is an author.

Willow
English, from the tree of the same name. Famous celebrity children called Willow include Willow Smith (Will and Jada Pinkett Smith's daughter) and Willow Hart (Pink and Carey Hart's daughter).

Winifred
(alt. Winnie)
Old English, meaning "holy and blessed." South African activist Winifred "Winnie" Madikizela-Mandela was once married to Nelson Mandela.

Winona
(alt. Wynonna)
Indian, meaning "first-born daughter." Famous Winonas include actor Winona Ryder and singer Wynonna Judd.

Winslow
English, meaning "friend's hill."

Winter
English, meaning "winter."

Wisteria
English, meaning "flower."

Wren
English, meaning "wren."

Wynne
(alt. Wynn)
Welsh, meaning "white."

X Girls' names

Xanthe

Greek, meaning "blonde." The name of several ancient Greek mythological characters.

Xanthippe

Greek, meaning "nagging."

Xaverie

Greek, meaning "bright."

Xaviera

Arabic, meaning "bright."

Xena
(alt. Xenia)

Greek, meaning "foreigner." The title character from the TV sci-fi series *Xena: Warrior Princess*.

Ximena

Greek, meaning "listening."

Xiomara

Spanish, meaning "battleready."

Xochitl

Spanish, meaning "flower." Queen Xochitl was a legendary Toltec ruler.

Xoey

Variation of Zoe, meaning "life." Spelling alternative for Zoey or Joey.

Xristina

Variation of Christina, meaning "follower of Christ." Singer Christina Aguilera often spells her name Xristina.

Xylia
(alt. Xylina, Xyloma)

Greek, meaning "from the woods."

Girls' names

Yadira
Arabic, meaning "worthy."

Yael
Hebrew, meaning "mountain goat."
A figure in the Bible.

Yaffa
(alt. Yahaira, Yajaira)
Hebrew, meaning "lovely."

Yamilet
Arabic, meaning "beautiful."

Yana
Hebrew, meaning "the Lord is gracious." Yana Rudkovskaya is the wife of figure skater Evgeni Plushenko.

Yanira
Hawaiian, meaning "pretty."
A character in ancient Greek mythology.

Yareli
Latin, meaning "golden."

Yaretzi
(alt. Yaritza)
Aztec, meaning "forever beloved."

Yasmin
(alt. Yasmeen, Yasmina, Yasmine)
Persian, meaning "jasmine flower."
Yasmine Bleeth is an actor.

Yelena
Greek, meaning "bright and chosen."

Yesenia
Arabic, meaning "flower."

Yetta
English, from Henrietta, meaning "ruler of the house."

Yeva
Hebrew variant of Eve, meaning "life."

Ylva
Old Norse, meaning "she wolf."

Yoki
(alt. Yoko)

Native American, meaning "rain." Yoko Ono is an artist and peace activist.

Yolanda
(alt. Yolonda)

Spanish, meaning "violet flower." Name of reality TV star Yolanda Foster.

Yoselin
English, meaning "lovely."

Yoshiko
Japanese, meaning "good child." Princess Yoshiko was an important Empress of Japan.

Ysabel
English, meaning "God's promise." Spelling alternative to Isabel.

Ysanne
Contraction of Isabel and Anne, meaning "pledged to God" and "grace."

Yuki
Japanese, meaning "lucky."

Yuliana
Latin, meaning "youthful."

Yuridia
Russian, meaning "farmer."

Yvette
(alt. Ivette, Ivonne, Yvonne)

French, meaning "yew." Yvette Nicole Brown is an actor.

Z Girls' names

Zafira
Arabic, meaning "successful."

Zahara
(alt. Zahava, Zahra)
Arabic, meaning "flowering and shining." Name of Angelina Jolie and Brad Pitt's daughter.

Zaida
(alt. Zaide)
Arabic, meaning "prosperous"; Hebrew, meaning "loved grandfather."

Zalika
Swahili, meaning "well born."

Zaltana
Arabic, meaning "high mountain."

Zamia
Greek, meaning "pine cone."

Zaneta
(alt. Zanceta, Zanetah, Zanett, Zanetta)
Hebrew, meaning "a gracious present from God."

Zaniyah
Arabic, meaning "lily."

Zara
(alt. Zaria, Zariah, Zora)
Arabic, meaning "radiance." A fashion brand.

Zaya
(alt. Zayah)
Tibetan, meaning "victorious woman."

Zelda
German, meaning "dark battle." Associated with the hugely successful video game series *Legend of Zelda*.

Zelia
(alt. Zella)
Scandinavian, meaning "sunshine."

Zelma
German, meaning "helmet."

Zemira
(alt. Zemirah)
Hebrew, meaning "joyous melody."
Title of the opera *Zemira* by
Francesco Bianchi.

Zena
(alt. Zenia, Zina)
Greek, meaning "hospitable."

Zenaida
Greek, meaning "the life of Zeus."
Associated with physician Saint
Zenaida.

Zenobia
Latin, meaning "the life of Zeus."
Zenobia was a queen of ancient
Roman Syria.

Zephyr
Greek, meaning "the west wind."

Zetta
Latin, meaning "seven."

Zia
Arabic, meaning "light and splendor."

Zinaida
Greek, meaning "belonging to Zeus."

Zinnia
Latin, meaning "flower."

Zipporah
Hebrew, meaning "bird." Zipporah
was one of Moses' wives in the
Bible.

Zita
(alt. Ziva)
Spanish, meaning "little girl." Saint
Zita is the patron saint of maids and
domestic servants.

Zoe
(alt. Zoi, Zoie, Zoey, Zoeya, Zooey)
Greek, meaning "life." Famous Zoes
include actors Zoe Saldana and
Zooey Deschanel.

Zoila
Greek, meaning "life."

Zoraida
Spanish, meaning "captivating
woman."

Zosia
(alt. Zosima)
Greek, meaning "wisdom." Zosia
Mamet is an actor.

Zoya
Greek, meaning "life." Zoya
Kosmodemyanskaya was a Soviet
Union heroine.

Zula

African, meaning "brilliant."

Zuleika

Arabic, meaning "fair and intelligent." Zuleika was the name of Potiphar's wife in the Bible.

Zulma

Arabic, meaning "peace."

Zuzana

Hebrew, meaning "lily."

Zuzu

Czech, meaning "flower." Susan (Zuzu) is a character in the movie *It's A Wonderful Life*.

A name for all seasons

Spring	Summer	Fall	Winter
April	August	Autumn	January
Cerelia	June	Demetria	Neva
Kelda	Natsumi	September	Neve
May	Persephone	Theresa	Perdita
Primavera	Soleil	Tracey	Rainer
Verda	Summer		Tahoma
Verna	Suvi		